THE CRIMSON AND GOLD

THE
CRIMSON
AND
GOLD

FOOTBALL AND
INTEGRATION IN
ATHENS, GEORGIA

MARK CLEGG

THE UNIVERSITY OF GEORGIA PRESS ATHENS

© 2024 by the University of Georgia Press
Athens, Georgia 30602
www.ugapress.org
All rights reserved
Designed by Kaelin Chappell Broaddus
Set in 10.5/13.5 Miller Text Roman by Kaelin Chappell Broaddus
Printed and bound by Sheridan Books
The paper in this book meets the guidelines for permanence
and durability of the Committee on Production Guidelines for
Book Longevity of the Council on Library Resources.

Most University of Georgia Press titles are
available from popular e-book vendors.

Printed in the United States of America
24 25 26 27 28 P 5 4 3 2 1

Library of Congress Cataloging-in-Publication Data

Names: Clegg, Mark, 1958– author.
Title: The crimson and gold : football and integration in Athens, Georgia /
Mark Clegg.
Other titles: Football and integration in Athens, Georgia
Description: Athens : The University of Georgia Press, [2024] |
Includes bibliographical references and index.
Identifiers: LCCN 2024009244 | ISBN 9780820366982 (paperback ; permanent
paper) | ISBN 9780820366999 (epub) | ISBN 9780820367002 (pdf)
Subjects: LCSH: School integration—Social aspects—Georgia—Athens.
| Football—Social aspects—Georgia—Athens. | High school athletes—
Georgia—Athens—History—20th century—Interviews. | High schools—
Georgia—Athens—History—20th century. | School sports—Social
aspects—Georgia—Athens. | Athens (Ga.)—Race relations—History—20th
century. | Athens (Ga.)—Social conditions—History—20th century.
Classification: LCC LC214.23.A84 C54 2024 | DDC 379.2/630975818—dc23/
eng/20240318
LC record available at https://lccn.loc.gov/2024009244

Carry each his burden, we are young despite the years
We are concern, we are hope despite the times

—from "These Days," by R.E.M.

Well, son, I'll tell you:
Life for me ain't been no crystal stair.
It's had tacks in it,
And splinters,
And boards torn up,
And places with no carpet on the floor—
Bare.
But all the time
I'se been a-climbin' on,
And reachin' landin's,
And turnin' corners,
And sometimes goin' in the dark
Where there ain't been no light.
So boy, don't you turn back.
Don't you set down on the steps
'Cause you finds it's kinder hard.
Don't you fall now—
For I'se still goin', honey,
I'se still climbin',
And life for me ain't been no crystal stair.

—Langston Hughes, "Mother to Son"

CONTENTS

Preface ix

INTRODUCTION 1

CHAPTER 1. The Schools 4

CHAPTER 2. The Town 26

CHAPTER 3. The Gown 45

CHAPTER 4. Violence and Hope 67

CHAPTER 5. The Season 121

CHAPTER 6. The Game 152

CHAPTER 7. The Gladiators 179

EPILOGUE 214

Notes 225

Bibliography 241

Index 243

PREFACE

I have lived in Atlanta for almost fifty years, which auto-
matically disqualifies me from ever attaining the status
of an Athenian. I was, however, influenced by the four years
I spent in the Classic City as a young boy in the 1960s, attending the Athens YMCA, running through the forests and
creeks of a still largely undeveloped area on the outskirts of
town, and watching the Athens High Trojans perform in
front of a boisterous crowd at Death Valley on Friday nights
in the fall. My father wore the black and white stripes of a
Georgia High School Association referee, and he would occasionally allow me to tag along to the games he helped of-
ficiate. In addition to watching the battle on the gridiron, I
tried to position myself—without success—to catch one of
the coveted maroon-and-white plastic mini-footballs the
cheerleaders tossed out to spectators. I would also look for
loose change that might have fallen beneath the grandstands
or play a game of touch football with other unattended boys
on the barely lit edges of the end zone.

Sometimes my father refereed games at the Black high
school, Burney-Harris, and he would regale me with mes-
merizing accounts of the high-flying Yellow Jackets, who
played a wide-open, exotic style of football that relied heav-

ily on long passes and trick plays. This sparked my interest—the high school and college football I watched in person featured no African American players, but professional sports, which had just arrived in Atlanta, introduced me to a world in which integration was accepted and encouraged at a level that was still fiercely resisted in the Deep South.

By the late 1960s, the situation had started to change. I still remember my Little League baseball coach in Greenwood, South Carolina—a grizzled, leather-faced, chain-smoking mill hand who was thirty-five years old but looked sixty—calling his players together after a practice to announce that we would soon be adding our first Black teammate: "If any of you say anything bad to Clarence, I will kick you off the team." No one challenged the coach on his threat, and in fact players went out of their way to accept and be cordial to Clarence. This was, for me, an unforgettable example of leadership determining the environment.

In today's atomized society, the community bonds that once held us together have largely disappeared, with sports supplying one of the last (largely) benign links to group affiliation. Sports have held an outsized importance in America for the last century, and the community connectivity is strongest at the high school level, where the young men and women who participate are not strangers to their teams' fans and supporters; that's in contrast to sports at the professional and collegiate levels, where, as the comedian Jerry Seinfeld famously observed, we're just "rooting for the clothes"—that is, for whichever assortment of players happens to wear our tribe's "colors" at any point in time. In contrast, high school athletes are sons and daughters, nieces and nephews, cousins, friends, and classmates. Thus it is not altogether surprising that over fifty years ago, one of the largest impediments to the successful consolidation of the Black and White high schools in Athens, Georgia, was a battle over symbols—what colors the combined athletic teams would wear, what the mascot would be, what the new high school would be named.

This book tells the story of a decade of integration, as reflected through the prism of high school football in one medium-sized Piedmont city that fiercely supported its two high schools—one Black, the other White—and suffered through the trauma of losing deeply held traditions that had been established and cherished over generations. One quote from Michael Thurmond, an African American student and football player during that era, particularly resonates with me: "We were children asked to resolve adult issues." As a society, we placed an unfair burden on our youngest, both Black and White, to help us atone for centuries of racial sins. They were marching into the unknown, with little guidance or practical advice from the adults whom they respected and admired. For the most part, they navigated the journey as best they could, with frequent missteps—as would be expected—along the way.

This work draws on extensive archival research and interviews of those who lived through a transformational era and provided firsthand accounts of their experiences.

The book would not have been possible without the time and memories shared by so many current and former Athenians: Dr. Walter Allen Sr., Walter Allen Jr., Richard Appleby, Woody Chastain, Mac Coile, Bobby Cross, Ken Dious, Doc Eldridge, Mike Epps, Maxie Foster, Paul Gilbert, Barbara Hartman, Bill Hartman Jr., Robert Hawkins, Bill King, Horace King, Jimmy Klein, Rand Lambert, David Lester, Chris Lloyd, Chris and Stacy Mallet, Pete McCommons, Elizabeth Platt, Frank Platt, Clarence Pope, Bobby Poss, Terry Smart, Aleck Stephens, Lawton Stephens, Mary Stephens, Winston Stephens, Michael Thurmond, Bonnie Hampton Travis, and Gary Travis.

I am especially appreciative of the support provided by the staff of my publisher, the University of Georgia Press, and in particular that of my editor, Nate Holly, who dispensed sage advice and displayed consummate professionalism through several revisions of the book. Arthur Johnson did a spectacular job with copyediting. I would also like to extend a special thanks to the staff at the Athens-Clarke County Library's Heritage Room.

Also offered is a special acknowledgement to the staff of the University of Georgia's Hargrett Rare Book and Manuscript Library. Thank you, Mary Palmer Linnemann, for your unending patience and courtesy.

Others whom I would like to thank are Buck Belue of 680 The Fan; Becky Taylor, sports editor with the *Tifton Gazette* and researcher with the Georgia High School Football Historians Association; Terry Daniel of the Valdosta Touchdown Club, who sent me a CD of the 1969 Athens-Valdosta game; Charlie Strong (my cousin), who played quarterback for Gainesville High School in 1969 when the Red Elephants faced off against both Athens High School and Burney-Harris; Bertis Downs for granting me permission to use lyrics from the R.E.M. song "These Days"; and photographer, mapmaker, and fellow Appalachian Trail hiker extraordinaire Ken Young.

Finally, thank you, Athens, Georgia, the best damned midsized city in this country if your idea of a spiritual experience is indulging in a unique blend of pure and quirky music, delightfully ambitious food and drink, and top-notch football—all wrapped up in a genuinely laid-back southern vibe that is as warm and cozy as the inside of a wool blanket while attending a nighttime game in November.

ATHENS
GEORGIA
CIRCA 1960

199 PRINCE AVE BUILDING

THE VARSITY

ATHENS HIGH SCHOOL

YMCA

BURNEY-HARRIS HIGH SCHOOL

CENTER MYERS DORMITORY

ATHENS CITY HALL

SANFORD STADIUM

LINNENTOWN

ATHENS BEN EPPS AIRPORT

PRINCE AVE

BOULEVARD

PULASKI ST

DOWNTOWN

THOMAS ST

BROAD STREET

BAXTER STREET

ATLANTA HWY

RIVER

LUMPKIN

EAST CAMPUS

MILLEDGE AVE

UGA CAMPUS

MIDDLE OCONEE RIVER

NORTH OCONEE RIVER

1 MILE   2

THE CRIMSON AND GOLD

INTRODUCTION

Heading northeast from Atlanta, one has to drive more than half the seventy-two miles of roadway distance to Athens before the Gwinnett County suburbs finally exhaust themselves and the land no longer yields to endless development. The landscape around Braselton changes to lush, overgrown pine and hardwood forests, twisting, coffee-colored creeks and rivers, and more subtle, gently rolling hills. But there is always the tireless vegetation choking the red clay hills that seem to shimmer like a mirage in the thick of the summer heat—former University of Georgia art school professor and Athens music scene guru Jim Herbert called this riotous explosion of emerald foliage the defining feature of the region, one that works its way into the soul of the primitive artists and edgy poets and musicians who have shaped pottery, warbled songs and hymns, splashed paintings, or fashioned objects such as clay face jugs and whirligigs by hand from the modest materials available to them.

Sixty years ago, driving the slow, two-lane state highways to Athens was a journey back in time to an unhurried place that was unburdened by the disturbing headlines that were rattling the country to its core in the early 1960s. The city was comfortable with its 140-year past and was in no rush to embrace an increasingly uncertain future.

Vestiges of that past are still visible today, from the old brick storefronts downtown to the fiercely protected and preserved Greek Revival and Victorian homes of South Milledge and Cobbham and Boulevard. Just off busy West Broad Street, where the H. T. Edwards Teaching and Learning Center is now housed, is an annex containing a museum dedicated to Burney-Harris, the storied Black high school that shut its doors in 1970. Relics of its proud sports past—a battle-scarred plastic football helmet, a fading blue-and-gold letterman's jacket—and yellowing yearbooks provide a fascinating glimpse into the school's rich athletic history. There is no sign of the small stadium behind the school where, in the 1950s and 1960s, a 125-member marching band and an adoring crowd shook the ground in raucous support of the pride of the Black community, the Burney-Harris Yellow Jackets football team.

Further out Broad Street, near where it morphs into the Atlanta Highway, is Hilltop Grille. In the autumn, Hilltop is a favorite Sunday morning brunch haunt for hungover out-of-town Georgia Bulldog football fans seeking to fortify themselves with a last taste of Athens before reluctantly driving back to the drudgeries of home. A local radio station holds a "live remote" at a table set up on the edge of the dining area, where its sports personalities take phone calls from Bulldog fans gloating over victory or grumbling over a coach's decision that led to a disheartening defeat. The show's background music comes in the form of clanging dishes and Bloody Mary–fueled laughter.

The restaurant's walls are adorned with Bulldog memorabilia, including rare signed prints of artwork by the famed cartoonist Jack Davis, the late father-in-law of Hilltop Grille's owner, Chris Lloyd. But just behind the host station—in what is perhaps a nod to the aging former players who are patrons of the restaurant—is a framed black-and-white photograph of the 1969 Athens High School Trojans football team. The team depicted in the photo is distinguished by several features: there are only thirty-three players; they are all small in stature—only one player appears to weigh as much as two hundred pounds; and they are all White. This more-than-a-half-century-old photograph captures a transitional moment in the history of Athens: the very next year, the mostly White Athens High School would be forced into a merger with its equally reluctant partner, the all-Black Burney-Harris High School.

Absent from the walls of Hilltop Grille are any monochrome images of the Burney-Harris football team that played with a verve and high-octane style otherwise unseen on the prep gridirons of northeast Georgia in that era. Memories of the 1969 team—the last one to wear the gold and royal blue of the Yellow Jackets—are still shared on Facebook and at the reunions of the last few Burney-Harris graduating classes, whose members all express an enduring love for their alma mater, which once personified the fierce pride and tight-knit culture of the Black community of Athens.

CHAPTER 1

THE SCHOOLS

Ef you strike a thorn or rose,
Keep a-goin'!
Ef it hails, or ef it snows,
Keep a-goin'!
'Taint no use to sit an' whine,
When the fish ain't on yer line;
Bait yer hook an' keep a-tryin'—
Keep a-goin'!

—"Opening lines from "Keep A-Goin'!,"
a poem by Frank Lebby Stanton that Dr. Walter Allen Sr.
learned from his mother when he was a young boy

In 1960 the population of Athens and Clarke County was
about forty-five thousand, an increase of almost ten thousand over the 1950 census results. The Black citizenry con-
stituted some 25 percent of the total population, a decline
from 40 percent in 1930; this decrease had more to do with
an influx of Whites—professors, students, and administrative staff of the University of Georgia ("UGA" or "Georgia"),
and workers attracted by higher-paying industrial jobs—
than it did with an exodus of African Americans.[1]

The city initiated the public school system in Athens in 1885 when it passed a $20,000 bond issue to build two 10-room, two-story schools—one on Washington Street for White students and one on Baxter Street for Black pupils. Both schools proved to be very popular, and they were soon forced to search for more space to accommodate the flood of eager students. The Baxter Street location was remodeled and expanded for White students, while their Black counterparts were moved to two different 6-room schools on the east and west sides of Athens.[2]

In 1913, what would become the town's first Black public high school—Athens High and Industrial School (AHIS)—was built at the corner of Reese and Pope Streets. Its first principal was Professor Samuel F. Harris, who saw it as his mission to offer a combination of the teaching philosophies espoused by two of the most influential Black scholars of the day, Booker T. Washington and W. E. B. Du Bois. Washington stressed a practical industrial education for Black students, with a focus on trades such as woodworking, cooking, and bricklaying. Du Bois, on the other hand, emphasized a classical Eurocentric curriculum, including the study of both Greek and Latin. In 1922, AHIS became the first Black public secondary school to be accredited in the state of Georgia.

In 1960, like school systems throughout much of the South and the country at large, the Athens-Clarke County school system was segregated. (The county and city school systems had merged in 1956, thirty-five years before the county and city governments followed suit.) There were few private schools in Athens-Clarke County in 1960; the larger private schools that exist today—Athens Academy, Athens Christian, and Prince Avenue Christian—were started in the latter part of the 1960s or in the 1970s, concurrent with or shortly after the integration of the public schools.

In the early 1960s, the two public high schools were all-White Athens High School and all-Black Athens High and Industrial School, the latter of which changed its name to

Burney-Harris High School (BHHS) in 1964 in honor of the school's first two principals, Samuel F. Harris and Annie H. Burney. Both schools had moved from their original locations in the 1950s and were less than a mile apart, within walking distance of each other. Both high schools were also just off main thoroughfares—Athens High School was a block behind venerable, old-money South Milledge Avenue, while AHIS/Burney-Harris was one street away from one of Athens's main commercial arteries, West Broad Street.

AHIS/Burney-Harris had a proud sports history. In the 1920s, the Yellow Jackets of AHIS developed a formidable reputation in football against rival Black schools. Harry "Squab" Jones—who coached Union Baptist Institute, the county school for African Americans, before serving as the UGA football team's legendary athletic trainer for over forty years—lamented the fact that his team "never could beat that crowd from Athens High and Industrial."[3] (Union Baptist merged with AHIS in 1956 as part of the city/county school consolidation.)

Football at AHIS/Burney-Harris was a major event for the Black community, with games drawing big crowds from alumni, neighbors, and family members of players and their friends. Even practices drew large crowds, with many former players gathering on the sidelines to watch the action. The team played its home games in the small stadium behind the school, a two-story brick building with twenty-eight classrooms and a spacious cafeteria built in 1956 off Dearing Extension in the Rock Springs neighborhood. Due to segregation, African Americans typically had only two options for large social gatherings—church and school. "We couldn't use other facilities like restaurants or hotels, so we had all of our school activities here," recalled Elizabeth Platt, a 1967 graduate of Burney-Harris High School. "Although I did not have a lot of material things that money could buy, I had some of the best high school experiences anyone could ever have and would not change that for anything. Almost all our events were held at the high school, either in the cafeteria or our gymnasium, including prom and graduation exercises. In the cafeteria we held Christmas Cantatas (choir), Valentine Balls, Sadie Hawkins dances, Homecoming dances, and many other fun activities."[4]

The greater Black community also used the cafeteria and gymnasium for events. Trophy cases lined the school's hallways, and the lobby was decked with blue and gold, the colors worn by the Yellow Jackets.[5]

Teachers, administrators, and coaches at Burney-Harris —many wore all three hats—represented, in the words of Robert Hawkins, who grew up on Billups Street near Burney-Harris, "the top of the Black social hierarchy." Not only were they authority figures, but they also, just as importantly, were neighbors and highly respected members of the community. Eugene T. "Doc" Holmes, the AHIS and BHHS head football coach, lived two houses down from the school. Paul Troutman, the longtime industrial arts teacher, lived on Billups Street; Mrs. C. B. Smith, the English teacher, lived on Reese Street; and the principal, Professor Homer T. Edwards, lived a few blocks up from the school, next to the funeral home on Broad Street.[6] Former students often became teachers at Burney-Harris; it was, in every sense, a community school. After graduating from AHIS in 1936, Elizabeth King received her bachelor's degree from Spelman College in Atlanta and then returned to her high school alma mater to teach and coach women's basketball for twenty-five years. Elizabeth Platt remembered Ms. King, who died in October 2021 at the age of 103, as "someone I shared a very close bond with. She was my neighbor, fellow church member, and teacher. But most of all, she was my very special friend and stand-in mother."[7] Michael Thurmond reflected on Ms. King's tough but sound approach with her students—"Michael, if you want a textbook, why don't you go and write one?"—that helped influence his decision to write a book detailing the African American experience in Athens.[8]

Historian Alexander Stephens, who grew up in Athens, observed: "The Black community in Athens revolved around church, school, and home. It was not unusual for all three of these to intersect—a cousin that served as the deacon at your church might also teach your children at school."[9] The elite status held by African American educators, school administrators, and coaches was at least partially attributable to the lack of access that Black Athenians had to other areas of professional attainment, such as business, law, and government. As Dr. Walter Allen Sr., a longtime teacher, administrator, and bandleader at AHIS/Burney-Harris, succinctly put it, "There were not many places Black people could go. . . . They [Whites] didn't mind you teaching, because you were teaching Black kids."[10]

If a student misbehaved, either in or outside class, word quickly got back to the parents, and teachers were considered surrogate parents whose authority was never questioned. Horace King, who played football at Burney-Harris and later starred at UGA before moving on to a nine-year career with the NFL's Detroit Lions, recalled his mother warning him every time he left the house "to not do anything to embarrass me." He listened to her advice and called his teachers "ma'am" and "sir." Years later he remembered, well into adulthood, still calling his old coaches "sir" when he crossed paths with them in Athens.[11] Bobby Cross, a quarterback on the Yellow Jackets football team, recalled the humiliation of students walking to the principal's office, which would be followed by the sting of "two licks" from the paddle.[12]

Elizabeth Platt also recalled how much her Burney-Harris teachers emphasized proper deportment: "We were taught not only subject matters, but also how to carry ourselves as young women. We had to be taught how to sit properly in a chair, how to stand, how to enunciate, and to speak in front of others by our teachers."[13]

The emphasis on respect for authority, self-improvement,

and proper decorum—all enforced with the threat of punishment either at school or at home—was a constant at Burney-Harris, and the former students, all interviewed decades later, felt that they benefited from the tough discipline meted out by their instructors.

Burney-Harris ran its sports on a tight budget—unlike many of the White high schools, it did not enjoy additional funding from well-heeled booster clubs. Horace King remembered: "Coach Dooley at UGA would donate used equipment to our team. They would dump all of it out on the locker room floor, and you had to 'earn' the right to the best equipment. I was so happy one year when I got a pair of used high tops, one size eleven, the other size twelve."[14]

Another former student recollected: "The family and friends of AHIS students would repaint the old helmets and cleats and piece together uniforms from the hand-me-downs. Everyone got to wear the infamous [*sic*] Yellow Jacket blue and gold. However, some first stringers would wear blue tops and gold pants, others would wear yellow tops and blue bottoms, and others would wear blue tops and bottoms with yellow streaks."[15] Due to a scarcity of resources, Yellow Jacket substitute players on the sidelines would grab a helmet from a player leaving the game before running out on the field. Coaches and players took care of field maintenance—from mowing the grass to laying down lime with wheelbarrows for the gridiron boundaries.

The head football coach and biology teacher in the early 1960s was Doc Holmes, a wily figure who could always be spotted on the sideline chewing an unlit cigar. He forged close relationships with coaches Wally Butts and Vince Dooley at UGA, which not only led to the donation of athletic equipment to AHIS/Burney-Harris but also allowed the Yellow Jackets to play at UGA's Sanford Stadium on Thanksgiving Day against their Black county school rival, Union Baptist. Holmes also worked out an arrangement with the UGA athletic department that allowed Black boys to earn pocket money by selling trays of Coca-Colas at Bulldog football games. Holmes was a role model to African American boys and young men in Athens, and they felt he would always "[go] to bat for anybody who played for him."[16] He was a constant presence in their lives and would play basketball after school with children as young as eight years old—his goal was to keep them "off the street."[17] The AHIS/Burney-Harris coaches kept a close tab on their players, and those who missed a class were not allowed to practice. Both teachers and coaches would telephone—or, in some instances, show up at the front door—to talk to parents about their child disrupting or skipping class.

While nurturing and empathetic, Doc Holmes could also be a stern disciplinarian who would rail at his players for being "cry babies." One player was so intimidated by Holmes that he played the second half of a game with a broken leg rather than apprise his coach of the injury.[18] "You did not want to go back to the sidelines if you messed up," recalled former player Leonard Champion. The slap on the side of the helmet was not nearly as hurtful as the disgusted look Coach Holmes would give the offending player. The emotional pain of disappointing a "second father" was worse than the physical punishment.[19]

Clarence Pope, who played at Burney-Harris and would later join teammates Horace King and Richard Appleby as three of the first five Black players to win scholarships in football at UGA, recalled that "games at Burney Harris were the greatest show on earth. The fans loved it; there was an excitement and an atmosphere that could not be matched."[20] Paul Gilbert, a White football player who starred at quarterback at Athens High School and the University of Georgia, attended Burney-Harris football games on Saturday nights with his father and recalled a more entertaining style of football compared to the more conservative version that prevailed at the White schools: "They threw the ball all over the place," he remembered in amazement almost sixty years later.[21]

Burney-Harris played in the Georgia Interscholastic Association (GIA), the organization that governed Black high school sports in the years before integration. The Yellow Jackets competed in GIA Class AA, known as the "Big 7"—the highest classification among the Black schools—and would typically play four to eight games a year against Carver (Columbus), Booker T. Washington and Archer (both Atlanta), Lucy Laney (Augusta), and other Black schools. With only about 500 students, Burney-Harris had a much smaller student population than did its rivals—Washington High had more than 3,000 pupils, and Laney around 1,700—but Coach Holmes trained his players to believe in each other, and they knew "he was always there for them." Doc Holmes never coached an undefeated team and finished with a relatively modest win-loss record when he retired from coaching after the 1965 season, but he achieved that record with teams that almost always played against much larger schools. Still, his proudest achievement was mentoring seven players who eventually became medical doctors.[22]

During each Yellow Jackets game, the energetic blare from the brass section and the percussive thump from the drum line in the 125-member marching band—which included younger musicians from middle school—kept the crowd pumped up and engaged throughout. The signature cheer was a simple but infectious chant supported by the swaying horn section:

Let's Goooo Yellow Jacketttts . . . dah dah
Let's Goooo Yellow Jacketttts . . . dah dah
Let's Goooo Yellow Jacketttts . . . dah dah, DAH DAH DAH!

The school, the football team, the surrounding Rocksprings neighborhood, and the greater Athens Black community were as one when Burney-Harris took the field. After the game, a "sock hop" would be held in the school gymnasium or at the nearby Black YMCA branch, named for Samuel F. Harris, in Rocksprings Community Center. Disc jockey Raymond Roundtree spun 45s, or local groups like the Charms, the Grains of Sand, and Leaves of Grass—which included Burney-Harris band director Bennett Johnson—played popular rock and Motown covers.

Over the years, Burney-Harris was, for many players, a pipeline to the powerhouses of the HBCUs (historically Black colleges and universities) such as Grambling State, Southern, Fisk, and Fort Valley State Universities. The names of many who starred at AHIS/Burney-Harris are still seared in the memories of the older residents of Athens's Black community. Leonard Champion was a football and basketball star whose gridiron prowess attracted the attention of UGA head coach Wally Butts, who told the young Black quarterback that he "wished he was another color."[23] James Fair starred at Southern University as a linebacker and later was instrumental in forming the Athens Athletic Hall of Fame. Aaron Heard was a standout in both basketball and football and went on to star at Southern University before playing in the NFL for the Dallas Cowboys and Washington Redskins. Walter Rittenberry was so swift as a boy that he was once stopped by a policeman for sprinting down Broad Street—the cop assumed that someone moving that quickly had stolen something.[24] He was a gifted athlete who earned all-conference honors as a freshman running back at Fort Valley State before becoming homesick and returning to Athens. Rittenberry would later own Walter's Barbecue on West Broad and achieved a degree of immortality as a restaurateur with an "M.B. degree—Master of Barbecue" in a cameo appearance in the 1987 Athens-music-scene cult classic movie, *Athens, GA: Inside/Out*.

Terry Green was a star wide receiver on the BHHS football team but was better known for his basketball talents. He led the state in scoring with a forty-four-point-per-game average as a senior and was also near the top in the state in rebounds and steals. In consecutive games, he scored sixty-two and seventy-three points. He had a "following" at Burney-Harris that showed up at all his practices and games just to watch him dominate on the court.[25] Charlie Strong, who played basketball for Gainesville High, remembered the night Green scored sixty-four points against the Red Elephants—"he fouled out three people trying to guard him, including me. If the three-point shot had existed back then, he would have scored eighty."[26]

In April 1966, four-year captain and lineman Ken Dious was the first Black football player to try out for the University of Georgia football team. He never played for the Bulldogs—he was deeply shaken when his father unexpectedly passed away on the first day of spring practice, and he did not suit up with the team in the fall. While his father's untimely death was a terrible blow to Dious, his decision to quit the team was ultimately due to the reluctance of ever-cautious head coach Vince Dooley to include a Black player on the roster. UGA was not prepared to field the first integrated team in the SEC; it would be another year before the University of Kentucky would integrate the conference when Nate Northington played for the Wildcats.[27] Dooley noted at the time that Dious, who would go on to become a highly successful attorney in Athens, was a "fine prospect."[28]

┼┼┼┼

In 1913, the Clarke County Courthouse moved from its original location on Prince Avenue to its present location on East Washington Street, and the vacated space was repurposed as Athens High School. The imposing, French Second Empire–style building with an eighty-five-foot cupola would add matching wings on both ends to accommodate the expanding needs of Athens's White students.[29]

By the early 1950s, the aging building on Prince Avenue could no longer hold the ever-growing White student population, and a new facility was constructed. The "new" Athens

High School was nestled within a leveled-off section of hills behind the sorority houses on South Milledge Avenue. The school was a sprawling two-story brick structure, fronted by a long grass mall with a flagpole at the end that was perfectly centered against the columned and recessed entrance behind it. A bandbox gymnasium anchored one end of the school, and the Mell Auditorium was attached as a wing on the opposite side. The building still stands today, with additions and an extensive renovation completed in 2016, and is now home to Clarke Central High School.

While entirely White in the early 1960s, the student population of Athens High School (AHS) had social strata, with a mix of preppy teenagers—the sons and daughters of doctors, lawyers, university professors, and other professionals—and tough working-class kids, largely from East Athens. As with characters in an S. E. Hinton novel, their style differences immediately identified the male members of the two tribes. The working-class boys greased their hair back and wore hooded coats or jackets, blue jeans, and shirts with the collars up. They had packs of cigarettes rolled up inside the sleeves of their shirts, and they rode Cushman motor scooters. Preppy boys lathered on English Leather cologne, shopped at George Dean's, Gunn's, Dick Ferguson's, and John Q. West, and wore button-down collar madras shirts, khaki pants, crewneck sweaters, and tasseled loafers. The preppy young women favored traditional outfits from Heery's Clothes Closet and Baxter's.

Athens High graduate and journalist Bill King felt that AHS was in many ways trying to emulate UGA with its cliquey "clubs." The all-male Key Club was an exclusive organization dedicated to developing skills among students deemed future leaders in the community. The Pre-Debs promoted civic involvement among aspiring female students. Athens High School also had two social organizations: the Sweet and Pretties (SAPs) sorority and the Beta Alpha Tau ("BATs") fraternity. The SAPs were an exclusive organization, and those unlucky girls who were spurned by not receiving bids were as devastated as the women not selected to their preferred sorority during college sorority rush. The BATs had a paddling initiation rite and a bouillon-cube-eating ritual, which dissuaded some potential members from joining. They threw band and "make out" parties—fueled by cheap beer purchased in nearby Arcade—at Lake Yamacutah in Jackson County.

King's depiction of AHS as largely a public prep school for the UGA-bound White Athens elite is borne out by numbers: as late as 1970, Athens High contributed more than twice as many entering freshmen—107 in total—as any other high school in the state of Georgia.[30] Once at Georgia, the graduates from AHS largely gravitated to the most exclusive fraternities—Kappa Alpha and Sigma Alpha Epsilon—and sororities—Phi Mu and Kappa Alpha Theta—where they jockeyed for leadership roles in both student and interfraternity government. Upon receiving their diplomas after four or five years at UGA, they would go on to assume positions in local government, medicine, law, or family-owned businesses. They would marry, raise families, and progress in their careers while sipping cocktails and playing golf and tennis at the Athens Country Club and participating as movers and shakers in the Chamber of Commerce, the Rotary and Kiwanis Clubs, and other civic organizations.

There was a clear delineation in social strata among the White students at AHS. The working-class kids occupied the bottom rung of the social ladder, the children of university professors and administrators clung to the middle rung, and the offspring of the ancient, pre–Civil War Athenian families rested at the top. The system was, however, somewhat fluid—football players were considered the elite of Athens High School, and a working-class football player could vault to the top of the social pyramid if he wore the maroon and white on Friday nights. Mike Epps, a football player who was the son of a postman, felt awkward about his elevation in social status, which included an invitation to join BATs, in which he enjoyed a brief membership. "I always felt uncomfortable, like a bit of an outsider," recalled Epps, and his sense of estrangement was heightened by the fact that he did not drink alcohol.[31]

To let off steam or to celebrate football victories, students gathered to soak in the music at the Moina Michael Auditorium or at Charlie Williams's Pinecrest Lodge, a restaurant and event venue where bands like the Shirelles, Doug Clark and the Hot Nuts, and the local ensemble the Jesters—led by Athens High graduate and lead singer Ed Saye—would perform. During breaks in the performances, the students would sneak out to the parking lot and drink beer and smoke while sitting on the hoods of their cars. Ronnie Milsap, a young blind man living in Gainesville, would also perform at Charlie Williams's Pinecrest Lodge, and Gainesville football players would show up and mingle with their rivals to hear their local boy perform. Those caught drinking and driving were more likely to be escorted home by a friendly Athens cop rather than hauled off to jail.

More G-rated entertainment options for AHS students were available at the popular Lucky Wishbone diner on West Broad and later on Baxter Street, which, according to a former AHS student, could have been the setting for the 1970s TV series *Happy Days*.

As the football team of the largest public high school in northeast Georgia, the Athens High School Trojans developed into both a regional and statewide powerhouse, going undefeated and winning state football championships in Georgia's highest classification in both 1941 and 1955. They considered themselves, in the words of AHS graduate Bill Hartman Jr., "the power of North Georgia," a competitive counterweight to the undisputed dominant program of South Georgia, Valdosta High School. Clad in maroon and white—in the late 1960s, the school softened the maroon to a lighter crimson or cardinal shade—the Trojans played their home games at UGA's Sanford Stadium, typically "under the lights" on Friday night, and attracted crowds in excess of ten thousand for big games. By contrast, the University of Georgia football team, which experienced relatively lean years during the 1950s, would sometimes muster crowds only about twice that size for its Saturday afternoon games in the forty-thousand-seat stadium.

Bobby Poss, who played football for Athens High School in the 1960s, sold peanuts and Cokes at Sanford Stadium as a boy and recalled the atmosphere at Trojans games in the 1950s: "Those players in their maroon-and-white uniforms coming out of the dressing room to the concrete walkway in their steel cleats sounded like a bunch of stallions. I knew I wanted to play for them some day."[32]

Woody Chastain, who also played for Athens High in the 1960s, remembered the 1955 state championship game, played on a freezing and windy December night in Sanford Stadium against perennial Georgia football championship finalist Valdosta High School: "The Valdosta players were so cold that they wore sweatpants and sweatshirts under their uniforms. Fans built fires inside metal trash barrels to stay warm. We beat 'em 41–20, and Fran Tarkenton, the future UGA star and NFL Hall of Famer, only threw one pass the entire game."[33]

Weyman Gray Sellers took over the head football coaching job at Athens High in 1952. Raised on a farm in Albany, Georgia, Sellers played end in football for Coach Wally Butts at UGA from 1945 to 1948 and was cocaptain of the 1948 SEC championship team. After the Green Bay Packers selected him in the fifth round of the 1948 NFL draft, Sellers snubbed the NFL and instead signed with the Los Angeles Dons of the upstart All-America Football Conference. A persistent back injury prematurely ended his professional football career after one season, and he took a job as a crop duster pilot before switching to coaching after a close friend died in a plane crash.[34]

Always well conditioned, Sellers was avid about lifting weights, a form of exercise that was not nearly as widespread in the mid-twentieth century as it is today. He was, even in his old age, a chiseled and intimidating physical presence. He was "a huge man," noted *Atlanta Constitution* columnist Lewis Grizzard when Sellers was forty-six, "broad of chest with massive limbs."[35] My father, who played opposite Sellers in church league basketball, once told me, "You never wanted to guard Sellers when he had the ball down low—he was all elbows."

In 1949, Sellers married Jackie Wells, the daughter of Athens mayor Jack Wells. Sellers enjoyed horseback riding with his father-in-law in the hilly, sparsely developed area of North Athens off Tallassee Road. Weyman and Jackie had three children—two daughters, Weymanda and Donna, and a son, Gray. In addition to raising a family and coaching and teaching physical education at Athens High, Weyman also started Trojan Laundry on West Washington Street in downtown Athens, which, as late as 1966, offered dry-cleaned shirts at "$.20 each for orders of five or more."[36]

Wally Butts had a profound influence on Sellers. The notorious Butts was known as "the Little Round Man"—he resembled Humpty Dumpty with his moon face, short stature, and protruding belly—and reigned over Georgia football for over twenty years using a combination of physical and psychological intimidation. Ralph McGill, the famed editor and publisher of the *Atlanta Constitution*, described the always animated Georgia coach thusly: "Mr. Butts . . . is almost the Barrymore of the sidelines. His face reflects joy or despair. His muscles leap. If he sits, his legs jerk and flip as if some invisible physician were tapping him on the knee with an unseen rubber hammer, testing his reflexes. . . . If he walks he is often humped like Atlas, bearing the world on his back. Now and then he may be moved to snatch his hat from his head and slam it to earth."[37]

Butts was the very definition of hard-nosed (and hard-headed)—during his playing days as an end at Mercer University, he once played an entire game without a helmet to impress his girlfriend and future wife, Winnie. Even after almost losing an ear, Butts refused any cranial protection.[38]

Butts hounded his players relentlessly on the practice field. One former player recalled the fiery Little Round Man chasing a Bulldog placekicker around the field, "repeatedly trying to kick him in the butt," after the kicker had missed several extra points in a practice. Athens High star quarterback Fran Tarkenton went on to play for UGA from 1958 to 1960 and recalled Butts's "dehumanizing coaching tirades" after a less than stellar performance the previous Saturday: "In practice the following Monday, Butts gave me the full barrage—language I just didn't think a coach was capable of using on a football player. Some really awful stuff. . . . Here was my head coach calling me names I had only seen on the washroom walls."[39]

Butts enjoyed playing mind games with his players, and he inexplicably benched Tarkenton after several sparkling performances in which the scrambling quarterback came off the bench to rally his team. Finally fed up with his abusive head coach, Tarkenton quit the team and was joined by his good friend (and future Auburn head football coach) Pat Dye. The two players had to be talked into reversing their decision to leave and returning to Georgia by freshman football coach Quinton Lumpkin.[40]

Coach Sellers, like his mentor, Wally Butts, demanded perfection from his players. He was harshly critical of mistakes made on the field, and his Sunday afternoon film sessions were legendary, with unlucky players forced to watch their miscues four, five, or even six times as their coach repeatedly rewound the 16mm film spool. He never complimented players for good or even great performances because, in the words of former Trojan Gary Travis, "that was what you were supposed to do."[41]

Former players described Sellers-led practices as being

more physically demanding than anything else they had done in their lives, including college and professional football, Army basic training, and Marine Corps boot camp at Parris Island. "Put a hat in his chest!" the coach would scream during drills as he urged his defenders to "form tackle." Bobby Poss recalled his drill sergeant at Fort Benning asking him how he achieved his excellent physical condition, and Poss credited Sellers's training regimen.[42]

Players ran from one drill to the next in practice. Describing his coach's hard-nosed approach, Fran Tarkenton said that Sellers "wrote the book on how to be a tough football coach. . . . If you lost a ball game Friday night, Weyman Sellers was the kind who would bring you back on the field Saturday morning and scrimmage you for four hours. At practices we would run a mile, take our exercises, run ten fifty-yard wind sprints, and *then* start playing football."[43]

Other players who committed real or imaginary transgressions were summoned back to an "extra practice" after the other players had headed to the locker room. These included the "dissipators"—players who had been caught smoking—who were forced to run until they dropped.

"He was the meanest man I have ever met," recalled Mike Epps, who played for Coach Sellers in the late 1960s. "He would be put in jail today. But it built a bond between the players, a close-knit fraternity for those who managed to live through it." Epps remembered one particularly harsh punishment meted out to a substitute named Stan Satterfield: "The game field was terraced above the practice field. Stan missed a block and had to stand behind the visitor's grandstand and hold the ball above his head in a 'Statue of Liberty' position, and eleven unblocked defensive players hit him. All twelve players tumbled over the side of the small cliff down to the practice field below. It was a miracle that no one was hurt."[44]

Coach Sellers would never cut players from the team. If,

for whatever reason, he did not want to keep a player, he would challenge the player by giving him extra work in practice and isolate the player from the rest of the team by prohibiting him from "dressing out" for games, excluding him from team meals, and not allowing him to ride the team bus to away games.

Bobby Poss recalled one Friday night away game that Athens won, but Sellers was dissatisfied with his team's performance. After the bus ride back to Athens High, Sellers turned on the stadium lights and held a practice that evening. After a particularly lackluster performance in the first half of another game, his players were heading to the dressing room at halftime when Sellers halted them and made them line up outside the door: "Whoa, whoa!" he screamed. "You are going to have to come through me first." Sellers, wearing a white short-sleeved dress shirt with a tie, khaki pants, and rubber-soled shoes, ordered each player to line up and rush at him. The coach delivered a forearm shiver to the pads and helmet of each onrushing player, and after the line was finished, he had a bloody forearm and a smashed wristwatch crystal.[45]

When confronting a player after a botched play, Sellers would grab the offender by the face mask and pull him into his face for a serious "chew-out session." Unlike Butts, he never really cursed out his players; his most used profanity was the relatively mild "Gosh Almighty, damn!" He gave almost every player a nickname—"Orangehead" or "Copperhead" for a ginger-haired player, "Pygmy" for a short one, and "Bobbycue" for Bobby Poss, whose family ran the iconic Poss' Barbecue on the Atlanta Highway.

Like Butts, Sellers was an offensive genius. Butts ran the traditional "T" formation at Georgia, but unlike other coaches of the era, he loved the forward pass. During UGA's national championship season in 1942, the Bulldogs passed a then-unheard-of thirty times in their Rose Bowl victory over UCLA. During his twenty-two-year tenure as UGA's head coach, Butts tutored future NFL quarterbacks Johnny Rauch, Zeke Bratkowski, and Fran Tarkenton.

While Sellers was more run oriented than Butts, he also was an innovator. He employed multiple offensive sets and was an early proponent of "hurry up" offenses, in which his team would quickly line up after the whistle had blown to end a play to catch the opposing defense off guard and out of position. His team's superior conditioning and tight discipline allowed the Trojans to thrive with the accelerated pace of action, and Sellers would scream from the sidelines at referees for not lining the ball up quickly enough. Poss recalled that Sellers never used a blackboard to diagram plays; he "just explained them."

He also ran an innovative defense, an early version of "Cover Two" that allowed defensive safeties to line up "in the box" and drop back into zone coverage in passing situations. Although he had both offensive and defensive coordinators who ran their respective teams in practices, Sellers took complete charge of both units during games.

Despite Athens High being a large school—it had an average enrollment of around one thousand students in the early 1960s—Sellers fielded teams that typically had fewer than forty players. Everyone knew how rigorous practices were, and this had the effect of weeding out many potential players who never bothered to try out. Others quit in the preseason rather than continuing to endure the hell of August two-a-days.

Practices were held at "the Ponderosa," the shade-free practice field down the hill from the high school. For a time a large oak tree at the end of the field provided some cover from the relentless sun, but it was cut down as part of a senior prank in 1964. Black residents of the adjacent Rocksprings projects would line the fence bordering the field to watch practices.

Water breaks were a luxury for football players in the

1960s—rehydration was a concept that did not break through the coaching ranks until a decade or two later. Athens High used a "filthy old garden hose that ran for five minutes before cold water would come out," remembered Doc Eldridge, who played for AHS in the late 1960s.[46] Players would get two or three gulps before they would have to pass the hose to a teammate. Salt tablets were taken before practice to restore the body's sodium/water equilibrium disrupted by the loss of fluids from massive perspiration. Paul Gilbert remembered that Sellers's practices were so intense that an *assistant coach* once vomited on the field.[47] One player, Morry Collins, threw up so frequently during practices that Sellers nicknamed him "uvula."

Mike Epps remembered that injuries infuriated Coach Sellers and were brushed aside unless bones were broken. "If your head hurt, you took an aspirin," agreed Bobby Poss. "If you hurt below the neck, you took a whirlpool bath or deep needle pain shots that scraped bone—Novocain, Xylocaine, and Cortisone."

Helmets were not the highly engineered versions of today that offer much better (albeit still imperfect) protection against hard hits to the head. Football helmets in the 1960s were made of hard plastic, with canvas suspension hanging from the inside and thin layers of covered foam on the interior to cushion blows to the forehead and the base of the skull. Almost all the players wore double-barred face masks that did not adequately shield the face and nose from errant or intentional flying elbows and churning knees. A concussion was brushed off as "getting your bell rung," and a player who suffered one walked it off or went to the sidelines for a few plays before returning to action.

It was not uncommon for Coach Sellers to become physically involved in practices. David Lester remembered a play when he was backing up in coverage on defense. Unbeknownst to him, Sellers was behind him and, feeling that Lester was out of position, delivered a ferocious forearm to his player's back, knocking Lester face down onto the turf. Terry Smart recalled a practice in which he took a handoff at running back and burst through a hole, seeing only open field ahead until Sellers hit him with a forearm to the chest: "I saw nothing but daylight until Sellers knocked the daylights out of me."[48]

For a team with a small number of players in an era in which most players played "both ways" (on offense and defense), superior conditioning was one of the most important weapons in the Athens High arsenal, particularly in the early games played in the September heat, when fatigue would often determine the outcome. Lewis Grizzard, who started his career in journalism covering Athens High sports, noted, "A Sellers-coached team could double time to Macon and back and never miss a beat. He was a D.I. in shorts."[49]

Weyman Sellers was a man who craved control, and smaller-sized squads allowed him to exert it more easily. The numbers on uniforms were specific to position groups—guards had numbers in the sixties, tackles had numbers in the seventies, and so on, with no deviations—and certainly no single-digit number would ever appear on a Trojan jersey. Sellers's grueling practices ran like clockwork. And the comportment of his players—who always walked rather than ran to the sidelines after finishing their pregame warm-ups, so as to exude a businesslike nonchalance—was designed to strike uncertainty and even fear into the hearts of opponents. Players stood on the side of the field with their helmets on; kneeling or sitting on the bench was not permitted.

Coach Sellers was viewed as much more than a high school football coach in Athens; as was typical for someone who held that exalted position in a small city of that era, he was also considered a role model and a pillar of the community. His name and image appeared regularly in the Athens newspapers, and frequently in the Atlanta newspapers as well, and he had a forty-five-minute "coach's show" on local radio station WRFC on Monday nights. Sellers was also an active member of Beech Haven Baptist Church and, through his ownership of Trojan Laundry, a businessman, and he was closely connected to the town's power elite, many of whom were former players and contributing boosters of the athletic program at Athens High.

But as the 1960s began, Coach Sellers and the Athens business power brokers would soon be forced to grapple with the delicate issue of integration, which the city had postponed or ignored throughout the 1950s even as much of the country openly confronted its "separate but equal" demons of the past.

CHAPTER 2
THE TOWN

Athens didn't experience the sixties until the seventies.
—Pete McCommons

In the early 1960s, the boundaries of Athens consisted mainly of a hilly inverted triangle of land in the Middle Piedmont nestled between the North Oconee and Middle Oconee Rivers, their murky waters stained a deep rusty hue by the iron ore found in the ubiquitous North Georgia clay. These boundaries did not, of course, include East Athens, the flatter, more rural, and less populated area of town, which is bisected by Highway 78 (the "Lexington Highway") and is home to the city's airport, Athens–Ben Epps. In the 1950s and early 1960s, East Athens was still largely rural, with textile mills hugging the fringes of the riverbank and farmland stretching eastward toward Madison and Oglethorpe Counties.

A series of north/south ridgelines that unfold eastward from the North Oconee River geologically define the heart of Athens. Each ridge is interspersed with ancient narrow creek or river valleys that make driving west along Broad Street until it becomes the Atlanta Highway feel like an extended roller-coaster ride. The north/south ridges are flanked by one western ridge on Washington Street that peaks at 761 feet above sea level; this is the city's highest point, atop of which sits the Beaux-Arts-style Athens City Hall, guarded by the famously defective double-barreled Civil War cannon.

The "town and gown" were largely indistinguishable in the early 1960s, when the University of Georgia was easily the largest employer in Athens and Clarke County. On an absolute basis, UGA still remains the biggest job engine in the city and county, but Athens is no longer merely a "company town" almost entirely reliant on the growth prospects of the state's flagship university.

Outsiders still largely define the city of Athens as the University of Georgia campus and its thriving downtown. The far end of North Campus, where the famous Arch is located, spills directly onto Broad Street and the southern edge of downtown, and the western and eastern borders of downtown are the well-trodden stretch between Pulaski and Thomas Streets; the northern border of downtown is generally regarded as Dougherty Street. In 1960, the rather staid downtown area was cloaked in an Eisenhower-era grayness, a far different world from the bustling restaurant, bar, and boutique entertainment center that downtown Athens is today. There were few places to eat—the iconic fast-food eatery the Varsity, at College and Broad Streets (where a Chick-Fil-A is located today), the Snack Shack, and Tony's, a diner that served breakfast and a $2 dinner plate of spaghetti for hungry students (in a space later occupied by Rocky's Pizzeria and Amici's). Other than those choices, the downtown eating options were limited to a handful of "meat and threes," like the Mayflower (which sadly closed in the autumn of 2023). According to Pete McCommons, who attended UGA in the late 1950s and early 1960s, there was "nothing to do downtown, no hangout spot. It would be years before UGA students would remain in Athens after graduating to open small businesses in the downtown area."[1]

Architecturally, the heart of the commercial downtown district in 1960 featured most of the landmark structures that are still present today, including the Neo-Classical Revival Georgian Hotel, the Morton Building, the nine-story, 168-room Holman Hotel (now the Bank of America building), the Streamline Moderne–style Greyhound bus station (now a seafood restaurant), and the Farmer's Hardware building. Other architectural styles on display ranged from Renaissance Revival, Second Empire, and Greek Revival to the more functional late nineteenth-century and early twentieth-century adjoining two- and three-story brick buildings that still command steep rents from small businesses in the 2020s.

Downtown was dominated by four massive department stores—Davison's, J. C. Penney, Sears, Roebuck, and Gallant-Belk. These stores extended in a north-south direction across entire city blocks and on a hot day offered air-conditioned shortcuts to those wishing to avoid the walk all the way to College Avenue to reach the east-west arteries of Broad, Clayton, and Washington Streets.

There were churches, law offices, banks, and the classic family-owned clothiers George Dean's and Dick Ferguson's. Horton's Drug Store was (and still is) across the street from the Georgia Theatre, which featured newly released movies and matinee specials for the children on weekends. McGregor Company on Clayton Street, in business since the early twentieth century, supplied Athens with printing services, stationery, and other business supplies.

The nation's third-oldest chartered YMCA covered a city block at Broad and Lumpkin. Built in 1919, the sprawling, fortresslike structure with athletic fields in the back was where thousands of young, White male Athenians were initiated into sports. The building featured a 1,200-square-foot swimming pool, where swimming trunks were prohibited. The gymnasium included a running track slung low above the basketball court. In its early years both the University of Georgia and Athens High School basketball teams played their games in the YMCA gym, and they enjoyed a distinct home-court advantage—due to the overhanging balcony, shots at the basket had to have low-trajectory arcs.[2]

As in many cities in the United States, both man-made and natural barriers—railroad tracks, main thoroughfares, deep valleys—isolated Athens's African American population from the surrounding White neighborhoods. The Black population in Athens was also diffused into different areas of the city based largely on proximity to work and the lack of private or public transportation options. The African American neighborhoods clustered off Hancock Extension mainly housed the domestic workers who labored in the White homes in adjacent Cobbham; the Black side streets off the historic streetcar suburb of Boulevard provided easy access to the nearby century-old White-owned homes. Linnentown, up Baxter Hill from Sanford Stadium, was within walking distance for the custodians and maintenance workers who toiled on the ever-expanding North and South Campuses of UGA. Black families working in agriculture tended to cluster in the still largely rural spaces of East Athens.

Located on the "Hot Corner" at the intersection of Washington and Hull Streets in downtown Athens was the four-story Morton Building, built by Black entrepreneur and local postmaster Monroe Morton. At one time considered "the largest Black-owned building of its kind in the world," the Morton Building was the center of Black business and culture in Athens for decades—the first floor offered office space to Athens's Black doctors, dentists, jewelers, and other small businessmen, and the second and third floors housed the five-hundred-seat Morton Theatre. After it opened in 1910, the Morton Theatre initially drew vaudeville acts before later bringing in top jazz and blues names like Cab Calloway, Ma Rainey, Louis Armstrong, Bessie Smith, and Duke Ellington. The theater had long been shuttered by the early 1960s, but the building still provided office space to Black professionals and businessmen.[3]

In addition to the concentration of Black-owned businesses at the Hot Corner, pool halls and bootleggers offered entertainment to African American customers in the north downtown neighborhood known as "the Bottom," where Bethel Homes now stands.[4] There was also a cluster of Black-owned businesses at Pope and Hancock, including Charlie Morton's poolroom, renowned for the pig ear sandwiches served there. The White businesses downtown allowed Black customers, "as long as we didn't try to get something to eat or drink," recalled Elizabeth Platt. The downtown Varsity restaurant had a walk-up window for African American patrons, who were not allowed to dine inside.

Flanking the Bottom on the downtown side was a row of five Texaco gasoline storage tanks. Storing seventy-five thousand gallons of gasoline next to a heavily populated area dotted with old wood-framed homes was a disaster waiting to happen, and in the summer of 1970, the disaster occurred. Three of the five tanks exploded when a Gainesville trucker was transferring gasoline from his truck to a tank and fumes were ignited by a pilot light, sending flames five hundred feet into the night, injuring forty people, and causing over $1 million worth of damage. Luckily, almost all the old "shanty" houses built as far back as the Reconstruction era had been replaced a year earlier by the newly constructed Bethel Homes Apartments, which were much sturdier and less flammable but still were rendered uninhabitable until the blown-out windows and damaged walls could be replaced and restored.[5]

Owned by Armell Stroud. a Burney-Harris High School art teacher who also owned a liquor store on West Broad, the House of Blue Lights in East Athens attracted Black customers looking to "drink, carouse, and dance." On Saturday nights, overflow crowds packed the Black VFW (the "V") for a drink and spilled out onto Glen Haven Avenue when the crowds inside grew too dense.

Unlike today, downtown Athens was ringed by industry. Fronting Thomas Street—where the Hilton Garden Inn is currently located—was the massive Benson's Bakery, which wafted a fresh-baked-bread aroma through downtown. Founded in 1918 by W. Howard Benson, the company had expanded into fruitcake in the 1950s and built a new facility in nearby Bogart to produce the candied fruit holiday treat. As part of a fifteen-year partnership with the university, hundreds of UGA students earned extra money during the holiday season by fanning out across the country selling Benson's fruitcakes to churches and other nonprofits.[6]

Downhill from downtown, toward the river and railroad track, were the Hanna Manufacturing Company baseball bat factory, a warehouse district, and Chicopee Mills.

The Hanna bat factory took up two city blocks and also housed the ticket office for the Central of Georgia Railway. The factory's best-known product was the "Batrite" bat, made from ash wood transported by rail from the forests of the Northeast. Baseball players such as Babe Ruth, Lou Gehrig, Johnny Mize, and Mel Ott visited the plant and ordered custom-made bats from Hanna, and at its peak, the factory employed 125 workers.[7]

Chicopee Mills' history could be traced back to the earliest days of Athens, when four men formed the Athens Manufacturing Company in 1828. The company eventually owned textile operations on both sides of the North Oconee River. Johnson and Johnson purchased Athens Manufacturing in 1950 and produced cotton and wool yarns used for medical gauze and diapers.[8]

Most of the textile manufacturing occurred in East Athens, where Chicopee had its largest mill in the old Cook and Brother Confederate Armory at Cedar Shoals. East Athens—east of the North Oconee River—resembled a typical mill town, with small "shotgun" houses built close together and the mill providing everything from schools to cemeteries. Some mills set up schools on-site for the children they employed—child labor was widespread until 1938, when Congress passed the Fair Labor Standards Act. Notwithstanding the daily grind of physically demanding work in dark, loud, and sometimes dangerous facilities, mill workers and their families experienced a sense of togetherness, where "everyone looked after each other's kids," and community life was centered on local churches, sports, and shops. Although segregation was strictly enforced—Chicopee did not integrate its mills until the 1970s—White and Black families lived close to and knew each other.[9]

As Calvin Trillin noted in his book *An Education in Georgia*, the city of Athens had always been more progressive minded than the university.[10] The members of the Board of Regents and the segregationist governors who appointed them could not resist meddling with the state's flagship university. In 1941 Governor Eugene Talmadge fired Walter Cocking, the dean of UGA's School of Education and a popular Athenian, due to his support for integration, and the Board of Regents members who had supported Cocking were also fired. This blatantly political move cost the university its accreditation. But Athens was, by the standards of the time, an isolated liberal bastion in northeast Georgia; since 1932 it had voted, usually overwhelmingly, against the staunchly segregationist Talmadges—first Eugene and then his son, Herman—in their gubernatorial contests.[11]

To foster a more favorable business climate, local Athens businessmen like John P. Bondurant II and Howard Benson and others active in business-oriented civic organizations like the Athens Chamber of Commerce and the Athens Area Industrial Management Group—a group of top managers from thirty different companies—began to acknowledge the creeping reality of school integration. Bondurant, who headed the Athens Lumber Company for decades and served on the Athens City Council, spoke bluntly in a 1959 letter to Georgia's segregationist governor, Ernest Vandiver: "I do not believe that we can remain completely segregated, whether or not that is our desire. . . . I was brought up in a segregated society and have never known any other. However, I am a realist and I am one of the millions of Georgians who do not expect to see the schools of Georgia remain closed for any period of time."[12] (Georgia law at the time required a cutoff in state funding to any school system that permitted integration.)

Starting in the 1950s, local business and civic leaders began actively courting large-sized light industrial and manufacturing companies to build new plant facilities in or near Athens. These firms had headquarters located in the Midwest and Northeast, and they had transitioned decades earlier to an integrated workforce using skilled and semiskilled Black workers, many of whom had moved from their homes in the South to pursue greater economic opportunities in the North as part of the "Great Migration." School integration in Athens was therefore in alignment with the commercial goal of convincing northern firms to bring higher-paying jobs to the city, and the possibility of school closures would have offset all the positive attributes that the city fathers had to offer, such as proximity to a major university and an increasingly educated but nonunionized labor force.

Many northern firms were convinced by the sales pitches of the business elite and the small-town charm of Athens and built plants in the area. In 1951, Dairy-Pak, a Cleveland, Ohio, company, opened a factory on the northern outskirts of town that made juice and milk packaging. In 1954, the General Time Corporation, a manufacturer of alarm and wall clocks, opened a $2.5 million facility that employed six hundred men and women. The Westinghouse Electric Corporation built a plant to manufacture electrical transformers on the north side of town in 1957, and seventy-five technicians and executives moved their families from Sharon, Pennsylvania, to Athens.[13]

Like their counterparts in Atlanta, the business and civic elite in Athens were also concerned about the image of their city, and the lawlessness promoted by demagogic White segregationist politicians appalled them, as did the threat to public education posed by the nightmarish scenario of the state cutting off public funding to schools that integrated. They were also undoubtedly acting from a standpoint of pragmatism and out of concern for their own commercial interests, which were now inextricably linked with integration. They realized that shutting down UGA—which appeared to be a real possibility, as Black student applicants and their attorneys slowly chipped away at the legal defenses that blocked the students from admittance to Georgia—would have created an economic and public relations disaster for Athens at the very time they were seeking to attract more outside investment to the Classic City. Later in the early 1960s, John Bondurant and R. B. Hally, head of the General Time factory and leader of the Athens Chamber of Commerce, would publicly praise Dean William Tate for his efforts in ending segregation at UGA.[14]

One of the main charms of today's Athens—its inclusive and tolerant culture, with a thriving arts and music scene—was slowly starting to emerge in the 1960s, and decades later it would be touted by Chamber of Commerce pitchmen as a key quality-of-life selling point to those considering a move to the Classic City.

But in 1960, Athens did not unabashedly exude much of the hedonistic vibe that it does today. Liquor was not available for sale in the Classic City in 1960; the town's Baptist and Methodist churches kept a watchful eye on any local politician foolhardy enough to suggest permitting the legal sale of spirits. Liquor by the drink was not approved in restaurants and bars until 1969. Those who wanted to buy the "hard stuff" would drive an hour across the South Carolina border to McCormick or Calhoun Falls. It was also important to have friends who journeyed frequently to Atlanta, and good friends would take multiple orders and bring back a trunk full of bourbon.

Beer was available for purchase at "$5 a case" in Arcade, a small Jackson County hamlet fifteen miles north of Athens that for years was able to offer cheap beer due to minimal local taxes on alcohol sales. In the 1950s and 1960s, Arcade was a sudsy oasis in a desert of dry counties in northeast Georgia. For instance, Gainesville, the largest city in northeast Georgia after Athens, did not legally go "wet" until the mid-1970s. Arthur Parr's package store in Arcade off the Gainesville Highway did a booming business with college kids from Athens; saving a dollar on a case of beer was well worth the gas money for the thirty-mile round trip. Some estimate that 95 percent of the beer shipped to Arcade never went into a retail establishment but instead went directly onto trucks serving the dry counties of North Georgia. Even trains passing by on the tracks that ran parallel to the Gainesville Highway would make unscheduled stops to load up on beer at Parr's.[15]

While the Arcade-based racket of distributing beer to dry counties was relatively benign—it simply reduced the inconvenience for buyers stymied by the restrictive laws in their own counties—the crime problem both in Athens and in the surrounding counties of Barrow, Jackson, and Banks was much more sinister in the early 1960s.

The "Dixie Mafia," a loose confederation of rural White thugs, entered the public consciousness in the 1960s. The Dixie Mafia was indifferent as to which type of illicit activity it engaged in, as long as it was profitable. Its criminal pursuits ranged from moonshine production and distribution to loan-sharking, contract assassinations, arson, narcotics trafficking, prostitution, car theft, and running "chop shops."

Perhaps the best-known member of the Dixie Mafia in Georgia was Billy Sunday Birt of Winder, which is just a fifteen-mile drive from Athens. Birt's favorite Athens hangout was a notorious bar owned by Reese Spencer, the Night Owl Lounge, on the Atlanta Highway. Birt spent his time at the smoky, dimly lit lounge gambling huge sums of cash in high-stakes poker games, drinking, dancing, and carousing.[16]

Birt thundered through Athens in his Mercury Cyclone, which could reach speeds of more than 160 mph and could outrun any police car in North Georgia. His son Stoney loved Lum's hotdogs—their famous "hot dogs steamed in beer" were wildly popular for a brief time in the 1960s, and the Lum's franchise in Athens was owned by Dixie Mafia cohort C. W. Royster. When the public's ardor for beer-steamed hot dogs—with "sherry-flavored sauerkraut" available as a side item—inevitably faded, the downtown restaurant mysteriously burned down.

Another Dixie Mafia kingpin was A. D. Allen of Commerce, about twenty miles north of Athens. His specialties were moonshine, stolen cars, and chop shops. Local Jimmy Klein recalled Allen racing his "stolen '55 and '56 Chevys up Tallassee Road in Athens until it ended, and he would turn right and head to Commerce."[17]

Lifelong Athens resident Bobby Poss needed a 3-deuce manifold for the 1964 Chevy he had received from his parents on his sixteenth birthday. Thurmond's—the used parts dealer off the Atlanta Highway that sold auto parts with the "serial numbers shaved off"—did not have the part he needed, so he drove to a "chicken farm" in Pendergrass owned by Dixie Mafia chieftain A. C. "Cliff" Park. "Those chicken houses," Poss recalled, "were filled with nothing but auto parts." Poss paid the chop shop for his manifold and left without asking any questions.[18]

In 1967 Cliff Park paid $5,500 for the contract killing of Jackson County solicitor general Floyd Hoard, who had raided one of Park's moonshine warehouses. The contract killer hired by Park wired as many as twelve sticks of dynamite to the ignition system of Hoard's Ford Galaxie; Hoard was killed instantly in his garage while his wife and children were inside their home. Hoard's wife had planned on taking their children in the car that morning to run errands; it was only a fluke that prevented an even greater tragedy—Hoard typically drove the Galaxie to work each day, and by force of habit, he cranked it up that morning.[19]

Before being arrested, Park showed up at Hoard's funeral and signed the registry.[20]

The lawlessness in Jackson County was so distressing in the 1960s that the two U.S. congressmen representing northeast Georgia, Phil Landrum and Robert Stephens, would half-jokingly argue with each other during redistricting about who would have to absorb the county into his congressional district.[21]

By 1960, corruption and lawlessness in Athens had also reached crisis levels. Not trusting his own police department, Mayor Ralph Snow pleaded with *Atlanta Constitution* investigative reporter Jack Nelson to come to Athens to report on prostitution, gambling, and illegal liquor sales.

Athens had developed into the illegal slot machine center of Georgia, and an Athens businessman operated an illegal slot machine factory at Chambers Music Company, a front where between five hundred and six hundred slot machines were manufactured and stored, awaiting distribution to private clubs in Athens and to other locations in Georgia. Some of the most prominent citizens of Athens, including businessmen and university officials, belonged to the private clubs that allowed gambling and underage drinking. Nelson was able to capture on film a uniformed Athens policeman talking with a slot machine repairman inside the Chambers Music facility.[22]

The situation with prostitution had also reached a boiling point. Mayor Snow told Nelson that the four houses of prostitution in Athens had offered him $400 a week to look the other way and allow them to stay in business. "I rejected the bribe," said Snow, "and informed the man who offered it—a prominent Athens businessman—that I would do everything in my power to keep the houses from operating."[23]

The prostitution business was so well developed that cab drivers would pick up customers across the street from the Athens Police Department and drive them to the "River Street cathouses." Each customer would pay the cabdriver in full for his visit; the cabdriver would in turn direct the customer to tell the greeter at the door of the brothel that "driver number 'x'" had sent them, so that he could be reimbursed.[24]

Athens leaders had for years looked the other way when it came to prostitution. One former Athens mayor confided to me in a private conversation, "The prostitutes kept the sailors over at the Naval Supply Corps School out of trouble."

The local brothels were also a haven for young men attending the University of Georgia, who outnumbered female students by a ratio of two to one and were under the watchful eye of the university's dean of men, William "Bill" Tate, who was dedicated to his *in loco parentis* role as guardian on behalf of his beloved university. He was even known to barge into off-campus motel rooms if he suspected his students of shacking up.[25]

Effie Matthews owned the city's best-known bordello, a rambling two-story structure with wood-burning stoves anchoring both ends. (One former UGA assistant football coach regaled his physical education students with stories of how he worked out a barter deal with Effie: he chopped and split Effie's firewood for the winter in exchange for "services.") UGA fraternities would "pass the hat," with each participant chipping in a dollar, and the brother drawing the lucky number would win a trip to Effie's. A wooden covered bridge, on which the words "UGA Students Vote Yes for Effie" were painted in red, led to Effie's four houses on

Elm Street, and a well-known drinking song celebrated the charms of the famous rite-of-passage establishment:

> Down around the county line
> There's a great big neon sign
> Saying "Everybody welcome. Come on in."
> If you stop in for a while
> You will come out with a smile.
> It's that little place called Effie's House of Sin.

Another Athens native recalled spending an afternoon at Effie's before playing a football game for Athens High School on a Saturday night: "Coach Sellers told us to stay off our feet during the day. . . . I did that over at Effie's, for $7.50. . . . I learned that there was no truth to avoiding sex before games, because it might waste your energy. . . . I won offensive player of the game after my performance on the field that night."

Effie was a woman of mystery. She was from the Midwest and "just showed up in Athens on a train one day." She generally maintained a low profile, except for occasional random and unannounced visits to Athens Little League baseball games. She was an anonymous donor to the Little League program and would show up for games "dressed like she was at the Kentucky Derby."[26] When she passed away in 1966 at age 79, she allegedly left a large estate.

Jack Nelson's investigative work led to eight indictments and the temporary closure of Effie's. Slot machines disappeared from Athens, and sales of alcohol to minors dropped dramatically after a police crackdown. This happened even though Mayor Snow, under public pressure, turned on Nelson and accused him of "trying to picture Athens as a Phenix City," referring to the Alabama city across the Chattahoochee River from Fort Benning, Georgia, that was a notorious den of vice during the 1950s.[27]

After it reopened, Effie's managed an uneasy coexistence with city officials until it was shut down in 1974 by a reform-minded district attorney. In 1977, the Athens Fire Department burned down the building in a training exercise, and an enterprising former postal worker gathered the bricks and sold them as tagged and numbered souvenirs that quickly became coveted collector's items. The city's recycling center now stands where Effie's was once located, much to the hilarity of its aging former patrons.

╫╫╫

Autumn was ushered in each September by the first appearance of the garish posters announcing the return of the Clyde Beatty and Cole Brothers Circus. The circus was held at a huge fairground on Hawthorne Avenue, and the main attraction was the two-hour-long "Big Top" show featuring the standard lineup of clowns, performing elephants, jugglers, and trapeze artists. There were also sideshows featuring human physical oddities such as "Princess Anne," the world's smallest woman, and a much-whispered-about "hoochie koochie" show.

The circus was followed in late October by the county fair, which drew long lines for whiplash-inducing rides such as the Octopus, Twirler, Skyway, and Toboggan. The fair also featured sideshows, including a preserved corpse that was allegedly that of the world's largest man, an "Amazon" who was 9'2" tall and weighed four hundred pounds. As was the case for the circus, African Americans and Whites attended the county fair on separate days. Richard Appleby, a young African American adolescent who lived in the nearby Brooklyn Apartments, was keenly aware of the injustice of segregation, but he still enjoyed the charms of the fair as any young boy would, especially the food: "Cotton candy, hot dogs, candied apples, I ate it all!" he recalled.[28]

The Downtowner Motor Inn in the Five Points area had an unofficial "titty bar" that attracted big crowds of people, many of whom would head across the street after the show to Harry's Drive-In (where Five Points Bottle Shop is now located) for burgers, with carhop service in the front and beer sold—if you knew the right person—in the back. Some nights, local legend Terry "Mad Dog" Melton—who starred as an athlete at Athens High School in the 1950s—would sit on the hood of his 1956 Corvette in the parking lot of Harry's and drink beer while singing and playing guitar in front of small crowds. Other nights he would play at "the Canteen," a teenage club in Memorial Park, or at Allen's, the hamburger and beer joint in Normaltown later memorialized by local group the B-52's in their hit song "Deadbeat Club." Melton passed on a football scholarship to UGA to concentrate on his true love, music; he played in local bands such as Dixie Grease and was later instrumental in the formation of the Normaltown Flyers and in starting Athens's first live concert venue, the Last Resort.[29]

Eccentric attitudes flourished in Athens, and "look the other way" libertarianism coexisted uneasily with the more traditional mores that typically defined the surface values of a midsized southern city during that time. Several individuals from that era personified the unconventional behavior that most Athenians tolerated, if not fully embraced.

Ed Weeks, a World War II veteran and former track athlete at UGA, was known as the ubiquitous "Sandwich Board Man" who walked the streets of downtown advertising local businesses. Rain or shine, he could be spotted wearing his trademark fedora and mackintosh, and he would perform impromptu poetry readings on the courthouse steps when the mood struck him. Dubbed "the People's Poet," Weeks set out on a walk from Athens to New York City to generate publisher interest in his book of poetry. While the walk did not result in a book contract, his dispatches to the *Athens Observer* included the unforgettable headline "Weeks Weak After Week's Walk."[30]

Fred Birchmore was a talented musician and gymnast who graduated from UGA with a master's in English and a law degree. While studying abroad in Germany in the 1930s, he traveled to Egypt on vacation and lost his identification papers while there. Knowing that the German authorities would not readmit him without his papers, Birchmore bicycled across the Sinai Peninsula, through Iran and Afghanistan, down the Khyber Pass into India, and from there to Southeast Asia. While in Manila, he booked passage to the United States and then piloted the ship after the crew went on strike. His parents were waiting for him in San Francisco, lest he try to bicycle across the country back to his home in Athens. His bicycle, which he dubbed "Bucephalus," is held at the Smithsonian Museum. His two-year journey, which was prolonged by a bout of malaria, left him with one habit he could not part with—sleeping outdoors. He was able to accommodate his newly adopted nocturnal slumber routine by sleeping on the roof of his house in Athens, which he named Happy Hollow. He celebrated his wedding by taking his wife on a 4,500-mile trip through Latin America on a "two-seater" bicycle. He later earned his pilot's license, served as a gunnery officer on convoy duty on the Atlantic with the U.S. Navy during World War II, and wrote several books about his traveling experiences. He also founded a highly successful Athens-based realty firm. Always seeking a new project, he enjoyed driving around Athens hunting for large rocks that were suitable for the massive stone wall he was building in his back yard. Birchmore died at the age of ninety-nine in 2012.[31]

Herschel Carithers was a World War II pilot who won multiple awards, including a Distinguished Flying Cross and an Air Medal with oak leaf cluster. After retiring from the Air Force, he took a job as an airplane pilot for Benson's Bakery, and one day in 1963 he decided to fly his plane through the Coliseum, the new arena under construction that would eventually replace the ancient Woodruff Hall. He passed by the massive construction crane and buzzed the floor of the new arena before ascending and flying the short distance back to Ben Epps Field. He was arrested as soon as he got off the plane and was stripped of his pilot's license. "It was worth it," he reportedly said. "I always wanted to do that."[32]

Alva "Bobo" Holloman moved to Athens when he was seventeen and became the most unlikely pitcher to ever throw a no-hitter in Major League Baseball. Pitching for the St. Louis Browns as an out-of-shape, overweight journeyman making his first appearance as a starter, Holloman became only the third pitcher in league history to hurl a no-hitter in his first outing. Exhausted and sweating profusely throughout a game that fewer than 2,500 fans attended, Bobo was bailed out by several miracle catches by teammates and some well-timed rain delays that gave him the chance to catch his breath and recuperate. Three months later, plagued by a sore arm, he was cut by the Browns and never played baseball again.[33] He moved back to Athens, where he worked as a truck driver and ran his own advertising agency. On weekends Holloman worked as a high school football referee, and after games he and his crew (which included my father) would gather at the Arctic Girl fast-food joint on West Broad. Glenn Harben, the owner, would set up a makeshift bar in the back after hours, and the referees would drink beer and roar with laughter as they recalled the highlights and miscues from that night's game. In those days, the GHSA—the organization governing athletics and activities for member high schools in Georgia—did not prohibit locals from officiating the games played in their towns. One night, Athenian Wilbur Paul officiated an Athens High School game against Georgia Military Academy; after a fumble, Paul looked into the pile of players and screamed, "Our ball!"

Every Southern town and smallish city had its own unique group of "characters," and Athens had the advantage of being home to a major university, which helped to incubate and develop quirky personalities. This insouciance toward nonconformists was also crucial in helping Athens transform itself from a sleepy southern town into a world-recognized alternative arts and music hub in the 1970s and beyond.

Arguably, the "live and let live" mentality and tolerance of most Athenians somewhat softened the ground for a progressive agenda stressing civil rights and anti-war politics that would increasingly shape the rest of the decade. Nonetheless, while these attitudes might have greased the wheels for change, there would be many rough days ahead as the local public schools began to wrestle with the arduous process of integration. Fortunately for both the town and its schools, the "gown" would soon break the first wall of resistance in the status quo that had fervently guarded a separate-but-equal status among White and Black students in Athens for almost a century after the conclusion of the Civil War.

CHAPTER 3

THE GOWN

The Court may force your school to enroll Negro students,
but it cannot alter your attitude towards the Negro. You can,
if you so desire, ignore his presence, refuse to accept him in
your fraternities, and make him feel completely unwanted as
a member of your group. Social ostracism, if implemented
without violence, is a most powerful weapon.

—O. C. Aderhold, UGA president, in a statement to students after
a federal court ordered immediate integration of his school

Omer Clyde ("O. C.") Aderhold, president of the University
of Georgia at the beginning of 1961, was "an engaging, sympathetic man who took a personal interest in his students,
his employees, and his many other friends."[1] He resembled
a more avuncular version of then vice president elect Lyndon Johnson, with his horn-rimmed glasses, wide, bulbous
nose, and thinning hair combed backward from the crown
of his head. Aderhold was also a cautious man, and he had
remained mostly silent in response to the dizzying sequence
of events that unfolded on his watch during the first two
weeks of 1961.

Like Georgia governor Ernest Vandiver, Aderhold, the son of a farmer, hailed from Lavonia, Georgia, a small town just across the border from South Carolina. Aderhold had graduated from UGA in 1923 with a degree in agriculture.

After obtaining his PhD from Ohio State University, Aderhold returned to Athens in 1947 to assume the role of dean of the College of Education. In 1950, he was named president of the university and almost immediately was confronted with the conundrum of integration.

Administratively, the University of Georgia was a very different place in the early 1960s from what it is today. Back then the thirteen schools were autonomous fiefdoms that operated with little oversight from the president; it was not until the late twentieth and early twenty-first centuries that power was heavily centralized in a top-down, corporate-type structure. The relative independence of the university's schools allowed a midcentury administrator like Aderhold—who was, in the words of former student and faculty member Pete McCommons, "courtly, kind, and bumbling"—to preside in a largely detached role overseeing the school's thirteen deans.

Nonetheless, Aderhold had notable accomplishments he could point to. For example, the percentage of professors on the university's faculty with a PhD had risen from 27 percent in the early 1950s to 47 percent ten years later.[2] The sleek and visionary new Georgia Center for Continuing Education—funded by a grant from the Kellogg Foundation—combined hotel, conference, and modern classroom accommodations and was considered both conceptually and architecturally groundbreaking. The massive Science Center, tucked behind the south stands of Sanford Stadium on "Science Hill," was completed in 1960, and more capital projects were underway on the university's South Campus. The university had also sold the fifty-eight acres of the old "Normal School" property off Prince Avenue to the U.S. Navy Supply Corps School, recently relocated from Bayonne, New Jersey, and the new Main Library, with its eye-catching blend of modernist and classical architecture, anchored the south end of the North Campus quad. The university was slowly climbing the ladder from sleepy southern land-grant institution to respectable, nationally recognized public university.

But the thorny issue of integrating the school had nagged Aderhold throughout his first decade as president. His situation was not unique in the South—only two of the twelve members of the Southeastern Conference, the University of Florida and the University of Kentucky, had successfully integrated their schools by 1961. The University of Alabama experimented briefly with integration in 1956 when Autherine Lucy was enrolled as a graduate student before being suspended three days later "for her own safety" due to rioting by opponents of integration.

In 1952, Horace T. Ward, a Black man from LaGrange, Georgia, sued for admission into the University of Georgia School of Law after his application had been denied. Aderhold spearheaded an effective delay strategy, the intent of which was to frustrate any African American applicant who hoped to be admitted to UGA until they ultimately just gave up. Bureaucratic roadblocks were thrown up, such as a requirement for new examinations, and the state's Board of Regents—the group of political appointees who govern the university system of Georgia—had helpfully installed new admission requirements: all UGA law school applicants had to have a letter of recommendation from a law school alumnus as well as a letter from a superior court judge in the area where the applicant resided. The stall tactics worked: shortly after the lawsuit was filed, Ward was drafted into the U.S. Army; by the time he completed his military service, he was eager to embark upon his career and accepted a spot at the Northwestern University School of Law. A federal judge subsequently threw out the lawsuit against UGA because, in his judgment, it had been rendered "moot" due to Ward's admission into another law school.[3]

Aderhold attempted the same strategy with African American students Charlayne Hunter and Hamilton Holmes after they applied to UGA in July 1959 and were denied admission. The two applicants sued the university, and Aderhold and UGA registrar Walter Danner simply brushed aside their complaints with the explanation that the applicants' objections were not in the "proper form." In subsequent applications, a transcript was missing, or the application was received past the deadline or simply "never received," or there were problems with transfer credits. Or there was no dormitory space available for Ms. Hunter—UGA required all women students under the age of twenty-three to live either on campus or in a sorority house. When something such as the alumni endorsement requirement was deemed unconstitutional, the university would appeal to a higher court until all appeals were exhausted and then challenge a different court ruling in favor of the applicants. During an interview for admission, Holmes was asked if he had ever been to a "house of prostitution" or a "beatnik place" or a "tea parlor."[4] He was judged by his interviewers to be evasive on a question about a speeding ticket. But the policy of obfuscation and the successful use of legal and administrative stall tactics would soon come to a head, as the calendar turned to what would be an epochal year for the university, Athens, and the state of Georgia.

On Tuesday, January 11, 1961, the University of Georgia Bulldogs played a game of college basketball against their ancient rivals from Atlanta, the Georgia Tech Yellow Jackets. The game was played on the campus of UGA at Woodruff Hall, the creaky, three-thousand-seat, multipurpose auditorium that was derisively referred to as "the Barn" due to its drafts and persistent problem with leaks. Adolph Rupp, the legendary basketball coach at the University of Kentucky, called Woodruff Hall "the only arena in the SEC where wind is a factor." Later in the 1961 season, during a game against Ole Miss, water dripping from holes in the rotting ceiling forced game officials to wrap the scoreboard at the end of the arena in towels, and players "cautiously avoided moving into that area [underneath the scoreboard]."[5]

Georgia entered play with an eight-game losing streak against Georgia Tech, but this miserable stretch of frustration seemed to be nearing an end as time wound down on the back-and-forth game. Georgia guard Allan Jackson hit a jump shot with twelve seconds left, giving the Bulldogs a two-point lead. On the ensuing inbounds play, Georgia tied up Tech on the far end of the court, and the Yellow Jackets were forced to frantically call a time-out, leaving Tech the near-impossible task of driving the length of the court to score with two seconds left in the game.

Many Athenians still say that the timekeeper, a local named Bob Bowen, was slow starting the clock after the inbounds pass. Maybe that half second or so of additional time was needed by Roger Kaiser, Tech's All-American guard, who grabbed a pass and threw up a desperation heave just beyond midcourt that made a perfect arc through the drafty, cold, and hazy air of the Barn before finding the bottom of the net. The forty-foot shot was worth only two points back then, so the game went into overtime, but the outcome seemed preordained after Kaiser's miracle basket. A dispirited Georgia team ended up losing by nine; that point differential also matched the Bulldogs' losing streak against the Engineers after their defeat that evening.

The crowd in Woodruff Hall was mostly students, who had just returned from Christmas break and had started their winter quarter classes. As they sat in stunned silence, a former Georgia football letterman yelled, "Let's go get 'em!" Everyone knew who "'em" were.

University of Georgia administrators were aware of the potential for violence that evening, and some had proposed cancelling the basketball game, seeing it as a potential staging area for rioters—it was a short walk up the hill from Woodruff Hall to Center Myers, the all-female dormitory where Charlayne Hunter had taken up residence just a few days earlier as a winter quarter transfer student from Wayne State University. She and her former classmate at Atlanta's Turner High School, Hamilton Holmes, a transfer from Morehouse College, were the first two Black students to attend the University of Georgia in its 160-year history. In the culmination of an eighteen-month legal battle, federal judge William Augustus "Gus" Bootle had ruled on January 6, 1961, that Hunter and Holmes were qualified to attend UGA, and both should be granted immediate admittance to the university. In more than a touch of karmic blowback, African American attorney Horace Ward—who had been denied admission to Georgia's law school in the 1950s—was part of the legal team supporting Hunter and Holmes in their successful federal lawsuit against UGA.

The night of Judge Bootle's decision, a crowd of about two hundred gathered at the famed Arch at the entrance to the university's North Campus, where they sang "Dixie" and hung an effigy of Holmes. They later tried to burn a cross on the front lawn of the Prince Avenue home of UGA president Aderhold.[6]

Rollin M. "Pete" McCommons knew there would be trouble after the basketball game. There was a buzz around campus, and a group of UGA law students and members of the school's pro-segregation Demosthenian Literary Society organized plans for a riot, with promises of legal immunity—based on surreptitious assurances from sympathetic state legislators—for those who participated in the protests and engaged in the violence that might ensue. Some students joked that they had a date to the "game and the riot." Earlier that day, the chapter adviser of Pete McCommons's fraternity, Phi Delta Theta, had collected the handguns and rifles of all the members who resided at the fraternity's red brick, two-story house off Lumpkin Street. McCommons remembered being surprised and amazed by two things: the sheer size of the arsenal of weapons, and the fact that so many of his "good ole boy" fraternity brothers willingly complied with the request to hand over their firearms.[7]

Pete McCommons grew up in nearby Greene County, which represented the unofficial northern border of Georgia's "Cotton Belt." The Cotton Belt was an area that relied heavily on mainly Black tenant farmers, who had, since the end of the Civil War, struggled to produce "white gold" due to the twin challenges posed by soil depletion and the devastation wreaked by the boll weevil. The exhausted farmland of the lower Piedmont was hauntingly and beautifully captured in Arthur F. Raper's book *Tenants of the Almighty*, which featured Jack Delano's stark Depression-era black-and-white photographs of Black tenant farmers with deeply lined faces living in their plantation shacks, struggling to eke out a living while choking on the debt they incurred to buy seed and fertilizer.

In his high school years, Pete's athletic ability in football, basketball, and track attracted the attention of the sportswriters of the *Augusta Chronicle*, who dubbed him "Fleet Pete."[8] In the autumns, he and his parents drove the thirty-five-mile distance from their home in Greensboro to Athens to attend Bulldog football games. Greensboro, unlike a lot of the neighboring county seats in east Georgia, had a well-educated cadre of municipal leaders; many of their families still lived off the residual wealth created from long-shuttered plantations, which allowed the children in those families to attend elite schools. As Pete was growing up, his parents stressed the need to treat everyone with respect, regardless of race. His father was a merchant who worked in both of the family businesses, a general store and a funeral home; on funeral days, the store's clerks would dress in black and walk across the street to assist with the memorial service, leaving a "skeleton crew" to mind the store. Pete's mother was a schoolteacher who became a full-time homemaker after the first of her three children was born.

In Pete's early high school years, a peculiar twelve-foot apparition appeared in a cornfield in Greene County. The "Iron Horse"—an abstract welded-steel structure crafted by Chicago artist Abbott Pattison under a Rockefeller grant—was planted just off Highway 15, facing toward the south and away from Athens and the University of Georgia. The horse's original home was the plaza next to Memorial Hall on the UGA campus. But the students at Georgia in 1954 were not prepared for cutting-edge contemporary art and immediately set out to deface and even destroy the structure. Students placed manure under the horse, and they later lit mattresses shoved underneath it in an unsuccessful attempt to burn it down. McCommons learned years later that a group of students even tried to purchase dynamite from Normal Hardware Store to blow up the indestructible equine figure. Fortunately, the owner turned down the disappointed students, who were told that buying dynamite, unlike the purchase of firearms, required a permit. Finally, UGA president O. C. Aderhold stepped in and ordered the horse's removal from campus.

After toying with the idea of attending Emory University, McCommons enrolled at UGA in 1958 after winning a General Motors scholarship to attend the state's flagship public university. By his junior year, he had already amassed an impressive record: a political science major whose intent was to pursue a career in one of his two primary interests, government or theology (he had attended church regularly in Greensboro and had been active in the Methodist Youth Fellowship), McCommons was a member of the university's lacrosse team and had racked up one service or academic honor after another—election as vice president of the student council, inclusion in "Who's Who Among Students in American Universities and Colleges," and membership in honor societies such as BIFTAD and the Philaretos. Every photograph of McCommons in the university's yearbook, *Pandora*, captured an image of stolid conservatism—suit and tie, close-cropped hair, and a square jaw with a serious, unsmiling expression. He was, at least on the surface, the embodiment of Eisenhower conservatism.

McCommons had, however, been attending meetings of the Westminster Disciplined Study Community, a group of undergraduates who met each morning at the "ungodly hour" of 7:15. The meetings were held at Westminster House, the Presbyterian Church's campus ministry, located a short distance up the hill from Center Myers. Each meeting was "disciplined" in the sense that if all members did not show up, the meeting was adjourned; the lure of sleeping in was thus more than offset by the risk of sparking the righteous indignation of the attendees who had managed to show at the crack of dawn for naught.

Winston Stephens, an undergraduate English major with a pre–Civil War Athens pedigree, joined McCommons at the disciplined study meetings. She had to be careful, because her father, Robert Stephens, was the U.S. congressman representing Athens, and his political enemies were already trying to position themselves as the "candidate for the White man" and would, if presented with the opportunity, use his daughter's activism against him. Like McCommons, she was involved in UGA's Greek system as a member of the Kappa Alpha Theta sorority, and she was the past president of the Women's Student Government Association. "I guess we [Kappa Alpha Theta] were a bit more liberal minded than some of the other sororities," she recalled years later. "No one in the sorority criticized me directly for my involvement in the Disciplined Study Community, but I knew there was only so much I could do before that would change."9

The quiet discomfort that led her to the Disciplined Study Community was kindled in 1960 during a court hearing that she wandered into during a break from classes on UGA's North Campus. From her seat in the viewing gallery, she watched as Walter Danner, the University of Georgia registrar, swore under oath that Hamilton and Hunter's race had no influence on his decision to deny them admission. This obvious and tortured twisting of the facts was particularly upsetting to Stephens because she was a member of the venerable First Presbyterian Church—also known as "First Church"—which was consecrated in 1820, allowing it to legitimately lay claim to being the oldest church in town. Danner was a member of "the Session," First Presbyterian Church's board of elders, and the idea that a highly respected pillar of her church and the greater Athens community would dissemble in court represented a turning point for Stephens—she would have to think for herself and would no longer simply accept what she was told.

She had another distinct memory from the court hearing, which was held in the old Federal Building, next door to First Presbyterian Church. A member of Hunter and Holmes's legal team was a "tall and imposing" Black female attorney from the NAACP: Columbia Law School graduate Constance Baker Motley, who performed with skill and poise. Stephens was first struck by the fact that a woman could be an attorney and was further amazed that she was African American.[10]

Campus minister Corky King, a young and charismatic former football player from Virginia, led the disciplined study group. In addition to discussing the works of contemporary liberal theologians, political leaders, and activists such as the Reverend Martin Luther King Jr., Reinhold Niebuhr, and Thomas Merton, the group debated the practical matter of how each member could help usher in an atmosphere of tolerance within the tense climate at UGA in the early 1960s, when state and university officials either tacitly or openly condoned discrimination. The thoughtfulness and "good works" nature of the discussions took hold with McCommons. These views were further strengthened in his meetings with a new wave of younger, more liberal UGA professors—most notably, George Parthemos, a political science professor and University of North Carolina graduate and a former World War II navy commander, and speech professor Joseph Popovich, both of whom had taken a keen interest in seeing the university integrated. These younger professors exuded charisma and energy and style and contrasted with the older, more sober UGA professors whom McCommons "could see coming from a mile away, with their horn-rimmed glasses, painted ties, and shoulder-padded suits from the 1940s."[11]

On the night of January 11, as a crowd assembled in front of Center Myers after the Georgia–Georgia Tech basketball game, McCommons met up with Calvin "Bud" Trillin, a young Atlanta-based reporter for *Time* magazine. Trillin had followed the court battles related to the admission of Hunter and Holmes to UGA, and he knew that their first days on campus would likely be newsworthy. McCommons, along with thousands of other students and faculty members, was worried that a negative and violent reaction to the admission of the two Black students would irreparably damage the world's impression of both the University of Georgia and Athens. In the days leading up to January 11, he had tried to use his role in student government to promote a more tolerant atmosphere at the university and was part of a group who secured the signatures of more than two thousand students—roughly one-third of the undergraduate student body—on a petition that demanded that the university remain open if integration occurred.

McCommons and other concerned students had met with Trillin in his room at the Holiday Inn earlier that week to try to convince the journalist that the university was an island of moderation in a roiling sea of racists; that premise would be seriously undermined by the events that were about to unfold. Shortly after 10:00 p.m., a small group of students at the edge of the Myers Quad unfolded a bedsheet with the scrawled message "Nigger Go Home" and shouted, "Two, four, six, eight, we don't want to integrate! One, two, three, four, we don't want no nigger whore!"[12] Another group broke away and rushed toward the dormitory, hurling rocks and bottles at Charlayne Hunter's window. Some have speculated that a fellow Myers resident told students in the surrounding rooms to turn out their lights so that Hunter's room could be easily identified.[13] Uninjured, Hunter left her bedroom and went to an adjacent office to wait out the attack. More objects were hurled, firecrackers were set off, and small brushfires were started in the woods that framed the quad. One rock struck *Red and Black* society editor Marcia Powell, who was observing the riot with McCommons and Trillin. This, remembered McCommons, more than anything else, infuriated Trillin, who hours later called his editor and reported: "President Aderhold, he's a shit. Dean [of students Joseph] Williams, he's a shit. Registrar Danner, he's a shit; no wait, hold that, he's just a clerk."[14]

The crowd grew to an estimated two thousand, and McCommons kept asking himself, "Where the hell is the state patrol?"[15] A group of state patrolmen were, in fact, in a barracks just five miles away, but they could not rush to the scene unless authorized to do so by Georgia governor Ernest Vandiver, who had earlier publicly mulled over the idea of going to jail before allowing the university to admit Black students.[16] An outmanned group of officers from Athens's tiny forty-man police force—many of whom who had been directing postgame traffic—arrived on the scene, and they discharged twenty-five to thirty canisters of tear gas and fired jets of water from fire hoses. Gradually, they pushed the crowd back and restored some semblance of order.

The legendary dean of men Bill Tate, carrying a bullhorn and wearing his trademark short-brimmed baseball cap, had followed the crowd from the basketball game and, with his disarming mixture of charm, threats, and humor, played the biggest role in defusing a situation that was on the verge of spinning out of control. One former student recalled, "He had a way with students even though they were scared to death of him. They respected him. He knew their daddies and their grand-daddies, and if a student was about to get in trouble, he would ask them their name, and it would scare them to death and when they told him, he would say, 'Oh yeah!,' and tell them their daddy's name."[17]

My father, then a graduate student at UGA, was on the periphery of the crowd and for years has told me that Dean Tate was the unsung hero of the evening. (I was two years old and sound asleep in our rented house behind the UGA baseball field, blissfully unaware of the fracas less than a half mile away.) His account was backed up by McCommons, as well as by Trillin: "The riot was finally broken up by the ar-rival . . . of Dean Tate, who waded in and started grabbing identification cards."[18]

Tate believed that the worst way to handle an unruly mob was to stay in front of it; instead, he strode into the midst of it and was struck by a brick. Tate later explained what hap-pened after he pulled a demonstrator off a policeman: "I pulled him off and he hit me. So I hit him and knocked out one of his teeth. Hell, I still have all my teeth."[19]

No one questioned the authority of Dean Tate, whose jowly and beady-eyed visage resembled that of the school's mascot, a bulldog. By the end of the evening, he had col-lected a large stack of ID cards, and those students unlucky enough to have surrendered theirs would at minimum face a tense meeting with the dean; at worst, they risked expulsion from the school.

Somewhat amazingly, the mob never attempted to over-run the small police force and rush into the Myers dormi-tory, which it easily could have done. Perhaps those in the crowd grew bored, or they feared that suspension from school would not play well with their parents back home. In any event, the mob slowly dispersed, and when the state troopers finally showed up an hour later, they found an empty quad littered with trash and broken glass.

In a curiously impromptu decision, Dean of Students Jo-seph Williams—under pressure from Governor Vandiver—suspended both Charlayne Hunter and Hamilton Holmes "for their own safety and the safety of thousands of other students." This was done despite the pleadings of Athens mayor Ralph Snow and Athens police chief E. E. Hardy, who felt that the danger had passed and worried that suspending Hunter and Holmes would only encourage similarly violent mob behavior in the future.

A weeping Charlayne Hunter, clutching a small Madonna statuette (she had recently converted to Catholicism), was led out of Center Myers by Dean Williams, who carried her suitcase. A teary-eyed Dean Tate rode with her in a state patrol car—part of a motorcade, with sirens wailing—to the off-campus home where Hamilton Holmes was staying. Holmes was not on campus that evening and was completely unaware of the riot until his state patrol escort arrived. The irrepressible Tate tried to lighten the mood with some levity as he rode with Hunter and Holmes back to Atlanta, spinning yarns on the drive along Highway 29; Hunter remembered that Tate "talked all the way back about the little towns we went through—things like why Dacula [a small town in Gwinnett County] is pronounced Da*cu*la instead of *Dac*ula."[20]

An exhausted and disheartened Pete McCommons went to his car around 2:00 a.m., slumped into the driver's seat, and turned on the radio, fiddling with the dial until he found a station delivering a speech by Peter Zack Geer, Georgia's arch-segregationist executive secretary to Governor Vandiver. The voice of Geer, who would be elected lieutenant governor in 1962, thundered over the crackling radio: "The students at the university have demonstrated that Georgia youth are possessed with the character and courage not to submit to dictatorship and tyranny."[21]

The brothers at the Kappa Alpha fraternity—whose spiritual founder was General Robert E. Lee—raised their huge Confederate flag above the portico of their house on South Lumpkin Street and shrieked rebel yells up into the sky on that cold, early winter night, and they partied into the early morning.

卌

On January 12, the leaders at the University of Georgia surveyed the damage.

Optically, the riot at Center Myers was very harmful to the school's reputation. Journalists had been on hand to record the scene, and their depictions of the previous night's ugly events were sure to grab headlines not just across the nation but around the world. Locally, the news was big enough to push the hiring of the new Georgia football coach, Johnny Griffith, off the front page, a seemingly impossible feat in football-crazed Athens.

But administrators also had reason to feel fortunate on several fronts. No one had been seriously injured—glass shards had cut one woman, and a few policemen suffered bumps and bruises. And there was a convenient outsider group to blame: eight Ku Klux Klansmen from Atlanta had participated in the riot and had been arrested. Their car was filled with firearms, but they had not brought any of their weapons with them to Center Myers. The administrators also had the disappointing outcome of the basketball game that they could partially (and inaccurately) blame for the riot. Finally, the quandary of integration had been firmly punted to the state legislature, which just happened to be in session. Like many other state legislatures in the South in the aftermath of the Supreme Court's landmark 1954 *Brown v. Board of Education of Topeka* ruling that made segregation in public schools illegal, the Georgia General Assembly, in a spasm of political posturing, had passed a law requiring the elimination of state funding for any public school that permitted integration. In 1961, the University of Georgia relied much more heavily on state funding for its budgetary needs than it does today, so the potential evaporation of its primary source of financial support could be wielded by an antagonistic state legislature like a cudgel.

Until 1963, when the Supreme Court ruled the practice to be unconstitutional, Georgia held statewide elections under the "county unit system," a sort of Electoral College on steroids; under this system, votes in rural areas were tremendously overweighted in statewide elections. The practical effect was to largely eliminate legislative accountability to urban voters, whose number was rapidly growing each year relative to the more sparsely populated areas of the state that were starting to experience either flat or negative population growth, particularly in South Georgia.

Given the outsize political importance of rural counties anchored by the county unit system, Georgia governors and legislators had wagered that any integration "test" would occur in Atlanta, where they (the politicians) would experience little blowback and might even enjoy a boost to their popularity. The closure of an Atlanta-based school would be an easy opportunity to score cheap political points back home; the only victims would be African Americans and a sprinkling of White, liberal do-gooders, punished by seeing the schools of their own children shut down due to lack of funding.

The plan backfired when the first test for integration was the University of Georgia. The composition of the school's student body was quite different in the early 1960s compared to today: 90 percent of the students were in-state, two-thirds of the student body was male, and a much larger percentage of students were from rural Georgia—unlike in the present version of the school, there was representation from each of the state's 159 counties. It would be more than three decades before the introduction of the HOPE scholarship, which resulted in tuition-free benefits for students with a B average or better and allowed the stronger Atlanta-area schools to dominate the enrollment statistics at UGA. But in 1961, in the words of Dean William Tate: "When integration came, the university was the one institution that could weather it . . . [because] a lot of people in the state love the university, and the university has always been tied up to the state. . . . It's not that way with [Georgia] Tech. The engineers don't drift back to these little old counties. There's not a soul in Meriwether County who gives a damn what happens to Tech."[22]

So when Governor Ernest Vandiver—who was himself a UGA graduate, and who had campaigned under the slogan "No, not one" (meaning not one Black child in a White school)—announced that he would be forced to cut off state funding to the university but would also ask the legislature to quickly repeal the law that required such a draconian reaction, the bluff of the segregationist politicians had been called. The law was changed, and a face-saving new law was introduced, one that allowed tuition grants for families who sent their children to private schools.

Events moved swiftly in the next few days after the riot. Four hundred members of the university's faculty met in the old Greek Revival Chapel on North Campus on January 12 and passed a resolution calling for the reversal of the suspension of Charlayne Hunter and Hamilton Holmes. Dean Tate reviewed his stack of confiscated student ID cards and cross-referenced them with his memory of the riot and then suspended the thirteen most egregious offenders involved in the mayhem in the Myers Quad.

Judge Bootle had quickly rescinded the university's suspensions of Hunter and Holmes, and when classes were resumed on Monday of the following week, the two students returned to school, accompanied by Georgia Bureau of Investigation (GBI) escorts "as a precautionary measure." One hundred state troopers and the Athens police stood by, on alert for any sign of a recurrence of the previous week's violence.[23]

Hamilton Holmes lived on Harris Street, in a Black

neighborhood, with the family of Archibald Roosevelt Killian, the owner of the popular Four Seasons restaurant. When warned that the Ku Klux Klan had threatened to burn down his house and kill all of its occupants, Killian organized a group of armed neighbors to keep constant watch on his home.[24] He also notified the Klan through informal channels that he might die protecting "Hamp" Holmes, but he would take some Klansmen with him.

Police chief E. E. Hardy was impressed with the determination and resolve of Archibald Killian, and a year later, in March 1962, Killian and his cousin Donald Moon were sworn in as Athens's first Black police officers. But the swearing-in ceremony could take place only after an administrative glitch was corrected: all police officers had to be registered voters, and Killian's name initially could not be found on the rolls, because the clerk who had registered the light-skinned Killian to vote had listed him as "white."[25]

The painful first step had been taken. Never again would violence or the threat of it hinder integration at the University of Georgia. Two Black transfer students had chosen UGA for practical reasons above all else: Hunter was drawn to the school's journalism program—there was no other comprehensive journalism program within the university system of Georgia—while Holmes came to UGA because its science facilities represented an upgrade for the future orthopedic surgeon compared to the more limited offerings on hand at Morehouse College. And Holmes was a football fan who closely followed the gridiron fortunes of the Georgia Bulldogs.

Some Black Athenians were initially skeptical of the two pioneering students; there was a sense that they were "handpicked" because they were well-spoken, light-skinned African Americans from Atlanta. For the most part, Holmes and Hunter rarely crossed paths with each other in Athens: she preferred to stay on campus, whereas Holmes became a fixture in the Black neighborhood of Rocksprings, where he enjoyed playing basketball with the boys at the community center—the locals still remembered his prowess on the basketball court when he played for Turner High School against Athens High and Industrial School. "It was," recalled longtime African American resident and future university professor Maxie Foster, "a 'tale of two cities.' Hamilton Holmes was part of the Black community in Athens, and we never saw Charlayne Hunter."[26]

The White students at UGA made a gradual if uneasy adjustment to the presence of two Black students on campus. "People don't notice as much if they see Charlayne or Hamilton on campus," Winston Stephens later told Calvin Trillin, "but they'll remark on it if they have a class with them, especially if they think it will mean some physical contact. . . . Most people feel they're here, and nothing can be done. There's no pressure against being normally friendly. I always say hello to Charlayne. I sat down in the library to study with her the other night and nobody said anything."[27]

┼┼┼┼

President Aderhold was under pressure not only from influential alumni but also from the Board of Regents, whom he reported to. One Board of Regents member, a racist firebrand from Augusta named Roy Harris, demanded a list of the four hundred faculty members who had supported the reinstatement of Hunter and Holmes. It is not clear what type of reprisals Harris intended to seek against the faculty members who had signed the petition—they represented about two-thirds of the professoriate at the university, and any move against them would threaten the school's accreditation, which had been revoked once before in the 1940s due to political meddling by then governor Eugene Talmadge.[28] Aderhold politely demurred, stating simply that he did not have the list, but advised Harris to could contact Dr. Kenneth Coleman, a history professor and the secretary for the meeting, if he wanted a roll of the attendees.[29]

President Aderhold meticulously catalogued every item of correspondence and newspaper article related to integration at UGA that passed over his desk, and the letters and telegrams he received from across the nation supporting the admission of Hunter and Holmes outnumbered those opposed by more than a two-to-one margin. An alumnus from Detroit wrote: "Your type of people have done a good job of letting the world know the ignorance prevalent in some of our elected officials, along with others, Governor Vandiver is a shining example." Another alumnus sent a telegram to Aderhold relaying his request that "you act firmly to lift our university from shame already brought to it by ignorant, vulgar Roy Harris and Vandiver. Their unjust and evasive schemes are ridiculous. Their defiance only brings chaos. Holmes and Hunter are not lepers."[30]

Those opposed to integration accused Aderhold and other university administrators not only of being complicit in the unpardonable sin of allowing Black students on campus but also of suppressing the First Amendment rights of White students. One transcript of an editorial broadcast from radio station WDMD ("The Big D") in Dawson, Georgia, read: "The Big D believes that Dr. Aderhold and other University officials are depriving white students at Georgia the right to express themselves. The Big D believes that the rights of 7,500 white students at the university are being abused, while two Negro students are given a royal welcome and reception by the faculty."[31] Roy Harris went one step further, claiming that Aderhold and Dean Tate had "brainwashed" the school into accepting Black students, and the Board of Regents member vowed to spend the rest of his life getting Aderhold "out of the university."[32]

The difficulties continued for Hunter and Holmes, as they experienced insults and ostracism from White students, the exact type of nonviolent resistance that Aderhold had earlier encouraged. But the overt threat of violence had passed. Mary Frances Early transferred to UGA from the University of Michigan for the spring quarter of 1961 and became, in 1962, the first African American to earn a UGA degree—a master's in music education. More would soon follow.

O. C. Aderhold had, more through happenstance than skill, threaded the needle on the issue of integration. He had spent years dodging the legal matter of desegregation, even swearing in court that UGA had no official policy of discrimination, but he realized that further resistance was pointless once a federal district court judge ruled that Hunter and Holmes had met the requirements for admission. He was not prepared to risk further damaging the school's reputation by defying the courts and forcing newly elected President John F. Kennedy to send National Guard troops to Athens, as Kennedy would later order at both the University of Alabama and the University of Mississippi when those schools defied court orders to desegregate. In a head-spinning twist, those who welcomed the long-overdue integration of the school now viewed Aderhold as the voice of reason, and those who opposed it reviled him.

In a letter to the University of Texas chancellor, Harry Ransom, in October 1961, Aderhold seemed almost apologetic about the integration of UGA: "As you know, we are operating under a Court Order, and must admit all applicants regardless of race who meet the academic requirements for admission to the university." On the issue of integrating the school's sports teams, Aderhold saw no reason to even address it: "The question of integrating the athletic squads has not become an issue. We will not deal with it until it does."[33]

When his tenure as president ended in 1967, O. C. Aderhold had still not had to deal with the equally perplexing business of integrating the school's athletic teams. But the toughest nut in the battle to integrate the schools in the state of Georgia had been cracked, and more and more schools recognized the folly of fighting a pointless rearguard action. The Atlanta public school system shortly thereafter announced its plans to integrate. Georgia Tech declared its intention to admit Black students in the fall quarter of 1961. Georgia State University—then called the Georgia State College of Business Administration—was integrated in 1962. The state of Georgia was finally, and largely against its will, marching toward the future instead of remaining moored to the past.

The Morton Building at 195 West Washington Street in 1921. Built and operated by local Black entrepreneur Monroe Morton, it was the anchor of the African American "Hot Corner" in downtown Athens. Its Beaux-Arts-style theater featured such acts as Duke Ellington, Ma Rainey, and Louis Armstrong. Photo courtesy of the Hargrett Rare Book and Manuscript Library.

Linnentown, circa 1935. Linnentown was a twenty-two-acre Black neighborhood located east of the UGA campus, on Baxter Hill. The homes in the area were condemned and destroyed in the early 1960s as part of an urban renewal project to make way for three high-rise UGA dormitories. This photo was taken from Sanford Field, where the Tate Student Center is now located. Photo courtesy of the Hargrett Rare Book and Manuscript Library.

The Athens High and Industrial School marching band, circa 1955, at the school's location at Pope and Reese Streets. The bandleader dressed all in white at front left is Dr. Walter Allen Sr., who taught music at AHIS/Burney-Harris before becoming assistant principal at Athens High School and Clarke Central High School. Athens High and Industrial School was the first Black public secondary school to be accredited in the state of Georgia. Photo courtesy of Walter Allen Jr.

Omer Clyde ("O. C.") Aderhold. President of the University of Georgia from 1950 to 1967, Aderhold oversaw a period of steady growth in the UGA campus and its student population. After fiercely opposing integration for a decade, he yielded to the inevitable in 1961 when the university accepted its first two Black students, Charlayne Hunter and Hamilton Holmes. Photo courtesy of the Hargrett Rare Book and Manuscript Library.

Rollin "Pete" McCommons was a student leader at UGA during the school's tumultuous integration in 1961. He went on to help start the *United Free Press*, a progressive newsletter in Athens, before cofounding the *Athens Observer*, and he is currently the publisher and editor of *Flagpole*, the Athens-based alternative newsweekly. Photo courtesy of the Hargrett Rare Book and Manuscript Library.

Clifford "Baldy" Baldowski cartoon in the *Atlanta Constitution* depicting an apprehensive Charlayne Hunter looking out through the broken windows at Center Myers and wondering whether UGA is sincere in welcoming her back to the campus after the riot on January 11, 1961. *Atlanta Constitution*, [18 January 1961], Clifford H. "Baldy" Baldowski Editorial Cartoons. Courtesy of the Richard B. Russell Library for Political Research and Studies, the University of Georgia Libraries.

"JEEPERS, I DON'T KNOW IF HE'S THE SAME AS HE USE TO BE OR NOT !"

Hamilton Holmes and Charlayne Hunter receive their diplomas in June 1963 on the field of UGA's Sanford Stadium. Holmes went on to be the first African American student to attend the Emory University School of Medicine and became a highly regarded orthopedic surgeon, while Hunter (later Hunter-Gault) has had a distinguished career in journalism. They are the namesakes of UGA's Holmes-Hunter Academic Building. Photo courtesy of the Associated Press.

William "Bill" Tate, dean of men at the University of Georgia from 1946 to 1971. Dean Tate played a leading role in defusing the riot that occurred at Center Myers in the wake of the January 1961 integration of UGA. Here he is pictured wearing love beads while sitting with students who were protesting the Kent State shootings in May 1970. Photo courtesy of the Hargrett Rare Book and Manuscript Library.

Athens High School coeds pose in front of the Varsity restaurant at the corner of West Broad and Milledge. The Varsity was the scene of protests in 1964, as African Americans sought to integrate the iconic eatery. Photo from *Trojan 1968*, accessed via the Athens-Clarke County Library Heritage Room.

Athens Klansmen Howard Sims and Cecil Myers celebrate with their wives after an all-White jury in Madison County, Georgia, delivered a "not guilty" verdict in the murder of Lt. Col. Lemuel Penn. The two men were later sentenced to ten years in federal prison for violating Penn's civil rights. Photo courtesy of the Associated Press.

Allen Morse, African American student at Athens High School. The highly talented running back was denied a spot on the Trojans' active roster in 1966 because the team supposedly ran out of uniforms. Photo from *Trojan 1967*, accessed via the Athens-Clarke County Library Heritage Room.

Burney-Harris Yellow Jacket mascot. Image courtesy of Elizabeth Platt.

CHAPTER 4
VIOLENCE AND HOPE

Alan Morse, who may be the first Negro ever to
play at Athens High, is currently a back too, but
Sellers is mulling moving him to the line.

—*Steve Teasley*, Athens Banner-Herald, *August 7, 1966*

In 1963, both the city of Athens and the University of Georgia were booming.

UGA was in the midst of an expansion that would see a tripling of student enrollment by the end of the decade. State funding for higher education, which had steadily increased during the post–World War II economic boom, exploded when a new, progressive governor, Carl Sanders, took office in early 1963.

Sanders was a "Double Dawg," the holder of both a bachelor's and a law degree from UGA. He was the state's first urban governor in forty years, having defeated the segregationist former governor from the 1950s, Marvin Griffin, in a landslide in 1962. Sanders's overwhelming victory was made possible by the first popular vote in the state of Georgia since 1907—in April 1962 U.S. circuit judge Griffin Bell issued an injunction against using the county unit system that overweighted the votes of rural counties, and the Supreme Court declared the system unconstitutional the following year. A young and charismatic believer in civil rights and higher education, Sanders was supportive of the presidential agendas of both John F. Kennedy and (later) Lyndon Johnson.

To support the rapid growth in student enrollment, the university built three high-rise dormitories on "Baxter Hill," the steep ridge that climbs up Baxter Street and crests at Milledge Avenue. The new multipurpose Georgia Coliseum, which was later renamed for Henry Stegeman, an early twentieth-century basketball coach at UGA, was touted as the "Jewel of North Georgia," and basketball games, rodeos, concerts, and graduation exercises would soon be held beneath its curved, barrel-shaped ceiling. The new Lamar Dodd School of Art, tucked into a corner of North Campus off Jackson Street, was completed in 1963. The futuristic and eye-catching white concrete building clashed with the sober, classical styles of North Campus, and many referred to it as the "ice plant" or "that monstrosity."[1] The Gillis Bridge, which skirts the western end of Sanford Stadium and connects North and South Campuses, was built in 1963. Prior to its construction, students were forced to walk the steps leading up and down the small valley that separated the two campuses. A campus bus system was also finally introduced, which eliminated the need to hitchhike between far-flung classrooms.

The year 1963 also featured the opening of the first stage of the city's new, modernized retail complex, Beechwood Shopping Center, built on the stretch of Alps Road that connected Broad and Baxter Streets, about a mile west of downtown. The shopping center was adjacent to the recently developed Beechwood Homes subdivision, which was filled with ranch-style homes occupied by the families of many managers and executives from northern companies that had relocated to Athens over the previous decade.

Sears vacated its store downtown to anchor Beechwood,

which originally featured fourteen stores and two thousand parking spots. As an added convenience, the sidewalks that snaked around the U-shaped complex had awnings that protected shoppers from sun and rain.[2] The success of the shopping center fueled a quick expansion to more than thirty stores by 1965, including the Beechwood Buffet, featuring ninety-seven-cent dinner specials.

The radial growth of Athens largely mirrored the patterns seen throughout America in the early 1960s. The automobile was now the unassailable chief mode of transportation in the country—over sixty million cars were on the road by 1960, one for every three citizens, and their widespread use allowed retailers to abandon downtown areas and offer amenities not available in central business districts, such as free parking and the convenience of shopping without the worry of bad weather.

The rapid success of Beechwood Shopping Center spawned further development away from downtown, such as the nearby Alps Road Shopping Center (built where a drive-in cinema had once been located) and the spacious Winn-Dixie grocery store off Prince Avenue. Fast-food chain restaurants appeared out of nowhere to meet the demand of hungry shoppers and nearby residents: a Burger Chef on Alps Road (the radio jingle bragged that a hamburger cost "a nickel and dime, 15 cents!"), a McDonald's on Prince Avenue, a Hardee's on Baxter Street, a Kentucky Fried Chicken on Milledge Avenue. Pizza had also arrived in the Classic City with Gigi's, a popular "date night" eatery on Baxter that offered piping-hot pies, served with romantic lighting provided by flickering candles placed inside the neck of straw-bottomed Chianti bottles on red-and-white-checkered tablecloths.

Residential growth kept pace with the rapid commercial development, as ranch-style subdivisions were built in quick succession further and further away from the fading downtown area. A newcomer's map from the mid-1960s showed new subdivisions in "Homewood Hills, Knottingham, Bel Air Heights, and Forest Heights to the northwest; Beechwood Hills, Timothy Estates, and Glenwood to the southwest; and University Heights, Green Acres, and Clarke Dale to the southeast."[3]

Slum clearance had become a major priority for the leaders of Athens in the 1960s. The 1960 U.S. census had determined that fully 27 percent of the city's housing units were in a "dilapidated condition." Under the Johnson administration's urban renewal program, matching funds were made available for slum clearance to those communities that provided updated, alternative housing to the displaced residents.

In most instances, the city's run-down housing was desperately in need of replacement. The "Bottom" neighborhood on College Avenue between the northern edge of downtown and the train station was a particular eyesore and an embarrassment to city leaders concerned about the impression it made on visitors who arrived in Athens via rail and walked the short distance from the station to the downtown hotels. The wood-framed housing with thin slats for planks often lacked indoor plumbing and electricity.

The university's three new high-rise dormitories—Brumby, Russell, and Creswell Halls—were built on Baxter Hill in Linnentown, named for Lyndon Row, a street that ran through a neighborhood of fifty Black families who had lived on the upper twenty-two-acre portion of the hill since the early twentieth century. About two-thirds of the families owned their homes; some, like Hattie Thomas Whitehead and her family, lived in newly built houses constructed with the help of neighbors, who provided free labor and materials. Residents could sit on their porches and watch UGA games in the fall, and many offered up their yards and streets to fans for game day parking.

The three streets that ran through Linnentown were unpaved, even though the residents were taxpayers who had received repeated assurances from City Hall that the dirt roads that turned into muddy quagmires after heavy rains would soon be covered with asphalt. Hattie Whitehead's family was issued a permit to build their new home and was told that the city would provide a sewage and water hookup, but the municipal government never followed through on its promises.

Mayor Julius Bishop named Paul Hodgson, the scion of a prestigious Athens family whose roots in the city extended to the pre–Civil War era, to head Athens's urban renewal efforts. This hybrid program—in which the federal government provided grants and loans to cities, which in turn allocated funds and oversaw implementation—was an important initiative in President Johnson's War on Poverty and was dedicated to replacing slums with modern, multifamily low-income housing.

Under the aegis of the urban renewal program, the city exercised its power of eminent domain and condemned and demolished the homes of Linnentown. The city then sold the land to the Board of Regents for a nominal amount of $216,935, a bit more than the total compensation of $195,500 awarded to all the Linnentown property owners. Individual homeowners were paid an average of $5,750 (about $20,000 in today's dollars), and most of the once close-knit community dispersed to East Athens or to public housing. It was, in the eyes of the city and the university, a "win-win": the university obtained land at a cheap price to expand student housing at a time when the need for it was exploding, and in turn, Athens would be relieved of an eyesore. In the words of Mayor Bishop, "the university . . . placed more than $12 million worth of improvements on this land which was formerly a slum in the heart of the City of Athens."[4]

The residents of Linnentown would have disputed the characterization of their neighborhood as a "slum." Although the mainly shotgun-style houses were largely unpainted and in need of repair, it was a community where people knew each other and cared for those who were sick or in need; where people took pride in their homes and planted flowers, raised chickens, grew vegetables, and held Easter egg hunts; where the children played in Tanyard Creek, which flows down Baxter Hill and underneath Sanford Stadium before it joins the North Oconee River.[5]

As historian Alexander Stephens noted, "The idea of moving residents from mainly substandard housing to new government-subsidized, low-income housing units might have been good in theory, but the execution was poor. No thought was given to social networks in the displaced communities that had been built over generations."[6] Logistics— getting to jobs and schools and shops that had been patronized for years—were disrupted, and support systems were destroyed. Residents of Linnentown and other displaced communities relied on each other through a mutual trust within their community, organically established over decades of segregation. After this social connectivity was broken, many Black residents suffered personal trauma—Hattie Thomas's parents divorced after struggling with the stress of leaving their Linnentown neighborhood for Rocksprings Homes.[7]

Post–World War II development in Athens reflected the uneven accrual of benefits to White and Black communities across the nation, as federal, state, and municipal governments rained cash on rapid highway expansion and other construction projects. More than seventy U.S. universities used urban renewal funds and condemnation to expand college infrastructure at the expense of African American communities; like UGA, both Georgia Tech and Georgia State University used urban renewal to grow their Atlanta campuses and displace adjacent Black neighborhoods. All too often, Black Athenians were given little or no voice when their communities and homes were threatened with redevelopment to spur economic growth.

North of downtown, more than three hundred homes and the town's only Jewish synagogue were razed (on combined acreage representing three percent of the total landmass of the city) as part of an urban renewal program dedicated to the construction of indigent public and elderly housing and the build-out of the first phase of State Route 10 Loop, a beltway known as the Athens Bypass. The three-story Bethel Homes Apartments were built as part of this program; the new low-income housing stock represented an upgrade in living conditions for most of the Black residents who had for generations lived in drafty shanties in the Bottom. But they were angered that they had had no voice in the condemnation of their former homes, many of which dated back to the immediate post–Civil War period. Like the residents of Linnentown, they were simply offered a price and not given the opportunity to negotiate conditions of sale. The fact that many residents lacked clear title to their property further exacerbated the problem. But once again, the City of Athens was relieved of a major eyesore.

A similar program in the late 1950s had seen the extension of Baxter Street through an African American neighborhood to Alps Road. Without the westward extension of Baxter Street, which had previously ended at Rocksprings Street, the future success of Beechwood Shopping Center would have been imperiled. The new St. Mary's Hospital was built on the Baxter extension in 1966, replacing the "old" St. Mary's that had operated for years in its buildings on Milledge Avenue.

The only setback to Athens's rapid growth was a once-in-a-generation storm that lashed the city early in the summer of 1963. Over a foot of rain fell on Athens in the last week of June, which raised the water level of the North Oconee River by twenty-six feet and caused the collapse of the Whitehall Bridge. Eight people drowned, including six children under the age of ten, when the station wagon they were in was tragically swept away after plunging into the flood-swollen river. Athens suffered massive damage to its infrastructure that week, including washed-out culverts and damaged drainpipes, and the storm destroyed sections of roads, forcing the city to bring in over a thousand tons of rock to help repair the damage.[8]

The alliance of business, university, and government interests had transformed Athens into much more than the home of UGA—it was now the undisputed commercial and retail center of northeast Georgia. The city was expanding in every direction and brimming with confidence. As another broiling Piedmont summer gradually eased its grip on the land, Athens turned to the much trickier issue of school integration.

╫╫╫

Almost three years after the integration of the University of Georgia, the Clarke County school system was integrated in the fall of 1963 when five Black students—Wilucia Green and Marjorie Green (sisters), Agnes Green (no relation), Bonnie Hampton, and Scott Michael Killian—began attending previously all-White schools under the "freedom of choice" plan. The plan as implemented by Clarke County allowed students of any race *on an individual basis* to transfer to the school of their choice. The NAACP carefully selected and vetted the five students (now often referred to as the "Forgotten Five," as a nod to their largely unacknowledged role in integrating the Athens-Clarke County school system) for both their temperament and their academic achievements, as it needed to minimize the possibility of failure for these young pioneers. The Green sisters were the daughters of Dr. Donarell Green Jr., the most prominent Black physician in northeast Georgia and the first African American doctor to serve on the staff at St. Mary's Hospital; Wilucia became the first Black student to attend Athens High School, while Marjorie began seventh grade at Childs Street. Agnes Green's father was a pharmacist, and her mother worked for Atlanta Life Insurance Company, the highly successful firm started by Atlanta's richest African American, Alonzo Herndon; Agnes joined Marjorie Green at Childs Street. Also enrolled at Childs Street was Bonnie Hampton, the daughter of Katie Hampton, secretary of the local NAACP. Scott Michael Killian, who broke the color barrier at Chase Street Elementary, was the son of one of Athens's first Black policemen, Archibald Killian, who also opened the city's first integrated business, the Four Seasons restaurant.

The NAACP's role in promoting school integration in Athens was not unusual. A decade earlier, future Supreme Court justice and attorney for the NAACP Thurgood Marshall had filed the successful *Brown v. Board of Education of Topeka* brief that eventually overturned more than a half century of "separate but equal" treatment of African American students in the nation's public school systems. But there were many in the Black community, including many teachers, who clashed with the NAACP and had long advocated for the existing post-Reconstruction structure of all-Black schools and teachers as cornerstones of racial pride and self-reliance.[9]

In Athens, however, support for school integration coalesced into a broad collective effort within the African American community, with the local Black churches taking a leadership role to ensure that the process would be smooth and unmarred by violence. Meetings were held with the children and their families before classes started to alert them to the reaction they might expect once they started attending the previously all-White schools. In a show of unanimity and resolve, an interdenominational group of five armed Black pastors—including those from Ebenezer Baptist Church West, Greater Bethel AME, and Hill Chapel Baptist, some of the most prominent churches in the Black community—volunteered to escort the students to and from school. It was a frightening time, especially for younger children like eleven-year-old Agnes Green, who still remembered the blare of sirens three years earlier when Charlayne Hunter and Hamilton Holmes were rushed out of town under the protection of a state patrol motorcade.[10]

While the first days of integration generated heavy media coverage, there were no arrests, and there was no violence, other than a few White students throwing "paper balls" at Black children as they arrived at school. The Black students could not help but overhear the "n-word" whispered by some of the White schoolchildren. Still, TV cameras and a strong security presence helped ensure that there would be no recurrence of the nasty first days of integration at UGA.[11]

As the novelty of having Black schoolmates gradually wore off, the insults and crude gibes subsided, though they did not disappear. But social ostracism was the less visible but no less disheartening challenge faced by the isolated Black students. Wilucia Green, who transferred from AHIS to Athens High School as a junior and would later become the first African American student to graduate from the previously all-White high school, described how all the White students would try to "blend" into the wall as she walked down the hall or would shun her in the school cafeteria.[12] As a Black student, she was not encouraged to participate in after-school activities, and even the White students who were friendly with Green could not breach the racial conventions of the time, which would have frowned upon inviting a Black classmate to such normal adolescent events as parties or sleepovers.

Bonnie Hampton, along with Agnes Green and Marjorie Green, integrated Childs Street School. She recalled the sidewalks crammed with curious and angry White parents, who shouted insults and jeered the arrival of the young African American girls. When the Hamptons' car arrived at school to drop Bonnie off those first few weeks, her entire focus was to make it up the steps and through the front doors. Once inside, the racist taunts were no longer audible, and the toughest part of the day was behind her. But by no means were her days at Childs Street easy.

The school cafeteria featured tables that spanned nearly the width of the room. Once Bonnie found a seat, the White students usually left a space open on either side of her, and the person who sat opposite her typically felt awkward sitting directly across from a Black student. One day, she had left a textbook in the desk of her previous class and received permission from her teacher to go retrieve it. She was standing at the open door of the classroom hoping to catch the attention of the teacher, who was lecturing the entire class, and Bonnie saw that many of the girls had removed the rubber bands from their teeth braces and were using them to wear their hair in pigtails; they did this to mock the three Black girls, all of whom wore their hair in the same fashion. The teacher did not reprimand the students for their cruel behavior; instead, she was angry at them for mimicking the appearance of the three Black girls, even if their motivation was scornful in nature. "Why would you want to be like them!" she admonished her students.

The teacher finally noticed Bonnie and granted her permission to enter the classroom. When Bonnie picked up her book, the White student at the desk took on a horrified expression when he realized that he was occupying the same space that a Black girl had sat in earlier that day.

Curious White students would ask the Black girls if they had been paid to integrate a White school, as if a shadowy, moneyed outside presence was pulling the strings of desegregation behind the scenes.[13]

Bonnie divided the White students into three categories: those who "did not know any better and had been raised that way," those who knew better but "wanted to be part of the crowd," and those who rejected the racism exhibited by their fellow classmates. There was a sizable correlation in the last group—those who were tolerant were usually the children of UGA professors or administrators or other professionals.

The racist taunts usually occurred in the anonymity provided by crowded hallways. Over time these taunts began to dwindle, however, and Bonnie was able to build a few casual friendships with White girls, many of whom gradually began to relax and invite her into their informal groups. On November 22, 1963, when the assassination of President John F. Kennedy was announced over the school's intercom system, one White girl told a group that included Bonnie that the president's death was not a cause for mourning because "he was just for the niggers." The other White girls quickly scolded her and demanded that she apologize to Bonnie.

Throughout her experience at Childs Street and later at Clarke Junior High School and Athens High, Bonnie Hampton never displayed weakness. She never wept, because she was "not a crier, never have been." Her best defense was to exhibit behavior that came naturally to her—directness and confidence when thrust into difficult situations.

At Clarke Junior High School, a math teacher asked the three or four Black children in her class if they knew where she could find "a good maid." Bonnie quickly made up a response that "she didn't know, but that her family was looking for one themselves." In a history class, the teacher assigned a Civil War project in which one group would advocate on behalf of slavery, and the other against the "peculiar institution." Bonnie was picked to participate on the proslavery side of the debate, and she delivered an accurate and chilling performance, built largely on repeating the comments she had heard from Whites her entire life. She was not going to grant the White teacher the satisfaction of losing her poise and crumbling during her presentation. Years later at a reunion, a White student remembered the insensitive and difficult role assigned to Bonnie and praised her for her composure and ability to rise to the moment with aplomb.[14]

After leaving middle school and moving on to Athens High, Bonnie Hampton experienced a racial environment that was still awkward but nonetheless represented an improvement over the daily tensions she experienced at Childs Street and Clarke Junior High School. She continued the behavior that had worked for her since her days as one of the Forgotten Five: striding confidently into every situation and never acting like she did not belong. More than fifty years later, that strength and confidence still were apparent when Bonnie Hampton Travis recalled her story in a phone interview.

While at Athens High, she became an officer for DECA (Distributive Education Clubs of America), a high school club dedicated to developing leadership skills for future entrepreneurs and business leaders. One morning, she was driving her car and went over a steep embankment into a ditch. One of her high school classmates—a White boy who had bullied her relentlessly at Childs Street—saw the accident, stopped his car, went into the ditch, and pulled her out of harm's way. In Bonnie's eyes, this Good Samaritan act marked a milestone—one of her previous tormentors was now willing to look beyond race and help a fellow human in need.

Mary Stephens was the daughter of U.S. representative Robert Stephens and typically split her middle and early high school years between attending school in Athens and—when Congress was in session—in Washington, D.C. The shuttling back and forth between schools in adolescence made her more introverted, and she felt later in life that this made her naturally more empathetic toward Marjorie Green, her Black classmate at Clarke Junior High School. Mary and Marjorie would meet up after school at the home of Margot Holder, the daughter of H. Randolph Holder, who owned the local radio station WGAU. They occupied themselves with typical teenage girl after-school activities like studying, sharing gossip, and watching television, and the racial differences between the three girls, two White and one Black, blurred over time.

There was no template for the successful integration of schools in the South or in much of the rest of the nation in the early 1960s. The Black and White populations of southern cities hardly interacted with each other; they attended separate churches, social clubs, lodges, and schools. Parents could offer their children little in the way of practical advice on how to navigate the rocky shoals of integration. Most of the parents were part of the "Greatest Generation," and many—both Black and White—had served in the armed forces during World War II. But the military did not end its practice of segregating troops until 1948, three years after the war ended, when President Truman signed an executive order requiring the immediate desegregation of the armed forces. For the children and adolescents who participated in the initial attempts at school desegregation, it was a bewildering experience, and they—the Black students especially—felt like "guinea pigs" in an experiment conducted by adults who had never been thrust into such uncharted territory themselves.

The common refrain for the Black students involved in integrating the Athens schools was an acknowledgment that the resources at their new schools—the textbooks, the facilities, and the supplies—were superior to what was available at the Black schools. But these enhanced tools were offset by the loss of something less tangible: the tough but nurturing relationship that existed between teachers and students at their former schools. Their Black teachers not only demanded excellence but also instilled a belief system for success, and since the teachers were highly admired members of the community, there was a partnership among school, parent(s), and child that did not exist at the predominantly White schools. Agnes Green, who was on the receiving end of perhaps the worst taunts because she was quite athletic and considered a "tomboy," missed the nurturing atmosphere and returned to all-Black Lyons Middle School after the end of the 1963–1964 school year. But she and the other members of the Forgotten Five had blazed the trail for integration of the Athens schools. Many would soon follow in their wake, but in the meantime, the Forgotten Five and other local successes with integration had stirred the dark forces of bigotry, and the racist backlash would be bloody.

卌

In the 1920s, nationwide membership in the second incarnation of the Ku Klux Klan reached an estimated five million, and fifty thousand Klansmen marched through the streets of Washington, D.C., in August 1925. In the decades that followed, the Klan saw a steady decline in its membership rolls after a series of corruption scandals and the introduction of tighter national immigration laws that reduced the worries of many of its supporters. However, a third iteration of the organization saw a surge in membership in the 1950s and 1960s as a reaction to the string of victories won by civil rights advocates in Congress and in courts across the United States.

The composition of Clarke County Klavern 244, the Klan's Athens headquarters, reflected many of the changes the Klan had undergone since its heyday in the 1920s, when membership in the Klan was seen as almost a respectable activity—sort of a social club for middle-class Whites. Support for the Klan had largely waned among the middle class as integration slowly gained momentum across the South, and the core members who remained were much more working class and more militant.

Today, the building at 199 Prince Avenue radiates a retro industrial cool. Two stories in height, the brick structure until recently housed the popular vegetarian restaurant the Grit on its bottom floor. Customers enjoyed coffee or mimosas while gazing at the pedestrian, bicycle, and automobile traffic along this busy stretch of Prince where downtown meets Cobbham, a spectacularly preserved neighborhood filled with Victorian, Queen Anne, and Greek and Gothic Revival homes. In the 1980s, several Athens-based bands held jam sessions and even impromptu small performances for their dedicated fans on the unoccupied second floor, and Michael Stipe, the front man of R.E.M., later purchased the building.

But in 1964, this stretch of Prince Avenue was down on its luck and still a few decades away from undergoing its transformation into bohemian hipness. Clarke County Klavern 244 rented the second floor on 199 Prince Avenue, which also housed a gas station on the ground level. The local chapter of the KKK had shrunk to twenty-nine members, including six hard-core members of its "security patrol."[15]

While Athens had experienced an economic boom in the previous fifteen years, this upturn did not raise the living standards and prospects of all its White citizens. As Bill Shipp described it, "Athens was also the home of textile plants, cottonseed oil makers and tire cord manufacturers. Those industries gave Athens and environs a slightly different face on close inspection. These industries often thrive on the sweat and brawn of poorly educated and poorly paid white workers, who in 1964 stood on a socioeconomic level only slightly higher than that of blacks."[16]

The Athens Klan members were the personification of Lyndon Johnson's famous quote, "If you can convince the lowest white man he's better than the best colored man, he won't notice you're picking his pocket. Hell, give him somebody to look down on, and he'll empty his pockets for you." The members of the Klan's security patrol included a gas station "grease monkey," a "mill yarn-plucker," and a machinist, all of whom felt their status threatened by the advances made by African Americans.[17]

After Hunter and Holmes integrated UGA in 1961, Black Athenians gained a newfound confidence and began to participate in sit-ins and protests at the city's segregated businesses, including the downtown Woolworth's. African American businessman Homer Wilson remembered: "At that time, the people were glad to see some things happening. We had been going into back doors, side doors, no doors, and all the rest. So, yeah, we were in the mood for change."[18]

In 1964, the Civil Rights Act was winding its way through the halls of Congress, and one integration barrier after another was collapsing. In Athens, Black citizens were ramping up their demands for equal rights and starting to show up in large numbers at area businesses to picket and protest. Alarmed by the growing clamor for equality, the Athens Klavern decided to fight back by using violence and intimidation.

The Varsity, founded and owned by Atlanta's Gordy family, had had a presence in Athens since 1932 with its downtown location just across the street from the Arch on College Avenue. In 1963, its much larger sister location, with its red accordion awning and dazzling red, black, and white signage, was built at West Broad and Milledge. By the standards of the time, it was a sui generis warehouse-style fast-food place, with its own lingo for ordering the restaurant's signature chili dogs, frosted orange drinks, and grease-drenched onion rings and fries. On UGA game days, it was not unusual to see lines backed up to the glass doors that opened on three sides of the structure. The restaurant featured a porcelain and stainless-steel ordering counter extending the length of the block-long building and offered three named TV-viewing rooms—"The Bulldog," "The Trojan," and "The Coed." Hungry patrons would take their orders and sit at student-like desks and watch sports on a small television perched high in a corner of each glass-walled room.

In 1964, the Varsity, like many restaurants in the South, would not serve African Americans, at least not in the dining areas. The new McDonald's franchise on Prince Avenue, by contrast, was integrated, and the owner let it be known that his restaurant was open to all customers, regardless of race. The Four Seasons restaurant, owned by African American Archibald Killian, was a popular chicken, fish, and shrimp eatery that was integrated by White UGA students who learned by word of mouth of the delicious recipes prepared by the Black owner. Business boomed for a while until White parents complained, and Killian was pressured to keep his restaurant segregated.

Local Black youth, assisted by the Athens chapter of the NAACP and advised by Athens's only Catholic priest, Father John Mulroy, began forming picket lines and protesting outside the Varsity. This attracted the attention of the Athens Klan, who showed up in hoods and robes to counterprotest. At one demonstration, the protesters also showed up robed and hooded to poke fun at the Klan members, who took umbrage at being lampooned by a group of "insolent" Black picketers. Guns were pulled out, and a Klansman struck a bystander in the face with his weapon. Athens mayor Julius Bishop was apprised of this close brush with tragedy but declined to act on the basis that the Klansmen were "within their rights" to carry guns in public, and he could take action only if violence ensued. The Athens radio stations and newspapers shied away from extensive coverage of the protests at the Varsity under the pretext that those Klansmen responsible represented only a "handful of troublemakers," and the issue would be settled soon.[19]

Emboldened by their repercussion-free performance at the Varsity, the Klan looked for other opportunities to engage in racially tinged criminal mischief and intimidation. Armed nightriders stopped Black drivers in Athens and cross-examined them about their destination. In March, James Potts, a Black man who worked in an auto repair shop owned by Klansman Herbert Guest, was accused by his employer of stealing money from the business; Potts was forced to lean over the hood of a car and endure a whipping from an estimated eighteen Klansmen. In June, Klansmen showed up outside a unit of the Broad Acres Apartments, a Black low-income residential complex, and fired a shotgun blast through the door. A nineteen-year-old Black man, John Clink, was permanently blinded in one eye, and two pellets struck the lip of Alice Farr, a thirteen-year-old Black girl.[20]

Although a tiny group, the local Klavern wielded an influence far beyond its meager numbers and enjoyed a friendly relationship with the Athens Police Department, with whom the Klansmen traded guns and information. On one occasion, an Athens policeman pulled over a Black couple. After questioning the couple and allowing them to drive on, a Klansman asked for and received the names and addresses of the car occupants from the helpful cop. On July 4, Klansman Joseph Howard Sims spotted an elderly Black couple with New Jersey license plates asking a policeman for directions to Atlanta. Sims walked up to the car and stuck his head through the open window and said, "Get your black asses back up North where you came from."[21]

It is unlikely that the Athens Klan had a particular plan. Its members were poorly educated—none had graduated from high school—and they were sloppy and brash in their piecemeal and uncoordinated vigilantism. But their overconfidence had been reinforced by their proven ability to act with impunity, as nobody—no members of the media or the police department, no one in city leadership—had held them accountable for their increasingly violent behavior. The *Athens Banner-Herald* reported only on the criminal trial of "seven Negroes" who had been found guilty on charges of criminal trespassing for entering the Varsity and falling to the floor after they were denied service.[22] By this time, Archibald Killian was no longer involved with his restaurant and was one of three Black cops in Athens. He pointedly refused to arrest Black civil rights protesters and tried to turn in his badge when Mayor Bishop ordered him to do so. No

Klansmen were arrested and no serious investigations were underway in the summer of 1964 to rein in this armed and dangerous group of homegrown terrorists.

By the late 1970s, Blanche's Open House, a restaurant on Hancock Avenue owned by Blanche and Herbert Guest, was the late-night haunt of overserved frat boys in need of a greasy antidote to the bourbon and cheap lager they had swilled over the course of an evening. Back in 1964, it was the favored hangout for Local 244. It was, as described by John T. Edge, a classic small-town diner with a certain run-down charm: "[Y]ears of cigarette smoke had rendered the white brick dining room walls beige. The floor was a checkerboard of red and white tiles. Seven red vinyl stools faced a scarred linoleum counter."[23]

On the night of July 10 and on into the early morning of July 11, 1964, the armed security patrol of Klavern 244 shuttled back and forth between the Guests' Open House restaurant on the western edge of downtown and the garage Herbert Guest owned on East Hancock Avenue. Three members of the security patrol—Cecil Myers, James Lackey, and Howard Sims—were driving a cream-colored Chevy II station wagon, and at around 4:00 a.m. they saw a Chevrolet Biscayne sedan stop and change drivers near the UGA Arch on Broad Street. The security patrol noticed that the car had Washington, D.C., license plates and realized its three occupants were Black. Later, a Klansmen would tell the FBI that they assumed the Black men were some of "President Johnson's boys" sent to Athens to cause trouble.[24] They immediately began trailing the sedan northward through Athens and onto State Route 172 as the two-lane road curved its way through the hamlets and dark forests of northeast Georgia. The world was shut down and in a deep and dreamy summer slumber, it seemed.

Lt. Col. Lemuel Penn, a decorated World War II veteran, was the assistant superintendent of schools in Washington, D.C. Mr. Penn and the two other Black reserve officers in the car had just finished their required two weeks of army reserve duty at Fort Benning in Columbus, Georgia. They had left Columbus the previous evening and took turns driving through the night—they were uncertain about the availability of motels in the Deep South that might accommodate Black travelers on the route back to D.C.

Just before crossing the bridge over the Broad River in Madison County outside Colbert, the station wagon driven by James Lackey pulled alongside the car driven by Penn. Sims, on the passenger side of the front seat, and Myers, in the backseat, leaned through their open windows and fired their shotguns at the Chevy Biscayne.

The first blast blew away the left side of Penn's face; the buckshot from the second shot narrowly missed the occupants in the back seat. Penn died instantly; his dazed and terrified companions were somehow able to take control of the steering wheel as the car careened off the guardrails of the bridge. The station wagon that had torn the night asunder with its sudden roar of death passed them, and its red taillights disappeared into the dark and humid Georgia night.

At the subsequent trial of Howard Sims and Cecil Myers in Madison County, an all-White jury deliberated for several hours before returning a verdict of not guilty on the charge of first-degree murder, despite a confession—partially retracted at the trial—by James Lackey. Jack Nelson, the intrepid *Atlanta Constitution* reporter who had earlier exposed the prostitution and illegal gambling rackets in Athens, tried to interview Howard Sims as he awaited the jury's verdict. Sims became enraged—not over the upcoming verdict, which he was sure would be in his favor, but at Nelson, whose exposé had damaged Sims's gambling business. "You stink," he snarled. "You ruined the best part of Athens! You destroyed some of the finest social and service clubs in town. I wouldn't talk with you about anything!"[25]

The 1964 Civil Rights Act had been signed into law just

days before Penn's murder, which allowed the Justice Department to prosecute Sims, Myers, Lackey, and three other men for violating Penn's civil rights. Otherwise, all the defendants would have walked free without any concerns about future legal action. In federal court, the two gunmen, Sims and Myers, were each sentenced to ten years in federal prison; Sims had an extra ten years added to his sentence for attempting to kill his estranged wife. In 1981 Sims was shot to death at a flea market outside Athens after he and a friend argued; the Klansman's life ended at the age of fifty-eight with a blast from the same type of weapon that killed Lemuel Penn—a twelve-gauge shotgun.[26]

╫╫╫

Most preteen boys are too busy with the joys and challenges of growing up to be more than vaguely aware of the momentous events swirling around them, such as the tragic murder of Lemuel Penn. That was the case in Athens with a group of boys, both Black and White, who would later experience and influence the course of integration in the Classic City. All were conscious of the two separate societies delineated by race that existed in Athens, and the Black youngsters were keenly aware of the institutional racism that sought to permanently consign them to second-class status.

Clarence Pope, Michael Thurmond, Horace King, and Richard Appleby grew up in separate parts of the city, but the four Black adolescents attended the same schools and gradually became friends as they played together in sports and made their way through the segregated school system. All four would later play groundbreaking roles in advancing the cause of their race in athletics and, in the case of Michael Thurmond, politics and government.

In July 1953, the Reverend John Henry Pope received a troubling phone call from Portsmouth, Virginia. His niece, whom he and his wife, Miss Janie, had raised, was in trouble with the law once again. This time the charges were serious enough that her two babies, a boy and a girl, would need to become wards of the state unless they were adopted by family members.

The Silver Comet passenger train made a daily stop in Athens at 9:28 p.m. on its way north. Reverend Pope boarded the train wearing his best set of clothes and settled in for the overnight, thirteen-hour journey to Portsmouth.

Both he and Miss Janie were born in Athens in the 1870s as the children of formerly enslaved people. In addition to his ministerial duties for the local Black church, Reverend Pope owned an East Athens farm on which he raised some livestock and grew vegetables. He was seventy-five years old when he received that phone call in the summer of 1953, and he had earned the right to spend his remaining years in peace, but he also knew that he had been summoned to carry out one more important mission—to raise the eight-month-old boy, Clarence, and his eighteen-month-old sister to the best of his ability in the years he had left. He was realistic enough to understand that he likely would be unable to see the small children into adulthood, and that left him even more determined to impart as many life lessons to them as he could before departing this world.

Clarence Pope attended East Athens Elementary and was teased by his fellow students, who called him "Farmer Brown" for wearing overalls. He was a big kid, and he enjoyed playing sports during recess and after school. His world was blown apart when Reverend Pope—whom he called "Daddy"—died at the age of eighty-four, when Clarence was just nine years old. The young boy felt like he would never again get the type of love and attention that he received from Reverend Pope, and he soon sought refuge in sports, in which he had always excelled. He honed his athletic skills by playing against the older boys in his neighborhood.

The house the Popes lived in, off Herring Street in East

Athens, was in a small valley just across the North Oconee River from Sanford Stadium. On Saturdays in the fall, an acoustical anomaly brought the sounds of UGA football games to his home. This allowed Clarence to hear all the band music and cheers and groans and even actual conversations funneled from the open east end of the stadium. The young boy would throw a football high in the air and catch it or sit on a large rock and imagine playing for the Bulldogs. Although UGA was still years away from allowing Black players on its football team, Clarence knew he wanted to play for the University of Georgia one day.

Clarence met a slight but smart and confident schoolmate named Michael Thurmond when they were competing in a drama contest in the sixth grade. Clarence was a member of his school's safety patrol, and this earned him his first trip away from home, when he and Thurmond rode the Silver Comet to Washington, D.C. The smaller Michael Thurmond was an easy target for bullies on the train, who were jealous of his smarts and self-assurance, but Pope took him under his wing and protected him, and a friendship was born.

Miss Janie was impressed with the courteous and intelligent young Michael Thurmond, and she would always encourage Clarence—who had an active social life and was never without a girlfriend—to be "more like Mike."[27]

Michael grew up in the Sandy Creek area east of the North Oconee River and was the youngest of nine children raised by Sidney and Vanilla Thurmond. Sidney worked in the fields as a sharecropper during the day and at a poultry plant at night. Michael's mother helped in the fields and looked after the children. In the little spare time they had available, the family earned extra income by selling fruit and vegetables.

Sidney Thurmond could neither read nor write, but he always encouraged his children to do well in school, and this, along with the positive example of several siblings who were studious, helped motivate Michael Thurmond to pursue his goal of attending college. "There was nothing [my father] wouldn't sacrifice to send my brothers and sisters and myself to college or wherever we wanted to go," Michael later reflected. "He knew that ultimately that's what would make the difference. That's the great equalizer in the world."[28]

Horace King was, in his own words, a "west side kid who grew up in Rocksprings, near the projects but not in the projects." His parents both worked hard. Horace's father held two jobs, working during the day as a custodian at Clarke Junior High School, and as a night watchman at the Athens Country Club. "I never understood why a country club needed a night watchman," King laughingly recalled years later.[29] His mother was a domestic worker at various homes in Athens and later worked as a custodian at Brumby Hall, the all-female high-rise UGA dormitory.

As a boy, Horace bicycled around downtown Athens and would sometimes stop outside the old fortresslike YMCA at the corner of Broad and Lumpkin. "Why can't I play here?" he would say to himself, as he listened to the shouts and splashes of the young White kids playing basketball or swimming in the 1,200-square-foot pool.

Horace learned to compete the hard-nosed way, by playing in pickup basketball games at the Rocksprings Recreation Center near Henderson Extension. A former Athens High and Industrial School sports legend named Leonard Champion meted out punishment on the court—elbows, forearms, even punches were allowed as players sought to gain any type of advantage. A brick wall stood just beyond the baseline on one end, and it was not uncommon to see a player get pushed into it as he attempted a layup. There was no animosity or cruelty to Champion's method of instruction; he wanted to teach the younger kids one of the tough lessons of competition—that those who wanted to win had to use every tool at their disposal.

As a young boy, Horace attended the neighborhood school, West Broad Elementary School, which was just a short walk from his home. So he felt like a "bit of an outsider" when he, like all Black students in Athens-Clarke County at the time, started attending Lyons Middle School in the seventh grade.

Lyons was in East Athens next to Ben Epps Airfield. With numerous stops and workday traffic along the way, the bus ride from West Athens to Lyons could take more than an hour. The bus driver, Mr. Garnell, tolerated no foolishness among his passengers. Children who misbehaved were forced to disembark and walk the remaining distance to school. "Don't be sticking your head out the window; no breaking the rules" was the constant warning shouted out by Mr. Garnell, who, like Horace's father, was an army veteran.[30]

Black students played a semiorganized version of football while at Lyons. Those who had parents who could afford to pay for them had full uniforms; those who did not had to improvise. The kids wore leather shoulder pads and helmets with a single bar or even no face mask. Because of the flimsy equipment, the boys played "arm tackle" football, with fewer than eleven players per side.

On autumn Saturdays as a young boy, Horace worked as a vendor at UGA football games at Sanford Stadium, selling Coca-Colas to the assembled crowd. After selling out his allotment of twenty-four drinks, he would put his tray aside and find an empty seat to watch the game. He dreamed of playing for the Bulldogs one day, but that dream seemed remote at the time as the first Black players had not yet begun to compete on the campuses of the SEC.

Horace realized early that he might be among a special group of athletes—his homeroom won the seventh-grade championship in basketball and then went on to whip the eighth-grade champions. With growing confidence, he began to believe that he might have a future in football or basketball, and he started putting in extra work and doing anything he could to "make himself better."

He also knew that a group of kids in his class was athletically blessed—especially a tall, wisecracking boy named Richard Appleby who lived off Hawthorne Avenue. Clarence Pope, Spurgeon Cross, Will Jones, and George Wingfield were also showing signs of their budding talents. Horace knew that if they stuck together, they would turn into something special.

Richard Appleby grew up north of town off the Jefferson Highway in Oconee Heights, a small neighborhood consisting of five or six Black-owned homes that lacked running water and electricity—"We lived out in the country," he remembered. He attended North Athens Elementary, situated next to the smelly Gold Kist poultry plant on Oneta Street. Richard was one of ten children—five boys and five girls; his father, a navy veteran, was a tailor who worked at a laundromat off Hancock Avenue. His mother was a homemaker, tasked with the joy and burden of raising her ten children. Richard was her sixth child, and he started earning money at age eight, making three dollars plus tips for caddying eighteen holes of golf at the Athens Country Club.

The family eventually moved from their home in the countryside to Lyndon Avenue before settling in the Brooklyn Apartments off Hawthorne Avenue. He met his friends and future teammates while attending Lyons Middle School and, like the others, began playing competitive sports at the middle school level. In his early teens, Richard Appleby went through a growth spurt, adding six inches in one year before topping out at 6'3". By the time he was in ninth grade, he could dunk a basketball.[31]

+++++

In different neighborhoods in different parts of town, a group of White boys were also climbing the rungs of adolescence, making their way through their separate YMCA camps, Boy Scout dens, schools, churches, and sports teams.

Their paths did not begin intersecting with those of young Black students until the Athens public schools began integrating in 1963, but these young men were also both witnesses to and participants in the painful integration efforts that would be widespread in Athens around the end of the decade. Andy Johnson would lead the last segregated team at Athens High School as its quarterback in 1969 and would welcome the first Black players (and fellow Athenians) to the newly integrated UGA football team. Doc Eldridge also played at Athens High School and, along with African American teammate Michael Thurmond, helped mitigate the racial tensions that beset the town's first integrated high school football team. Bill King recorded the first fitful attempts of full-scale school integration as a budding young journalist at Athens High.

Anderson "Andy" Sidney Johnson grew up off Whitehead Road, just inside the county line in the northernmost extremity of Athens. The families that lived in the brick, ranch-style homes in the Bel Air Heights neighborhood were an eclectic mixture of White blue-collar workers, university professors, and lower-level white-collar managers. This was a relatively new swath of development, and nature still encroached; the neatly cut yards were bordered by gullies infested with croaking frogs, menacing yellow jackets, and sunning snakes and interspersed with gushing creeks that slashed and tumbled over sharp granite as they made their way to the muddy waters of the North Oconee River.

Andy's father worked in the printing office of the University of Georgia, and his mother was an assistant at Hope Haven, a facility for those suffering from developmental disabilities. Andy was a middle child sandwiched between two sisters, and he was an athletic prodigy even at a young age, despite being one of the youngest members of his school class—he had an October 18 birthday, and October 31 was the cutoff for grade levels in Athens.

From the age of six, when sports competition started at

the YMCA, Johnson displayed his special athletic talents. Wearing his Washington Redskins uniform—before the Atlanta Falcons came into existence in 1966, Washington was the preferred NFL team of the Southeast—Andy dominated the local Punt, Pass, and Kick competitions, always winning in all three categories. My father coached him as a twelve-year-old in twelve-to-fourteen-year-old Pony League baseball, where Andy played every position except catcher. At tryouts, each player received three pitches, and Andy knocked all three of his over the centerfield fence. During the regular season, any kid who corralled a home run ball could exchange it for a free Coke at the concession stand. The kids used to line the outfield fence when Andy came to bat in hopes of winning a Coke.

He was, to borrow the hoary cliché, a "natural," and he combined his athletic prowess, wholesome good looks, and broad smile—in high school, Coach Weyman Sellers nicknamed him "Smiley"—with an authentic humility and modesty that lifted those around him. According to his lifelong best friend, Terry Smart, Andy went out of his way to make everyone feel better. Popular or unpopular, attractive or plain, Black or White—it did not matter; although introverted, Andy liked people and had a genuine interest in them.

When he was in middle school, Andy was already well known to the coaching staff at Athens High School, and Coach Sellers asked him to "suit up" with the varsity football team while he was still an eighth grader at Clarke Junior High.

Erwin James "Doc" Eldridge III was born three months after his family moved to Athens in 1952, thus tenuously attaining the status of "native Athenian"—though some half-jokingly claim that the measuring stick for securing that exalted position is having been both conceived and born in town. Doc (it is a tradition in the Eldridge family that all first-born sons are called "Doc") grew up at Milledge Circle and Fortson Drive in the Five Points neighborhood, which had (and still has) its own small commercial district. Always a haven for small family-owned businesses, in the early 1960s Five Points boasted a Bell's grocery store, an Elks Lodge, Andy Anderson's barbershop, Hodgson's Pharmacy, the drive-in restaurant Harry's, "Mr. Smith's" Standard Oil gas station, the New Way Laundromat, and ADD Drug.

Doc Eldridge's parents were both University of Georgia graduates—his father was a World War II navy veteran and a certified public accountant, and his mother served in a variety of positions at Beech Haven Baptist Church before becoming office manager. Doc "never left Baxter Street," progressing from Alps Road Elementary to Clarke Junior High School to Athens High School to the University of Georgia.[32]

Like most White boys in West Athens, Doc was first introduced to sports through the downtown Athens YMCA, whose youth leader was the charismatic, ukulele-and-organ-playing, devoutly Christian Cobern Kelley. Kelley was a World War II veteran who narrowly escaped with his life when he was almost trapped by a Japanese patrol. He pledged then that if he were to make it out alive, he would spend the rest of his life serving the youth of Athens, where he had attended UGA prior to the outbreak of war. Every summer, Kelley would pack his "Kelley's boys"—who ranged in age from third to eighth grade—onto an old Blue Bird school bus with no air-conditioning, and they would head out with an unknown itinerary; the only common thread to these annual three-week trips was that they always entailed a long, multiday drive from Athens. California, the Green Bay Packers' training camp (Kelley knew legendary head coach Vince Lombardi), Coney Island, British Columbia, and Juárez, Mexico, were some of the destinations. Kelley would pull over to a campsite in the evening, unload the trailer behind the bus that held cooking equipment, and prepare supper. After they ate, Kelley led the boys in singing hymns, shared life lesson stories, and read scripture. Everyone would then crawl into their sleeping bags and sleep under the stars.

Looking back from adulthood, many of the boys who went on the trips with Kelley reflected on how mothers would simply "pack their boys on the bus," expecting little or no communication from their sons while they were away, except maybe a postcard or two.[33] Similarly, boys attending a two-week or four-week session at the Athens Y Camp at Tallulah Falls were required to periodically drop off letters to their parents in the cafeteria line before they were allowed to eat.

Kelley built a youth camp in a cleared-out section of lush woods along the Middle Oconee River and named it "Pine Tops." The camp featured a small chapel built atop a section of jutting granite; next to the chapel were a gymnasium, a bunkhouse, and a cafeteria that served pancakes each morning to the hungry boys recovering from the previous day's activities—swimming in the river or pool, foraging in the forest, or playing basketball or dodgeball in the gym. Boys caught misbehaving received a warning for their bad conduct; a second offense meant induction into the "red bottom club," with one lick from the paddle, performed privately. A third offense involved a steep escalation in corporal punishment—five licks from the paddle, administered in public.

Kelley and his squad of youth volunteers taught the boys the rugged lessons of football on the hard, grassless football field behind the old downtown YMCA. Metal pipes from the sprinkler system jutted out in certain sections of the field, and discarded tires were placed around them to prevent injury. On Saturdays in the fall, lucky players would make the short trek from the Y building to Sanford Stadium, where they would perform before the slowly assembling crowd at UGA home games. After their scrimmage "between the hedges," they sat in the end zone grandstands or on the grassy banks next to the reserved seats to watch the Bulldogs. The boys who played sports, went to school, and grew up together—Andy Johnson, Terry Smart, Rand Lambert, Doc Eldridge, Gary Travis, and many others—forged a close-knit connection that endured through the last second of the last game they played together in high school.

As the boys grew older, their Y team would travel by bus to surrounding counties and play the best teams the locals could muster. Paul Gilbert, who spent most of his boyhood in Morgan County, remembered the thrashings the Athens Y would administer to his team. He was delighted and relieved to start playing for the area's youth football juggernaut after his family moved to Athens for his sixth-grade year. Middle-school-age players at the Y, wearing mismatched uniforms, would compete against nearby high school junior varsity teams and beat them with regularity.

Weyman Sellers would sometimes show up at Y practices to watch the older boys perform—he wanted an idea of whom he should keep an eye on once the boys moved on to Athens High. By the mid-1960s, he knew something special was brewing.

Like Eldridge, Bill King also grew up in the Five Points area, on Hope Avenue, before moving to Homewood Hills, near the country club, when he was fifteen. Bill was born in the old Athens General Hospital, the first of three sons born to William Dabney "Bill" King and Mollie Parry King. His father, a native of Colbert in Madison County, had met his Welsh wife in 1944 while serving in England and France during World War II. He brought his "war bride" back to Athens in 1946 and started a thirty-seven-year career at C&S Bank.

Mollie King worked in sales at Michael Brothers Department Store in downtown Athens, where her expertise in fine china earned her the respect and friendship of many of the Athens elite. Very active in the neighborhood, she was known affectionately as "the Mayor of Homewood Hills." She also served as a volunteer librarian at Whitehead Road Elementary School and was a progressive-minded "professional letter to the editor writer" to the local newspapers, according to her son Bill. She was a voracious reader and reserved a special love for journalism. She later became a contributing columnist at the *Athens Observer*, a weekly alternative periodical cofounded by Pete McCommons, where she wrote columns on a wide range of topics; she was best known for her special and very vocal disdain for the British royal family. McCommons remembered Mollie King thusly: "She was the ideal columnist: witty and opinionated, but not close-minded."[34]

Mollie brought her classic British skepticism to America and was not impressed when she met the charismatic Cobern Kelley, who tried to convince her to send her boys to the YMCA. "I don't see a need for them to attend the Y," she dryly observed. "They have a father who plays with them."[35] Her personal mission regarding athletics and her sons was to ensure that they never drowned; this meant continual swimming lessons at Legion, Stegeman, and other area pools to ensure that the boys were always safe in the vicinity of any body of water.

As a young boy, Bill King developed an interest in "newspapering" in general and started several neighborhood newspapers. He would further develop his skills as a writer at Athens High, where he became a news, column, and editorial writer for the school paper, the *Thumb Tack Tribune*.

All the White youngsters were aware of the separate and unequal status of African Americans in Athens, but that was more of an abstraction—Jim Crow laws did not directly affect them. As they grew older and institutionalized racism slowly loosened its grip on Athens, they became unexpected participants in the drama that unfolded.

᠁

Although Athens High integrated in 1963, the football team remained completely White, and the first Black players would not try out for the Trojans until 1966. Many high schools and colleges in the Deep South followed this pattern of integrating the student body and then waiting years before allowing Black students to participate in sports; for some schools, particularly at the collegiate level, the time lag between the two milestones extended beyond a decade.

In 1964, Athens High School left UGA's Sanford Stadium and started playing football games on its own campus, on a field behind the school that was christened "Death Valley." Vince Dooley became the new football coach at the University of Georgia in 1964, and he, along with athletic director Joel Eaves, quickly looked at ways to upgrade Sanford Stadium. Over seven thousand bleacher seats were added to the open areas behind the end zones, and the stadium lights—which were perched atop poles placed inside the field's iconic privet hedges—were removed. UGA had not played a night game in years, and the poles supporting the lights were an eyesore that impeded the sightlines of spectators. Athens High was happy to accept the donated lights from UGA, as it allowed the Trojans to enjoy more of a Friday night home-field advantage in their newly built stadium.

The players' dressing room was on a ridge attached to the gymnasium that marked the far, southern end of Athens High School. The players would walk down the hill to Death Valley before the game, a tradition that was soon dubbed "walking down the pines," because the pathway down to the field was bordered by tall, skinny loblolly pines. The sight of the first uniformed Trojans walking down the pines would create a rumble in the crowd, leading to a loud roar once they all came into full view.

Athens High had a winning record in each season of the first half of the 1960s, although a region championship always eluded them. There were eight regions in AAA (the largest classification in Georgia at the time), and only the region winners advanced to the playoffs, which included quarterfinals, semifinals, and a championship game. The school's biggest rival was Gainesville High, which was the last game of the season. The two schools were forty miles apart, which represented the shortest distance between Athens and any regional opponent in 5-AAA. Both schools produced college and even professional-caliber talent, particularly Gainesville—Billy Martin and Billy Lothridge went on to star at Georgia Tech and in the NFL, while Preston Ridlehuber played quarterback at Georgia and running back professionally.

Sports are largely mythical in the sense that we lionize our team's heroes and sadly recall those who, like Icarus, achieve greatness before tumbling from the sky. Their triumphs and tragedies become even more Herculean with the passage of time as the distinct memories of specific games and plays slowly fade.

No film or radio recordings remain of the 1965 Trojans, a squad that has been exalted as legendary by older Athenians who played on the team or watched their local boys perform in front of sold-out Death Valley crowds. The roster brimmed with talent, including future college players Paul Gilbert, Jerry Cash ("the Bogart Bullet"), Ed Allen, and Bobby Poss. Gilbert in particular was a special talent—injuries to two quarterbacks thrust him into the starting role as a freshman, and he led Athens High to a couple of wins and a narrow loss to Gainesville at home. Recruited by every major college in the country, Gilbert was expected to lead the Trojans deep into the playoffs in 1965.

Athens High School dominated the regular season in the fall of 1965—the school's narrowest margin of victory was in the opening game of the season, a 19–7 triumph over Marietta High. Hart County fell by a score of 68–0, while Jonesboro High lost to the rampaging Trojans at Death Valley by an eye-popping score of 86–0. Paul Gilbert later coached for Jonesboro in the 1970s and recalled that their fans were still angry about that game. Years later, Bobby Poss, the team's center, remembered that some of the teams that they pasted on the road were so upset by the margin of victory that they turned off the hot water in the visitor's locker room.

Betting on Athens High to cover an unofficial point spread became easy money for local gamblers. Poss recalled that he was eating at the Beechwood Buffet early in the season when a local gambler named D. Allen sat at his table and asked him about the team's prospects against the upcoming weekend's opponent. Poss told Allen that Athens should win by three touchdowns. When Poss finished his meal and tried to pay the cashier, she told him his bill had been taken care of. Each week thereafter, Poss and Allen met and discussed the likely margin of victory Athens would achieve against the upcoming foe, and Poss would then earn his free meal. He was never asked to help throw a game—just to provide valuable information on the likelihood of the team covering the spread.

Athens High roared through the playoffs and played at home in the finals against Valdosta High School, the traditional powerhouse in Georgia high school football and the program against which all other schools were measured. By 1965, Valdosta had accumulated ten state championship trophies, winning three straight from 1960 to 1962.

Due to a quirk in scheduling, a relatively well-rested Valdosta Wildcat team arrived at the state finals having played only one playoff game, compared to the three playoff games Athens had played and won. Years later, Coach Sellers told journalist Lewis Grizzard that the unbalanced scheduling played a role in the outcome on that cold evening at Death Valley on December 4, 1965. But Valdosta was also loaded with talent, including future college players such as quarterback Glenn Davis (UGA), wide receiver Rhett Dawson (Florida State), and running backs Robert Strom and Kenny Bounds (both Georgia Tech).

With the game-time temperature at thirty-three degrees,

the bundled-up crowd was rocking for the final. Death Valley had a listed capacity of five thousand, but eleven thousand fans were in attendance. Earlier in the playoffs, AHS players had decided to forego playing in the more spacious Sanford Stadium to accommodate the anticipated overflow crowds; in its two-year existence, Death Valley and the raucous hometown supporters had already created a decided home-field advantage.[36] The fans would find a way to squeeze in.

Valdosta dominated favored Athens in the first half and led 14–0 at halftime. The Trojans could accomplish little on offense, and quarterback Paul Gilbert—still partially hobbled by a badly sprained ankle he had suffered several weeks earlier—was harried and sacked repeatedly by a strong Wildcat rush.

Wildcat quarterback Glenn Davis suffered a cracked rib early in the second half, and Valdosta shifted to a conservative strategy, relying almost entirely on its running game as it sought to run out the clock with a two-touchdown lead. Although Athens managed to score and cut the margin to 14–7 in the third quarter, the Valdosta plan of milking the clock was on the verge of success when the Trojans got the ball back with two minutes left in the fourth quarter on its own twenty-yard line. Athens had time to muster one last desperation drive in a game that Valdosta had statistically dominated.

Paul Gilbert lined up in the shotgun and led Athens quickly down the field, relying on midrange passes to carve up a loose Wildcat defense that was ceding yardage but determined not to give up the long "bomb." A young Mike Epps attended the game with his father, and years later he remembered the poise and composure of Gilbert: "He was smooth; I played with Andy Johnson, who was great, but Gilbert was really smooth."[37] It was a frenzied drive, and a malfunctioning stadium clock added to the confusion—at the end of each play, the referees would scream the time remaining to the two head coaches.

With the Trojans deep in Valdosta territory with less than a minute to go, student public address announcer Bill Hartman Jr. informed the tense crowd that in the event of a tie, the two teams would be declared co–state champions. Years later, Hartman regretted the possibility that his announcement might have played a role in the game-deciding play that would soon follow.

The Trojans scored on fourth down when Gilbert ran off tackle with five seconds remaining to make the score 14–13. Athens had covered the eighty yards in nine plays, and the extra point was almost an afterthought. By the standards of the era, before the advent of soccer-style kickers who improved both accuracy and distance, the Trojans' "straight on" placekicker, Chuck Perry, had been close to automatic all year—he had converted sixty-two of his seventy extra point attempts, including thirty-five of his last thirty-six, and had kicked the first Athens High field goal in five years. Perry, a senior, had unofficially compiled the most impressive set of statistics of any kicker in the state.[38] But there were several delays—joyous Athens fans rushed the end zone after the touchdown and shook the goalposts, and it took several minutes to clear them from the field. Then Valdosta coach Wright Bazemore called consecutive timeouts to freeze the placekicker by giving him several long and tortuous minutes to reflect on the gravity of the situation.

A placekicker, like a golfer, relies on routine and execution. Perry's routine was thrown off by several factors. For the first time all season, spectators were seated in the end zone to accommodate the overflow crowd. His routine was further disrupted when Trojans players stood in a huddle while the referees cleared the end zone of celebrating fans "shouting like wild men"; typically, the Trojans eschewed huddles for extra points and went straight into their kicking formation.

Four years later, in an honest and poignant column he wrote for the *Athens Banner-Herald*, Chuck Perry recounted the sequence of events:

I looked up at the line and all I could see was Wildcats, concentrating on the middle in hopes of blocking the kick. Wheels started turning. If they're going to stack the middle, I should kick the ball a little higher than usual and sacrifice the unnecessary distance. The snap came perfect from [Bobby] Poss, and [Paul] Gilbert set it down with the same precision he always managed. I stepped forward, keeping my head down and my eye on the spot, and kicked through. It felt funny from the start, like no other kick before. The tee moved forward a couple of feet. The ball went almost straight up, and there was a long period of silence. Nothing registered.[39]

A stunned crowd stared in disbelief before shuffling quietly out of Death Valley into the pitch-black December night.

Valdosta coach Wright Bazemore, perhaps still feeling the sting of the twenty-one-point loss to Sellers and Athens High in the 1955 state championship, was smug in victory: "We played seven teams down in 1-AAA [Valdosta's region] that were as good as Athens. Seven of our opponents down there were undefeated when we played them. We just had to work harder. . . . I am just sorry we couldn't give them a better second half. It wouldn't have been close if we had had Glenn [Davis]."[40]

Losing in the most excruciatingly painful way imaginable left the Trojans and their head coach inconsolable. The next day, the *Athens Daily News* reported that "Sellers, a brute of a man, fought hard to keep back the tears . . . [but] there wasn't a sadder man in the Trojan dressing room than Chuck Perry, who in his own mind, will take the blame for Athens losing. He shouldn't. Credit should go to a great Valdosta team that played inspired football and won it legitimately."[41]

"Choke" Perry—fans were just as merciless in the decades before social media—took the missed kick so badly that he had to sit out his classes for a while, and according to Bobby Poss, the local gamblers were furious with him. Lost in the drama was the fact that Perry had set school placekicking records during the season, and the straight-on style that he used required great precision, even in game situations not weighted with the hopes of an entire community.

Weyman Sellers was now 1–1 in state final games against Wright Bazemore and Valdosta. The Athens YMCA seventh-and-eighth-grade football team had just concluded a perfect season competing against older area junior varsity high school teams. Led by quarterback Andy Johnson, the undefeated team featured names that Sellers was already well familiar with from years of scouting the boys playing behind the old Y building off Lumpkin Street: Andy Johnson, Doc Eldridge, Terry Smart, Mike Epps, Gary Travis, Rand Lambert, and many others. The bevy of younger talent working its way through the youth football pipeline in Athens all but ensured that Sellers would have an opportunity for redemption against the Wildcats in the not-too-distant future.

But Sellers and Bazemore would soon take divergent paths in adapting to the growing trend of integration in Georgia high school football. Their differing philosophies would ultimately set them on a collision course four years later, in the waning days of the decade.

卅卅

After Wilucia Green integrated Athens High School in 1963, a steady trickle of Black students—taking advantage of the local freedom of choice policy—made their way to the formerly all-White school. Maxie Foster was one of them.

Maxie had grown up in Broad Acres Apartments, a public housing complex built in 1941 and considered one of the most downtrodden Black neighborhoods in Athens. But Maxie never felt deprived living in the "projects," where the units offered running water and electricity and appliances—an upgrade over the lack of basic amenities still denied to thousands of Black families across Georgia in the 1950s.

As a boy, Maxie worked with his siblings and his mother at the Broad Acres community dry goods store. He remembered a sense of community and an unwritten code that made theft from the store taboo. He liked to hang out with the older boys from Broad Acres like Valdon Daniel, James Fair, and Aaron Heard—Maxie was a fellow "projects kid," and that created a strong bond between them. His sisters supplemented the family's income by working at the Black cinemas owned by a kindly local Jewish businessman, Sol Abrams.

Maxie was one of eight siblings, and a single mother, Rose Rittenberry, raised them. Rose worked multiple jobs—in addition to her work at the Broad Acres community store, she also labored as a domestic worker in the homes of many White Athenians, including the families of University of Georgia professors. Over time, she made important contacts through her work, and she used those contacts to convince UGA professors to assist as instructors in evening adult education courses she helped set up in Broad Acres.

Maxie Foster had an early introduction to racism. His older sister Katie was married to a light-skinned Black brickmason from Thomson named Joe Hampton (Katie was the mother of Bonnie Hampton, one of the Forgotten Five). Hampton took a liking to his young brother-in-law and escorted him to Georgia games, where they attracted stares as they walked, holding hands, to their seats—the Sanford Stadium crowd assumed Hampton was White. In those days before integration, Black fans were forced to sit in wooden grandstands at the eastern end of the stadium. This Black-designated seating area was dubbed the "Crow's Nest"—sometimes referred to even more pejoratively as the "Niggers' Nest." Despite the less than welcoming environment,

Foster first realized that he wanted to attend UGA while sitting on the splinter-infested wooden benches in the segregated stadium.

Rose Rittenberry worked in the home of respected physician and fifth-generation Athenian Dr. Bolling S. Dubose Jr., who practiced internal medicine and served both the White and Black communities. Dr. DuBose referred Rose to other doctors and professionals who lived in the high-end Mathis Apartments off South Lumpkin. After the closing bell at school at West Broad Elementary, Maxie would walk to the Mathis Apartments and stare in amazement at the books that lined the walls while his mother cleaned the apartments. He made the connection that books were crucial to obtaining both wealth and respect, and he vowed to extract as much knowledge as possible from reading. His mother constantly encouraged him to study and continuously repeated the mantra *You are not better than anyone, and no one is better than you.* His mother also instilled in Maxie the sense of a larger responsibility: he was a representative of the Black community, and he had to be constantly cognizant of his actions, lest they reflect poorly on his race.

In his spare time, Maxie played with his two best friends, Allen (sometimes spelled Alan) Morse and Robert Hawkins. They would play basketball in the backyard of Allen's home off Billups Street or at the nearby Rocksprings Community Center. On one occasion, the three boys were walking down Billups Street and were chased without cause by a couple of Athens cops in a squad car. The boys tried to escape by sprinting into Allen's house; the White policemen entered the home in pursuit and beat them and Allen's father, Henry A. Morse, with billy clubs. Police chief E. E. Hardy, whom the local Black community had previously considered either indifferent to or complicit in the racially biased criminal justice system in Athens, apologized to Mr. Morse and other Black leaders for the brutality of his officers.

Foster entered Burney-Harris High School as a freshman in 1964, and while he felt comfortable with the mixture of warmth and discipline provided by his Black teachers, he also felt that something was missing, that everything about the school system in Athens relegated Black students to an inferior status. Even the locations of the African American schools were constant reminders to the Black students and their parents of the low esteem they were held in by the Clarke County Board of Education. North Athens Elementary was next to a malodorous poultry plant, and Newtown Elementary—like the pre-integration Black swimming pool—was adjacent to the city dump; West Broad Elementary was set back from busy West Broad Street across from Broad Acres Apartments, and there was no safe pedestrian crossing for the young children going to and from school; Lyons Middle School was located in a distant corner of East Athens, next to a quarry and the Athens airport, Ben Epps Field; and even Burney-Harris High School, set back one street from busy West Broad, was hidden from sight. In the judgment of many members of the Black community, this lack of visibility was deliberate—the city fathers did not want visitors who were driving on the busy thoroughfare into Athens from the west to see an African American high school.

Burney-Harris received hand-me-down textbooks from Athens High School at the end of the school year whenever AHS was scheduled to receive updated editions for the upcoming fall. Some Athens High students, knowing the next destination of their outdated books, would scrawl crude cartoons and racist messages in the margins of the pages. The racist taunts and jungle caricatures did not dissuade Maxie Foster from his decision, though—he had decided to transfer to Athens High for his sophomore year.[42]

His friends Allen Morse and Robert Hawkins joined Maxie Foster as transfer students to AHS in the fall of 1965. Black students at Athens High were still a small minority in the mid-1960s, representing less than 5 percent of the total student body. But the number had grown large enough in the opening weeks of the 1965–1966 school year to attract the attention of a group of bullies, who made it their mission to threaten and harass Maxie Foster and his friends.

Robert Hawkins was one of six children whose family never lacked for creature comforts. His father, an army veteran, stressed preparation and made sure money and food were never a source of worry for his large family. Each November, he would take his sons to the countryside to slaughter a large cow to keep his family fed for the winter. As a member of a respected Black family, Robert had never felt poor before transferring to AHS, but he was awed by the material wealth of many of the White students and their expensive wardrobes acquired at Dick Ferguson's or George Gibson's. The faded "Goldwater" bumper stickers on his White classmates' cars immediately caught his attention. Barry Goldwater had lost to Lyndon Johnson in a landslide in the previous year's presidential election but had carried the state of Georgia. Goldwater had run on a platform emphasizing states' rights and had refused to sign the Voting Rights Act of 1964, and he was opposed by the Reverend Martin Luther King Jr. Hawkins and other African Americans viewed the bumper stickers as another example of "Fergit, Hell!" defiance by a dominant White culture that remained steadfastly opposed to integration.

Hawkins's father was a skilled bricklayer whose specialty was installing glazed floor tiles. His talent was widely recognized, and he had been selected more than a decade earlier to lay the tile in the bathrooms of the newly constructed Athens High. The amount of material left over after the job was completed was large enough to tile the bathroom of his home off Billups Street. It was therefore more than a touch ironic that a small group of White students tried to block Robert Hawkins and his friends as they tried to enter the bathroom.

The intimidation had started at the beginning of the

school year, when a White student spotted the fifteen-year-old Hawkins—"who didn't weigh a hundred pounds"—and his Black friends and shouted, "We got us a goddamned nigger convention here!" Another time, Hawkins accidentally bumped into a White student, who jumped back in horror and began to brush at the skin that Hawkins had touched, as if to "rub the Black off."[43]

The incidents culminated in a confrontation one day as Hawkins, Morse, and Foster were walking down the hallway and found their path blocked by a group of White working-class students. The ringleader was holding a section of metal pipe and a length of chain. This was not the first encounter Hawkins and his friends had had with this group of toughs, who had denied Black students access not only to the bathrooms but also to the water fountains and the school cafeteria.

Allen Morse was stocky and strong, his muscles filled out by weight-lifting sessions and by helping his adoptive father, Henry Morse, in his cement finishing business. He had played first chair trumpet in the school band at BHHS, and one reason he transferred to AHS was that the Burney-Harris band director had refused to release the talented musician from the band so he could play for the Yellow Jackets football team. Slow to anger, Morse was a bull as a running back on the gridiron, where he earned the nickname "Night Train" because of his size and his resemblance to Dick "Night Train" Lane, a ferocious Black cornerback in the NFL whose specialty was making high clothesline-style tackles of opposing ballcarriers.[44]

On this day, Morse had had enough of the bullies, enough of the racist taunts, enough of the sneers and threats. He lowered his head and planted it in the chest of the ringleader—a boy related to the Klansman Herbert Guest—lifted him up, and planted him with a loud thud on the concrete floor. The Guest boy did not move for almost a minute, and those who had witnessed it feared that he was dead. He eventually recovered from the vicious takedown and dusted himself off, and he and his friends quietly slunk away. From that point forward, Allen Morse and his friends had no problems going to the bathrooms or cafeteria or quenching their thirsts at the water fountains.[45]

The administration of Athens High did not condone the intimidation and crude racist behavior exhibited by some White students. But Foster felt that he had been set up for academic failure; as a sophomore, the registrar's office had originally placed him in senior courses such as calculus and advanced Latin. Foster later changed his course selection to one more suitable for a tenth grader. The decision by the administration to place all the African American students in a single homeroom class might have been well intentioned, but it further fueled their sense of isolation and feeling of "otherness."

Both Foster and Hawkins acknowledged that it was also an awkward and even traumatic situation for the White students—nothing had prepared them for integration, and they felt helpless, like they were "guinea pigs." They had no frame of reference, and no one to whom they could speak for advice; their parents, teachers, and church leaders had only known segregation.

The Black students missed the camaraderie of their old school and did not feel comfortable approaching their White teachers for after-school help like they had done at Burney-Harris. Some grew discouraged and withdrew from AHS and returned to the all-Black high school. Sharing notes, seeking out lab partners, or studying with White students was not discouraged, but there seemed to be an invisible barrier that Black students were hesitant to breach.[46]

Incidents like those endured by Morse, Foster, and Hawkins made their way by word of mouth to the students at Burney-Harris, who mainly resisted the idea of transferring to Athens High under freedom of choice. Elizabeth Platt, who graduated from BHHS in 1967, remembered, "High school back then was such a wonderful time, and something I would never change; I loved those days. Even though integration to Athens High had started, I chose to remain at Burney-Harris with the students I had grown up with and gone to school with most of my life. I had no desire to attend the 'White high school.'"[47] Richard Appleby, who entered Burney-Harris in 1967 and at a young age was already fiercely proud of his Blackness, considered the African American students who left BHHS for Athens High to be "sellouts. . . . I changed my mind about that later in life; in hindsight I was being unfair, but that is how I felt at the time."[48]

Some of the White students were welcoming. Robert Hawkins remembered Bill Hartman Jr., son of UGA football legend Bill Hartman Sr., and Joel Eaves Jr., whose father was the athletic director at UGA; both students would make a point of being friendly and asking him how he was doing. Another White student gave him a tip about an open newspaper delivery boy position, and Hawkins soon became the first Black paperboy for the *Athens Daily News*. Yet another White student told him about an opening at the Winn-Dixie grocery store at Beechwood Shopping Center, and Hawkins became the store's first Black bagboy.[49]

Maxie Foster developed into a standout sprinter running track at AHS—his speed in the 400-yard dash later earned him the honor of being awarded the first athletic scholarship offered to an African American athlete at UGA—and he was named cocaptain of the varsity basketball team in his senior year. However, despite his success on the basketball court and the broad coverage of high school sports in the Athens media, Foster never saw his photo in the local newspapers. He could not attend the team's postseason banquet because the event was held at the Athens Country Club, which did not allow African Americans. He had to have a police escort to play a game in Oconee County and had a cup of ice water thrown at him during a postgame radio interview in Milledgeville.[50]

Robert Hawkins absorbed many hard lessons at Athens High, but the experience taught him how to be "bilingual" in the White world. The pain would never leave him, but his learned ability to make connections and adapt to difficult situations in an alien culture would ultimately prove to be beneficial, as Hawkins later applied these lessons as an adult to form and run a successful packaging materials distributorship in Atlanta.[51]

╫╫╫

In 1966, three years after the first African American student was admitted to Athens High, two Black student transfers from Burney-Harris decided to cross the invisible line of demarcation and try out for the Trojan football team. This development was inevitable—after all, the Black student population at AHS was steadily growing, and talented Black football athletes were destined to emerge at some point—after all, both the track and basketball squads at AHS were already integrated. But the resistance that would arise from their decision to don the maroon and white on the gridiron would be fierce.

Allen Morse and fellow Yellow Jacket transfer Stan Coleman were the young men who tried to break the color barrier in football at AHS in 1966. Both were gifted athletes, not only in football but also in track, where each excelled in the 100-yard dash and in sprint relay competitions.

Morse in particular attracted widespread attention in North Georgia. In the days before social media, and when there was limited traditional media coverage, Morse's unique combination of size and speed on the football field was spread by word of mouth throughout the region, and fans would line up along the fence surrounding the "Ponderosa" practice field to watch him scrimmage in Athens High's preseason practices.

With two African American players attempting to join his 1966 football squad, Coach Weyman Sellers was in a quandary. Like all coaches, he wanted to win, and he would seize any opportunity that would help him to achieve that goal. On the other hand, he was deeply prejudiced.

Racism was largely a feature, not a bug, among coaches in the Deep South and across the nation in the 1960s. Bobby Poss remembered visiting UGA coach Wally Butts at his home on Hampton Court on a Sunday afternoon in the early 1960s while Butts was watching an NFL game on television. "They are going to ruin the damned game!" Butts yelled, referring to the large number of Black players on NFL rosters.[52] Even the revered Cobern Kelley, who had nurtured hundreds of White male Athenians in his role as youth director of the Athens YMCA, was opposed to "race mixing." Several Y members who played football under Kelley remembered him driving the team on the bus to games in adjacent counties—and then ordering his players back on the bus to return to Athens once he realized their opponents had Black players on their rosters. The Athens YMCA did not integrate until after Kelley's death in 1968.

The views of conservative White coaches who supported separation of the races were not out of line with the prevailing attitudes of most of the White electorate. Politically, the state of Georgia remained very divided on the issue of desegregation. The four years of progressive leadership under the administration of Governor Carl Sanders were coming to an end—the laws of the state at that time prohibited successive terms for incumbent governors. In the 1966 gubernatorial contest, the Democratic Party nominee was Lester Maddox, who flaunted his segregationist credentials and was endorsed by the Atlanta Klavern of the Ku Klux Klan. "I certainly believe in separation of the races, in segregation," Maddox said. "I am not a racist, I am not a redneck, I am not a rabble-rouser, I'm a segregationist. When I go into the office of governor, I will be one. When I come out, I will be one."[53] Maddox went on to win the governorship in a race that the state legislature ultimately had to decide.

Sellers's nickname was "Zeke," and his White players had three theories regarding the derivation of that moniker and how it influenced his attitude toward African Americans. Some said a Black man named Zeke beat Sellers up badly in his early adulthood in a fistfight; others believed that an opposing Black player named Zeke physically manhandled him on the gridiron. There was also a flattering explanation for the name: "Zeke" was short for "'sique," a nod to the coach's chiseled physique. No matter what the derivation of the nickname was, Sellers hated it, and almost no one dared to use it in his presence.

In 1966, the earth was shifting under Sellers's feet. Earlier that year, an all-Black Texas Western basketball team defeated an all-White squad from the University of Kentucky to win the NCAA basketball crown. The Atlanta Braves professional baseball team had recently relocated from Milwaukee and featured many Black players, including all three starting outfielders—most notably, future home run king and Hall of Famer Henry Aaron. Similarly, Atlanta's new professional football franchise, the Falcons, were preparing for their inaugural season in an NFL that had integrated twenty years earlier.

At the University of Georgia, Vince Dooley's Bulldogs were beginning to play against teams benefiting from indisputable Black talent. The Bulldogs played SMU in the 1967 Cotton Bowl and were dazzled by the skills of the Mustangs' star wide receiver Jerry LeVias, who was African American. The following season, the favored Bulldogs were stunned in a one-point loss to a University of Houston team led by Black tailback Paul Gipson, who amassed 229 yards rushing for the Cougars in the newly built Astrodome. Houston's coach, Bill Yeoman, had integrated the team in 1964 and is often remembered for his humorous color-blind quote, "I am prejudiced—against bad football players."[54]

The Atlanta high schools had integrated in 1961, and Black students were participating on the schools' athletic teams by 1966. In the spring of 1966, the GHSA began allowing Black schools to petition for membership. In Valdosta, Sellers's rival Wright Bazemore had begun accepting Black players on his roster; one African American in particular, John Copeland, starred for the Wildcats in 1966. The Southeastern Conference was just one year away from allowing its first Black scholarship athlete—Nate Northington, a football player for the University of Kentucky—the opportunity to compete. Black southern football players continued to perform at extraordinarily high levels at northern and western colleges and universities; that autumn, Michigan State went undefeated due largely to the contributions of Gene Washington and Bubba Smith, two African American players from Texas.

Much closer to home, at Athens High School, Black athletes were beginning to participate in sports; that winter, Maxie Foster would play on the varsity basketball team for Trojans coach Marty Robinson, who welcomed the talented and quick guard onto his team and later named him cocaptain. By contrast, Foster remembered Coach Sellers as a "big, muscular, physically intimidating guy" who taught physical education and once shoved Foster into the padding behind the baseline during a basketball scrimmage as Foster attempted a layup.

As Sellers's squad gathered in August 1966 to begin preparing for another run at the state title, the local media took note of the two players who would try to break the color barrier at AHS—"Athens now has two Negro players, back Alan Morse and end Joe [sic] Coleman, either one of whom could become the first of his race to play for Athens."[55] Sellers mentioned that he was considering moving Morse to the line, despite the obvious gifts that Morse possessed as a runner—his reputation had spread across the state, and he was later invited to play as a running back in the Black high school all-star game at Herndon Stadium in Atlanta.[56] Late in August in a Trojan intrasquad scrimmage, Coach Sellers restricted Morse to playing defense and special teams, and Morse responded with two forty-yard returns on punts before scoring the only touchdown for his team on a sixty-five-yard punt return.

There was no further mention of Allen Morse in the local newspapers and no explanation for why he was no longer on the roster before the season kicked off on September 2 against longtime rival Gainesville. Both "Night Train" and Stan Coleman had been relentlessly hounded and abused by Coach Sellers throughout the August scrimmages. During summer two-a-days, they were forced to carry the ball with no blocking in seven-on-one or even eleven-against-one drills. As "deep men" on punts, they were chased and tackled by the punt coverage team with no blocking protection. Amazingly, on several occasions, Morse managed to dodge all his pursuers and score touchdowns. On another occasion, the players were dressed in helmets, shoulder pads, and shorts for "light touch" drills, but somehow the word was spread—to everyone except Morse—that full contact would ensue, and a surprised Morse was "lit up."[57]

"[Coach Sellers] wanted to run me off," Morse remembered, "but I was determined not to fall down—I would just run over whoever was in the way. I wasn't about to let them tackle me to the ground." On one occasion, Morse barely made it through practice but walked behind the gym before collapsing so that no one could witness his state of exhaustion.[58]

None of the White players felt good about being forced to use a Black teammate as "target practice," and many of them secretly despised Sellers for forcing them to try to hurt and humiliate a fellow Trojan. They were all familiar with

Sellers's harsh methods, but the treatment of Coleman and Morse had reached a new level of cruelty. But their queasiness over participating in the brutal drills was not enough to surmount the fear of voicing their concerns and the retribution that was sure to follow from a head coach whose authority was unquestioned and absolute. In the words of White teammate Mike Castronis Jr., "As football players we were always taught to do what the coach said—we never argued."[59]

Despite his ill treatment, Morse never walked out of a practice. Instead, when game jerseys were handed out shortly before the team picture was taken, Coach Sellers told him that he could stay on the team, but there were no more uniforms available. Sellers explained that if a player were injured, Morse could have that player's uniform, but in the meantime, although he could continue to practice with the team, he could not dress out for games. This represented the final straw for Morse, who told Sellers a few days later that he was going to focus on his studies: "I wasn't going to put in all that time and do all that practice, then sit around and wait for somebody to get hurt."[60]

Officially, he had not been cut from the team, but a shortage of uniforms—at a school with bountiful resources, in the highest athletic classification in Georgia—meant that there would not be a place for a very talented skill position player who would, along with fellow BHHS transfers Stan Coleman and Maxie Foster, go on to excel as a sprinter on the school's track team that finished fourth in the state.

The 1966 Trojans were loaded with talent, with many key returnees from the 1965 state champion runner-up team. They would finish the season 8–2, losing to Tucker 17–13 in a game that would cost them the Region 4-AAA title. They did not advance to the playoffs.

Valdosta captured yet another state title that year, beating Marietta High School 14–3 in the finals. The star player for the Wildcats in the championship game was John Copeland, the Black running back who had integrated the team; he scored on a seventy-four-yard touchdown run and was carried off the field by ecstatic White fans in the postgame celebration. In the long and proud history of Valdosta football, this remains one of the school's most iconic moments.[61]

Mike Castronis Jr. was a starting end on the 1966 AHS team and would later write a fictionalized account of a high school football team that overcame its racist coach and went on to win a state title. He thanked Allen Morse in the acknowledgments in his book:

> Thanks to Alan "Night Train" Morse. You gave yourself unselfishly throughout our final summer practice time in preparation for our 1966 season. You deserved to be a Trojan with the rest of us. To this day I believe had you been with us that year, our team could have won the state championship. Unfortunately, the time was not right nor were your teammates courageous enough to stand with you. I feel that lack of responsibility to the depths of my being. I wrote this story because of what happened to you. Fifty years is a long time to delay my apology, but it is sincere.[62]

CHAPTER 5

THE SEASON

They [Burney-Harris] are a better team than they were last year. . . . They surprised us with the amount of inside running they did. Their passing game is going to be good. They are going to sneak up on some people this year.

—Coach Sellers after Athens High and Burney-Harris faced off for the "City Title" in September 1969

Both the White and Black communities had a lot at stake in the September 12, 1969, game in which Burney-Harris and Athens High would clash at Death Valley, a contest that the local media billed as a battle for the "City Title." The parents and supporters of Burney-Harris were anxious about their boys "representing the community well," while their Athens High counterparts were more haunted by a fear that the local Black high school—scarcely a long golf tee shot down the ridge from Athens High, with only one-third of AHS's enrollment—had assembled a group of players who were fast and dangerous. Flashbacks of the previous year's game—ultimately won by Athens High, but not before Burney-Harris receivers had run wild and scored on five bombs of forty yards or longer—were very much seared in their collective memories.

The game assumed additional importance because it was becoming increasingly apparent that this would be the last year that the two schools would exist. In 1968, the Supreme Court ruled that freedom of choice was inadequate in achieving the integration of public schools, the intended goal of the Court's *Brown v. Board of Education of Topeka* decision. Under the steady drumbeat of pressure from the federal government's Department of Health, Education, and Welfare, Athens-Clarke County's elementary and middle schools were integrated through a system of targeted busing, and the long overdue consolidation of Burney-Harris and Athens High was nearly a fait accompli. Combining Athens High with Burney-Harris had boiled down to a matter of logistics—whether a new high school would be built or whether the Burney-Harris students would be absorbed into Athens High, and what grades would be included in the merged schools. One idea being floated was to keep the Burney-Harris building for a new tenth-grade academy.

With full-scale integration on the horizon, White attitudes toward Black students remained decidedly mixed at AHS. When Bill King entered Athens High as a sophomore in 1967, the school was integrated to the point that there were usually about "three Black kids in each class." By the time he became a senior in 1969, almost 10 percent of the student body was Black, and the school had a Black assistant principal, Dr. Walter Allen Sr., and an African American teacher of Spanish, "Señora Hawk." But King's characterization of Whites' treatment of African Americans in the late 1960s was not at all dissimilar to Bonnie Hampton's breakdown of the attitudes of Whites when she attended Childs Street School in 1963–1964: "The most virulently racist kids were usually working class and were prolific users of the 'n-word'; the slightly more refined students preferred 'nigra,' while the more progressive and tolerant sons and daughters of UGA professors stuck to the much more respectable 'negro,' or 'colored person.'"[1]

Similarly, Black students were largely ambivalent about or opposed to the idea of combining the two schools; they increasingly had agency when choosing between BHHS or AHS under freedom of choice. With each new school year, the African Americans who selected Athens High were less of a novelty, and while they remained a distinct minority in the school's overall student population, their numbers had grown to the point where they no longer felt completely isolated.

In 1968, a tower was built next to Death Valley with a bell that would be tolled after Trojan victories—another example of AHS trying to "emulate UGA, this time its North Campus Chapel Bell," according to Bill King. Before the opening game against Burney-Harris, a completely unfounded rumor spread among the White students at AHS that Athens police would be stationed at the top of the tower as "snipers" in case the visiting Black crowd from BHHS got out of hand.

This far-fetched threat of violence did not weigh on the players of either team as they prepared for the upcoming season. Their sense of dread was centered on the harsh reality of summer football practices. The "dog days" of August awaited, and preparation and conditioning would largely determine the outcome of the big rivalry game.

As August approached and the sun became an angry orange orb, guts tightened among thousands of young men around the South. Subtle changes in the weather would bring the first warning that "it" was around the corner—maybe the hiss of a sprinkler on a humid June morning, or the pungent aroma of freshly cut grass, or the first night that temperatures failed to dip below seventy degrees. "It" was summer two-a-day practices, and the young men wondered if they were ready—ready for the mandatory timed mile run, ready for the endless wind sprints, ready for the helmet-to-helmet brain scrambling from one-on-one "nutcracker" and "bull in the ring" drills. Ready for the pounds of weight that would be shed in the form of perspiration absorbed by heavy cotton, long-sleeved jerseys. Ready for the nausea and exhaustion and inevitable injuries caused by full-fledged combat in pads. Ready for the shouts and orders barked out by hard-nosed coaches. Ready for attrition, either through injury or quitting, as the ranks thinned in the slow march leading to the first September game.

The word *crossroads* is overused in sports parlance, but on the cusp of the 1969 season, Coach Weyman Sellers found himself exactly at that point.

The disappointing 1966 season, where Athens High fell to 8–2 and failed to make the playoffs—despite having many of the pieces in place from the previous year's team that had come within one point of a state title—was followed in 1967 by a 4–6 record, the first losing season for Sellers since 1959. As the losses mounted and his frustration grew, Sellers reacted the only way he knew how: by demanding even more from his players. Gary Travis remembered 5:30 a.m. practices that were followed by breakfast at the Chase Café; after they ate, the players would return for *yet another* practice before the school bell rang. A noisy protest from the players' parents ultimately put an end to the early morning sessions; three hours of grueling drills were draining their boys of all energy and causing them to lose concentration during school hours.

In 1968, Athens High moved to Region 8-AAA, where it was an outlier in a region that otherwise comprised Atlanta-area schools, predominantly from north DeKalb County. Some of those schools were newly formed or emerging challengers such as Lakeside, while others were traditional powers such as Decatur or Tucker, teams accustomed to making deep runs in the playoffs. Those schools were powered by the explosive growth of Atlanta, which opened Interstate 285 in the fall of 1969; the completion of "the Perimeter" turbocharged growth in the suburbs of Atlanta, and transplants from the Northeast and Midwest poured in, attracted by sunny weather, high-paying jobs, and affordable housing. The high schools in Region 8-AAA—Tucker, Lakeside, Decatur, Briarcliff, Sequoyah, Cross Keys, Druid Hills, and Chamblee—benefited from the influx of new blood and resources and were energized by the power vacuum in AAA football in North Georgia. Unlike in South Georgia, where Valdosta continued to be the undisputed king, there was no traditionally dominant power in North Georgia to block an aggressive usurper to the throne.

Led by junior quarterback Andy Johnson, the Trojans went 9–1 during the 1968 season; the only blemish was a loss to Decatur. But AHS was stunned in the first round of the playoffs, losing 26–3 at home to Forest Park. Valdosta ended up winning yet another state championship that year, defeating that same Forest Park team by three touchdowns in the final.

So Coach Sellers had serious concerns about the upcoming 1969 season. The heralded senior class that he had watched and anticipated since its remarkable YMCA days would soon be gone, and it had yet to produce a single playoff victory. Andy Johnson and his unique blend of passing, running, and leadership skills would be on display at the college of his choice the next season. Other heavily recruited players like Rand Lambert and Mike Nash were also wrapping up their careers at Death Valley. The entire offensive line was returning. The *Atlanta Constitution*, in its preseason poll for AAA, ranked Athens High number two in the state behind Valdosta and its unassailable coach, Wright Bazemore, who was coming off his thirteenth state title in twenty-seven years. But region foe Tucker was also ranked in the top five and was expected to challenge the Trojans for the 8-AAA crown, and several of the newer schools in the region, such as Lakeside, were climbing the ladder of respectability every season.

The 1969 team, like all of Sellers's squads, was all White. After the experiences of Allen Morse and Stan Coleman, no Black players tried out for the Trojans. Opposing coaches, on the other hand, were starting to welcome more and more Black talent; whatever their feelings about integration, most coaches wanted to win, and they recognized that the undeniable skills of Black players would help them toward that end. In a twist of poetic justice, Sellers's resistance to integration may have helped strengthen the Burney-Harris squads of the late 1960s—it is safe to assume that some of their talented players would have chosen to transfer to AHS under the freedom of choice plan had it not been for the racist reputation of the Trojans' head coach. In 1969, 120 of Athens High's 1,600 students were Black, and yet not one African American was on the football team.[2]

In 1966—the same year that Weyman Sellers welcomed his freshman class of highly acclaimed and undefeated YMCA players—Walter Jackson assumed head coaching duties at Burney-Harris after the highly respected Doc Holmes retired. Burney-Harris left the GIA—the Georgia sports league reserved for African American high schools—and was admitted to the GHSA in the spring of 1968. The Yellow Jackets were assigned to subregion 8-AA West, a collection of schools in northeast Georgia that included Athens High's chief rival, the perennial powerhouse Gainesville High.

In August 1969, the players at Burney-Harris High School were ready for a breakout season. The Yellow Jackets, in their first year of competition in GHSA against majority-White schools, were an impressive 7–2 in 1968. They had played Athens High in the first-ever meeting between the two schools, eventually losing in a shootout, 58–32. Athens dominated the line of scrimmage in that game, with all its touchdowns—three each by running backs Steve Tillitski and Terry Smart—coming on the ground, while Burney-Harris dazzled the packed crowd at Death Valley with its aerial attack, scoring five touchdowns on passes of forty yards or longer. Yellow Jackets receivers dropped several other long passes that would have tightened the score. Although Weyman Sellers was unavailable for comment after the game, the Yellow Jackets gained the respect of Trojan assistant coach Frank Malinowski, who praised the Burney-Harris players: "I doubt we will face another running back as fast as [Yellow Jackets running back] Joe Ford . . . their receivers dropped a few that could have been touchdowns. . . . They were continually behind our secondary."[3]

Burney-Harris's 1968 squad came tantalizingly close to capturing the region crown—something that was unthinkable for a Black school playing its first year in the GHSA—before falling to Gainesville 10–6 in a turnover-plagued, rain-soaked game at home. They later defeated a Lincoln High School team that finished runner-up for the state title in its classification in South Carolina. The Yellow Jackets went on to wallop all-White Forsyth County 67–0 and beat a tough South Hall team by two touchdowns to finish second in subregion 8-AA West.

A strong and tight-knit group of junior-year players at Burney-Harris—end Richard Appleby (playing just his second year of organized football), running back Horace King, and linebacker Clarence Pope—were attracting the attention of college scouts, as southern universities began taking the first awkward steps toward integrating their football teams. Tommy Bolton, the Yellow Jackets' talented 5'8", 150-pound quarterback, who had thrown five long touchdown passes against Athens High in 1968, was back for his senior year, as was Larry Sheats, a fierce nose tackle on defense. The offense also had two all-state weapons, running back Henry Terrell and end Richard Harris, and a lightning-quick, 125-pound junior scatback who was catching the attention of head coach Walter Jackson: "Michael Thurmond has really come on for us. . . . He's not very large, but he makes up for it in desire . . . he deserves to play."[4]

In addition to Walter Jackson, offensive coordinator James Holston and defensive coordinator James Crawford coached the Yellow Jackets. Practices were tough, but not as intense and exhausting as the "weed out" sessions conducted by Weyman Sellers. Horace King remembered preseason laps around a dirt path (the football field had no circular track around it) that ran through a graveyard beyond the sight lines of the coaches. King would sit down and take a break; after catching his breath, he would suddenly reappear with a group of runners that had passed by. He hated the salt tablets that were passed out before practice, and he would hide them in his pants rather than swallow the bitter pills that were the size of small jawbreakers. Water breaks did not occur until after practice; coaches feared that water consumed during practice would cause cramps. As was the case at most high schools at the time, no one lifted weights; the emphasis was always on cardiovascular conditioning.

The closeness that the boys forged at Lyons Middle School—when Richard Appleby, Horace King, Terry Green, and other ninth-grade boys whipped the seniors in intramural basketball—continued at Burney-Harris.

As difficult as it is to understand today, when the majority of players in top-level college and professional football and basketball are Black, African American athletes were widely considered to be inferior to their White counterparts in the late 1960s. Black athletes' raw skills were broadly acknowledged, but this grudging admission by White coaches and journalists was offset by the widely held convictions that African American players "lacked discipline," were "lazy" and "hard to coach," and were prone to "crack under pressure." Clarence Pope recalled, "At the time, young black youth were assumably inferior in not only education but also athletics— and that was mostly due to beliefs that black teams had inferior coaches. For example, black coaches were thought of as not teaching proper on-field techniques when compared to white coaches. When Burney-Harris was brought into the GHSA, we even saw newspaper clippings putting down techniques taught by black coaches, how black players were not properly coached, so to speak, as the white teams, etc."[5]

In the 1960s, Athens was the smallest city in the country to have two competing daily newspapers. The *Athens Banner-Herald*, the afternoon paper, was owned by the Morris family of Augusta, Georgia, and was known for its bland reporting. By contrast, the *Athens Daily News*, which was started in 1965 and was the morning daily, was an upstart broadsheet that liked to boast that it was "The People Paper." The *Daily News* introduced the first "Harry Dog," an overmuscled, slightly bemused cartoon version of the Bulldog mascot drawn by local adman Don Smith. Harry Dog, according to Bill King, "might be getting ready to greet a Gamecock with a frying pan, a bag of flour and some shortening, or wearing the Florida Gator mascot pinned to his jersey, asking, 'What d'ya think? Do I look too preppy?'"[6]

A sort of infectious goofiness pervaded the *Daily News*, which delved deeply into local news, including sports stories about Athens Little League and church league basketball. The *Daily News* enjoyed employing double-entendre headlines, such as "Clegg Hot, but Alone" to describe my father scoring fifty points in a losing church league basketball effort. Neophyte reporter Lewis Grizzard wrote a column for the *Daily News* that poked fun at Clemson football coach Frank Howard's thick country accent. In response, Howard threatened to sue both Grizzard and the *Daily News*, which resulted in the newspaper splashing the threat as its headline story.

The competitive rivalry between the *Banner-Herald* and the *Daily News* prompted both papers to beef up their sports reporting, and this filtered down to the prep level. It was not unusual for local subscribers to get daily high school *practice* reports, including quotes from players and coaches.

Black players felt slighted by what they viewed as unbalanced coverage in the city's two dailies. Even more galling was what the players viewed as a reluctance on the part of the newspapers to publish photographs of Black athletes. This was a valid criticism, although the gap between White athletes and Black athletes in terms of press coverage and photographs had narrowed considerably since Burney-Harris's admission into the GHSA in 1968. Athens High still commanded more print space and even had its own beat writers, but an increasing amount of ink was being devoted to the Yellow Jackets, even if they rarely appeared as the headline story on the sports page.

The media attention for Athens High extended into Atlanta, where all of AHS's Region 8-AAA opponents were located; naturally, coverage of the local Atlanta suburban schools also meant heightened exposure for Athens High.

Players from both the Trojans and the Yellow Jackets remember approaching the "City Title" game on September 12, 1969, without any additional racially tinged drama. While each team obviously wanted to win, neither viewed the other as a rival. The players simply did not know each other, except by reputation or by what they had read about each other in the newspapers. David Lester could recall only one occasion on which he had interacted with a Burney-Harris player before the "City Title" game: when Richard Appleby happened to be walking by Lester's house off Holman Avenue one day and joined in a game of touch football in the front yard.[7] The teams had just begun to compete against each other in sports—the two schools had faced each other in two basketball games the prior season, both won by Athens High. Burney-Harris had just completed its first year of baseball in 1968. And the schools had played only one football game against each other, the previous year's 58–32 shootout. The players sensed the extra importance that their respective communities placed on the game, but there was no feeling of mutual hatred typically found between heated rivals. In the words of Mac Coile, a sophomore who played for the Trojans, "I had gone to school with Blacks since fourth or fifth grade. I didn't even really think about the whole Black/White thing. . . . I just wanted to play; just wanted to win."[8] On the surface, Coile's comment might be difficult to believe, but in 1969, the players were not subjected to the constant bombardment of social media, with its attendant "hot takes" that would have further ratcheted up the pressure in what was already an eagerly awaited matchup between two talented teams. The task at hand for the players was not at all fuzzy or complicated by racial overtones; the job was simply to win and move on.

Unlike the 1968 game, when the two teams lit up the scoreboard for a combined ninety points, the 1969 game was a defensive struggle. The defensive deficiencies that the Yellow Jackets had displayed the previous year—when the Athens High running backs ran wild between the tackles— had been patched up. The Trojans drove deep into Burney-Harris territory on their opening possession, but the Yellow Jackets recovered an errant pitchout and stopped the Athens threat on the nine-yard line. Defensively, Burney-Harris fooled Athens with shifts on defense, particularly with the versatile Larry Sheats, who lined up in different spots along the line as well as at linebacker and would finish the game with ten tackles. A fierce Yellow Jacket rush led to several sacks of Trojans quarterback Andy Johnson in the first half. Sellers later commented, "They are a very unpredictable and unorthodox team."[9]

Athens High was expecting an aerial attack from the Yellow Jackets, but BHHS head coach Walter Jackson switched things up and ran the ball against the surprised Trojans, with Burney-Harris's undersized guards George Wingfield and Bruce Holt creating running lanes through the AHS defensive front. Running backs Horace King, Henry Terrell, and Chris Williams gashed the Trojans' defensive front with inside running, while quarterback Tommy Bolton hurt the Trojans on the perimeter by scrambling out of the pocket on passing downs. To the shock of a packed Death Valley, Burney-Harris marched down the field and took a 7–0 lead when Horace King scored after a short run.

The shock turned to disbelief when the Yellow Jackets scored another touchdown on a pass from Bolton to Terry Green just before halftime to take an apparent 13–0 lead. But a flag on the play—holding on Burney-Harris—nullified the touchdown. To this day, several former Yellow Jacket players swear that the holding call was a "phantom" penalty.

Athens received the kickoff to start the second half, and Sellers called a trick play; his son, Gray Sellers, corralled the kickoff and was heading toward the blocking wall that was forming on the sideline when he handed the ball off to Andy Johnson, who reversed field and raced down the sidelines. The speed of Johnson had been well chronicled by local scribes, but the Burney-Harris players were skeptical that a "White boy could run that fast."[10] Both Richard Appleby and Clarence Pope remembered years later that Henry Morse on the Burney-Harris kickoff team ran stride for stride with Johnson down the field. Pope believed that Morse could have tackled Johnson but became caught up in the footrace, curious to see if he could keep up with the AHS quarterback, who was timed at 10.1 seconds in the 100-yard dash in a track meet the previous spring. Morse's teammates later "got on him" for not making the tackle. The eighty-eight-yard kickoff return for a touchdown cut the lead to one point.

Athens went for two because Sellers thought that the Trojans taking the lead would break the spirit of Burney-Harris. In a statement that oozed with his dismissive and condescending attitude toward the Yellow Jackets, Sellers later said, "They are a front-running team, and we wanted to take some fire out of them."[11] The blow of falling behind by one point with an entire half left to play would seemingly, in

Sellers's estimation, be too difficult for the Yellow Jackets to overcome psychologically. In any event, the two-point conversion was unsuccessful, and Athens trailed 7–6.

Andy Johnson took over the game in the second half with both his arm and his legs. A seven-yard touchdown pass to Smart gave the Trojans the lead, and a twenty-seven-yard run by the six foot one, 185-pound quarterback led to Athens High's last score. AHS made adjustments at halftime on its defensive front to stymie the Yellow Jackets, who were unable to score in the second half. Johnson's aerial numbers were pedestrian—he finished 5–18 on his passing attempts—but Trojans receivers dropped a number of his tosses, and Johnson deliberately overthrew several passes when his targets were well covered.

Horace King recalled a relatively clean game free of cheap shots and trash talking. "Players didn't talk trash back then," he recalled. "The first time I heard players talking trash was in the NFL when we [the Detroit Lions] played the Oakland Raiders."[12] But with the last few seconds in the Trojans 20–7 victory ticking off the clock, an ugly incident broke out: an Athens High player was slugged in a pile after a play had ended, and a fight between the two teams ensued. Punches were thrown, and in a frightening escalation, some players removed their helmets and swung them like war clubs at the opposing team. Police came out on the field to help separate the two squads, and the players were sent off to their respective dressing rooms without shaking hands. Richard Appleby recalled that the Yellow Jackets felt that inept or biased officiating, like the first-half holding call that nullified a Burney-Harris touchdown, had robbed them of victory, and this probably contributed to the frustration that led to the ugly incident.

The total yardage of the two teams was almost even—242 for the Trojans, and 230 for the Yellow Jackets, whose normally potent passing attack was limited to just 21 yards.

The win was costly for Athens High School. Tackle Mike

Nash, who weighed over two hundred pounds and was the team's largest player, broke his ankle and was feared lost for the season. Fullback Rusty Russell, son of celebrated UGA defensive coordinator Erk Russell, badly sprained his knee and would miss some games. A weakened Trojans squad was suddenly plunged into self-doubt after the close call against Burney-Harris and the harsh postgame assessments of their coach. They had little time to get their mindsets straight—the next game was only a week away, just forty miles up Highway 129 in Gainesville.

Both Athens High and Burney-Harris had a game scheduled against Gainesville High. For different reasons, the outcome of those games would be a turning point in the season for each of the Athens-based schools. Athens High was positioned more favorably for its game against its longtime rival, who was by now a nonregion opponent. Burney-Harris, by contrast, was in the same subregion as Gainesville, and the outcome of its game in October against the Red Elephants would likely determine the team that would advance to the playoffs.

╫╫╫

Although they were now in different classifications—the Gainesville Red Elephants had dropped to AA in 1966—Athens High and Gainesville remained fierce rivals, with Gainesville holding a slight edge in the all-time series of 27–23–2 on the eve of their 1969 contest. The players knew each other, especially those who played American Legion baseball for Athens Post 21, which included Trojans Andy Johnson and Mike Epps from Athens and Steve Pierce and starting quarterback Charlie Strong from Gainesville. It was not uncommon for Gainesville-based players to stay overnight with their Athens baseball teammates in between practices or games at the field behind the old mill off Whitehead Road.

Gainesville was ranked number one in AA, and the previous week the Red Elephants had defeated the St. Pius Golden Lions, the team that had edged them in the AA 1968 state championship game. Gainesville was going to be a tough out, and Weyman Sellers studied game film and planned adjustments accordingly.

A few weeks earlier, Gainesville had begun its first year of mandatory integration. The former all-Black school on the south side of town, E. E. Butler, had largely consolidated into Gainesville High, and the Red Elephants featured a handful of Black players on its 1969 team, including fearsome defensive tackle Eddie Dean Lipscomb.

It was a rainy Friday night when the Trojans met the Red Elephants at City Park in Gainesville, and both teams struggled to hold on to the football. Gainesville was the most obliging, turning the ball over on fumbles five times in the first half alone, mostly when it was deep in its own territory. Athens High tried to return the favor, with two fumbles and an interception of a Johnson pass on a tipped ball. After eight combined turnovers, Athens led 3–0 at halftime thanks to a thirty-yard field goal by Bruce Williams.

Sellers had tried a variety of stylized offensive looks to catch Gainesville off guard in the first half. Despite the wet weather, Johnson had attempted a number of passes in an assortment of different sets—straight dropback, with Johnson backpedaling like Johnny Unitas; sprint-out run-pass option plays; and shotgun formations in which Johnson received the snap ten yards behind the line of scrimmage. The running game featured straight dives by Lambert up the middle, misdirection "counters" out of triple-option sets, and zone reads in which Johnson would sprint to the perimeter and either keep the ball or pitch out to a trailing running back.

The imaginative game plan did not work. Gainesville's gang-tackling defense, outside pursuit, and control of the line of scrimmage hemmed in the Trojan attack. Big number

75, Eddie Dean Lipscomb, one of several African American contributors to the Red Elephants' success that evening, was a constant presence in the AHS backfield, disrupting plays and creating havoc.

Gainesville was likewise stymied by the Athens defense and did not score until late in the third quarter after a long punt return put the Red Elephants in excellent field position. The score was 6–3 early in the fourth quarter when Athens mounted its longest sustained drive of the game, which ended—after a nifty run in which Terry Smart avoided several would-be tacklers—with Smart fumbling inside the Gainesville ten-yard line.

After the turnover, the Red Elephants failed to gain a first down and were forced to punt from deep in their own territory. Andy Johnson—in another of his multiple roles, this time as punt returner—mishandled the ball on the wet field, and Gainesville recovered at midfield. This seemed to break the spirit of Athens, whose sagging defense allowed Gainesville to cover the fifty yards for a touchdown in short order. Gainesville's last touchdown was set up by another Johnson interception. The game ended in a 20–3 win for Gainesville, and a jubilant crowd rushed the field. As colorful local journalist Phil Jackson—channeling his inner Grantland Rice—reported, "Tough as a barroom fighter and rough as a stucco bathtub, Gainesville's stubborn little Red Elephants stormed back in the second half Friday night to crack the bigger and favored Athens Trojans."[13]

A rival in a lower classification had destroyed Weyman Sellers's dreams just two games into the season. Sellers knew his team would crash out of the *Atlanta Journal*'s top ten poll the next week, and while that ranking was strictly a subjective beauty contest, he realized that his Trojans were on the ropes even before region play had begun. As the two teams' players met at midfield after the game and shook hands, Sellers grabbed David Lester by his jersey and ordered him into the locker room; Lester had committed the unpardonable sin of congratulating a Red Elephant player and friend whose family had moved from Athens to Gainesville several years earlier.

The coach stormed into the dressing room and confronted his players with a red-hot anger that was off the charts even by his own lofty tirade standards. He singled out players for their poor performance. He threw a plastic medical kit across the room. He called for a scrimmage on Saturday morning. He threatened to play the rest of the season with the B-team.

The rant session culminated with the coach calling out Andy Johnson, who had indeed suffered through a miserable performance: "Johnson, if you are an All-American, then the woods are full of them," he screamed before knocking his quarterback's cup of water out of his hand.[14]

Sellers had made a gross miscalculation in humiliating the most well-liked and respected player on the team. Most of the players had grown up with Johnson and had played football with him for ten years. He had earned the deep admiration of his teammates, not only through his prowess on the field but also for the way he treated everyone with kindness and respect. It was a decision that would backfire badly on Sellers. No one screamed at Andy Johnson. This was Sellers playing the role of the jealous John Claggart humiliating the beautiful sailor Billy Budd in Herman Melville's classic novel. Like Budd, Johnson quietly endured the harangue with his customary dignity and grace. But for his teammates who had grown up with Johnson—the leader of their teams starting with YMCA ball—Sellers had crossed a boundary that no one had ever dared to breach.

The only player who did not recall the incident was Rand Lambert, who had suffered a concussion in the first half and did not remember any of the second half, despite playing both offense and defense. The next morning back in Athens, when his mother walked into his bedroom, Lambert asked her, "Who won?"

HHHH

The day after the loss to Gainesville, a large group of disgruntled Trojans players talked to each other, and though estimates vary today on the number of players involved, the consensus more than fifty years after the event is that about half the team decided to quit. They had had enough of Sellers, enough of the abuse; most had suffered through it for three years—or for four years in Johnson's case, since he had joined the varsity as a freshman. The big tackle Alex Allen told Terry Smart he had had enough of football: "Let's go fishin'," he suggested to his friend.[15] The team was divided— some understood Sellers's anger and felt that it was just another example of a fiery coach bitterly disappointed in a loss. "We lost a game we should have won," remembered Mac Coile. "Coach Sellers was just extremely competitive."[16]

Two parents—Heyward Allen, father of Alex, and Marion Johnson, Andy's dad—decided to intervene. The players aired their grievances in the basement of the Allen home while the two dads listened. Marion Johnson told the players, "You boys can decide what you want, but you will have to live with it for the rest of your lives. Come on, Andy, we are leaving." Marion Johnson was not going to allow his son to quit and perhaps endanger his reputation when every major college in the nation was recruiting him. With that, almost as soon as it had started, the mutiny was quelled.

The next week, as the Trojans readied themselves for the start of region play with a game against Druid Hills, they enjoyed their best practices of the season. Senior player David Lester recalled that the team received a boost of energy that week when three enthusiastic sophomores were elevated from the junior varsity to the varsity. The crisis had been averted, and Sellers even cut back on one day of contact in the lead-up to the game—Thursday hitting was eliminated, a change in routine that he continued for the rest of the season. But racial tensions flared up once again, providing an ugly distraction for both of the Classic City's high school football programs. After the brief postgame scuffle between Athens High and Burney-Harris two weeks earlier, the two schools' junior varsity squads squared off on the Yellow Jackets' field. The "Baby Trojans" won a 7–0 battle, and another, even more regrettable incident occurred as the victors tried to board their bus for the short drive back to Athens High. Anticipating trouble before the game started, the AHS coaches instructed their players to keep their helmets on and sprint to the bus immediately after the conclusion of the contest. Their fears were realized, as the Trojans players were met with a barrage of rocks on the way to their bus after the game; Coach Sellers was struck in the head by either a rock or a football helmet, and windows on the bus were smashed.

Accounts differed on who was responsible. Weyman Sellers claimed that the attack was initiated by Burney-Harris varsity players, who were waiting on the edge of the field to practice at the conclusion of the junior varsity game. Walter Jackson claimed his players had nothing to do with it, and the only arrest made was of a twenty-four-year-old man who had no affiliation with the school.

Sellers told the *Daily News*, "I was running toward the bus and a member of Burney-Harris'[s] varsity team[,] which had been practicing, hit me over the head with a football helmet. I didn't take time to find out who did it because getting the buses out of the parking lot was more important. Naturally, there was a lot of blood and people thought I was hurt worse than I was." The cut required five stitches, said Sellers.[17] For his part, Burney-Harris coach Walter Jackson promised a full investigation and emphasized that his program would not tolerate this type of conduct.

The GHSA stepped in to investigate and leveled a one-hundred-dollar fine against Burney-Harris—not an insignificant sum in 1969. In addition, the school had to pay Sellers's medical bill and for the damage to the bus. That year's planned rematch of the two junior varsity teams at Death Valley was cancelled, as were all athletic competitions between the two schools for the remainder of the academic year. Interestingly, the possibility of cancelling all future athletic contests between the intracity rivals for the next year and beyond was also mentioned. In late 1969, there was obviously still some residual doubt about the pending merger of the two schools.[18]

Good football teams that experience an early setback follow one of several familiar arcs for the remainder of their season. The teams that rely on individual talent but lack cohesion or leadership will crumble and suffer more inexplicable losses. Other gifted teams will muddle through the rest of their schedule, disposing of the weaker opponents before falling to teams of equal or superior talent. The best teams absorb and learn the lessons from a loss and show gradual improvement that is rewarded with appearances in playoff and championship games.

Athens High and Burney-Harris followed the trajectory of superior teams that bounce back from a dispiriting early-season defeat to move on and have a successful season. Both teams began region play with their pride damaged but all their goals, according to clichéd "coachspeak," still in front of them.

Athens High's remaining eight games were against metro Atlanta region opponents. Ten-team Region 8-AAA was not split into subregions, so each game was essentially a knockout round in a tournament that would allow the survivor to fill one of the eight slots in the playoffs.

For away games in Atlanta—there were four in 1969—the Athens High team would board a bus that would first travel a short distance to Poss' Barbecue on the Atlanta Highway, where the players and coaches would enjoy their pregame meal. (If it was still open when they got back to Athens, the players would also stop for a postgame meal at the iconic restaurant.) The AHS fans traveled well, and the team typically brought a large contingent of supporters to away games, which was not a given since the remaining away games were on Friday nights, seventy miles away, in an Atlanta already renowned for its unbearable traffic.

As is often the case with teams that improve over the course of a season, help came for AHS from an unexpected source: a tough, brown-haired kid named Benny Edmondson was starting to emerge as a key player in the Trojans running attack—Coach Sellers singled him out for his strong performance against Druid Hills. Edmondson was one of only two players from East Athens, the "other side of the river," where most of the White working class earned their living in the dark and sometimes dangerous textile mills. Edmondson liked to fight other boys and usually won. He liked to fight so much at Athens High that several football players invited him to join the football team, where he thrived. A drill known as "bull in the ring" was popular in 1960s football; players formed a circle around a single "bull," who would run in place and signal for one player in the circle to meet him in the middle of the ring in a collision. "Bulls" soon learned to never pick Benny Edmondson out of the circle.

An undersized nose tackle was also an unexpected contributor thanks to his constant presence in opposing teams' backfields. One-hundred-and-forty-pound Mike "Rat" Epps relied on quickness and stunts to find gaps through blockers who typically outweighed him by forty to sixty pounds. He was a player special enough to persuade Coach Sellers to deviate from his strict numbering system—Epps was allowed to wear number 11 while playing on the defensive line.

In quick succession, the Trojans disposed of several of the lesser lights in their region without much drama, defeating North Druid Hills and Sequoyah before facing undefeated Chamblee High School, which had whipped perennial power Decatur 27–0 in its previous game.

In Death Valley, the Trojans shocked the Bulldogs by marching eighty-three yards for a touchdown on their opening possession. They tacked on an additional 17 points to take a 24–0 lead into halftime. The Trojans sat on their lead in the second half, and the Bulldogs fell 24–6.

++++

Burney-Harris coach Walter Jackson rued the 20–7 loss to Athens High School that was widely considered a moral victory for his underdog Yellow Jackets: "The score doesn't indicate what kind of game it was—you just don't get the picture from that. We have nothing to hang our heads about. This club has a lot of heart and a lot of talent, and it'll go a long way this year."[19] The Athens media fell in line with that narrative and acknowledged that the Yellow Jackets had demonstrated that they would be a handful for all their opponents the remainder of the year.

As AHS struggled in the rain in Gainesville, Burney-Harris traveled across the state line into South Carolina to play Lincoln, the state championship runner-up, whom the Yellow Jackets had upset by one point in the final minute of the previous year's game. The 1969 contest between the two schools would be different: Burney-Harris dominated from the beginning, with Tommy Bolton throwing four touchdown passes, and BHHS routed Lincoln 54–6.

Similar to what transpired with Athens High, the schedule eased off for Burney-Harris, whose next two games were against weaker competition, and the Yellow Jackets walloped Josey and Blakeney by a combined 81–6 before setting their sights on region play. One-hundred-and-twenty-five-pound running back Michael Thurmond, who had acquitted himself admirably in the JV game earlier in the week against Athens High, scored two touchdowns against Blakeney in his first varsity appearance.

The high-flying Yellow Jackets were increasingly garnering more attention from opposing teams. Phil Carpenter, head coach of their next opponent, the South Hall Knights, acknowledged that "Burney-Harris might be the best team we play this year," and he made that assessment with cross-county rival Gainesville still on the Knights' schedule. Walter Jackson went one step further in assessing his team: "We may have the material for a state title."[20]

The Yellow Jackets lived up to their increasingly high expectations by annihilating South Hall 42–0 at home. Once again, senior quarterback Tommy Bolton performed brilliantly, completing ten of twelve passes for 209 yards. South Hall was unable to complete a single pass and finished with only 130 total yards.

At the midway point of the season, Burney-Harris had accumulated almost two thousand yards of total offense and had outscored its opponents by a margin of 212–34. In an era well before the advent of sophisticated aerial attacks, the Yellow Jackets had amassed 843 passing yards; in comparison, the more rushing-oriented Athens High had managed only 316 passing yards at the same juncture in the season.

The Athens press was gushing in its praise of the Yellow Jackets' entertaining, foot-smashed-to-the-accelerator style of football: "Statistically, the Burney-Harris Yellow Jackets might appear even more awesome to upcoming opponents than they actually are, if that is at all possible."[21] For its part, the Burney-Harris defense was holding up its end of the bargain, pitching two shutouts and holding two other opponents to one score apiece.

Burney-Harris eagerly awaited its region matchup with Gainesville High at City Park in Gainesville. After routing Athens in September, the Red Elephants had lost consecutive games against strong nonregion teams before bouncing back to beat region foe Forsyth County 47–6.

The Yellow Jackets had accumulated gaudy offensive

statistics by the midpoint of the season and were primed to avenge the previous season's 10–6 loss to Gainesville at home, when a downpour had derailed Burney-Harris's high-powered offense. Once again in 1969, a heavy rain fell when the two teams met, and another turnover-plagued contest ensued.

Gainesville's swarming defense stifled the Yellow Jackets running attack, which was unable to reach the edges to utilize its speed. Tommy Bolton spent most of the evening trying to elude Red Elephant pass rushers, and a wet ball further hampered his ability to connect with his gifted receivers. On one of the few running plays that looked promising, Horace King found some open space but tripped over a referee and fell to the turf. He remembered that this was the only time that offensive coordinator James Holston lost his temper: "Are you blind?" he screamed at King when he returned to the sidelines.[22] Michael Thurmond, who played in the secondary for BHHS in the game, recalled the difficulty his team had in stopping the relentless toss sweep of the Red Elephants, whom he called "the thundering herd."[23]

Gainesville rolled up eighteen first downs and 268 rushing yards on Burney-Harris, which could muster only 115 yards of total offense. Bolton, forced out of the pocket all night and throwing on the run, connected on only seven of twenty-six passes. The Yellow Jackets fell 17–0. Like Athens High, Burney-Harris had fallen to Gainesville by seventeen points on a rainy night at City Park. With the head-to-head loss, BHHS would now need help from other teams if it hoped to still win the region. Bolton attributed his team's loss to poor execution: "With [proper] execution, we could have scored some points. I expected to get about four touchdowns against them. . . . It's the first time I have been shutout in football."[24]

Burney-Harris's next game was at Forsyth County High School. Not only did the Bulldogs have an all-White team, but *the entire county* was White and would remain so until the early 1990s, when encroaching growth from Atlanta transformed the sparsely populated, sleepy rural county into a booming exurban bedroom community.

Forsyth County had a well-deserved reputation as a bastion of White supremacy, dating back to the 1912 lynching of a Black man named Rob Edwards—accused as an accomplice in the rape and murder of a local White woman—and the subsequent forced removal of more than one thousand African American residents. Several Black players for Gainesville High, fearing for their safety, had earlier expressed misgivings about playing against Forsyth in the Bulldogs' stadium located deep in a "sundown county." The term *sundown county* or *sundown town* originated earlier in the twentieth century and referred to communities with no Black residents that posted signs advising any "colored" visitors to be gone by sundown. Whether these warnings were backed by discriminatory laws or local customs, violators risked threats and violence—and, in some cases, lynching.

If the Yellow Jackets were intimidated by their surroundings on the night of the game, they did not show any hint of it on the field. Tommy Bolton connected on two early long touchdown passes to Richard Appleby, and BHHS never looked back. The Yellow Jackets rolled up nearly five hundred yards in total offense and destroyed Forsyth County 67–0.

In its next game, Burney-Harris was matched up at home on a drizzly and windy Halloween night against the Winder-Barrow Bulldogs, who were 4–0 in subregional play. The Yellow Jackets' only hope for advancing into the playoffs was to defeat the Bulldogs and then pray that Winder-Barrow would in turn beat Gainesville in its last game of the season. This would create a three-way tie for the 8-AA West subregional crown between Gainesville, Burney-Harris, and Winder-Barrow. The ultimate winner would then be decided by a tiebreaker.

As they had done the previous week against Forsyth

County, the Yellow Jackets took the game by the throat early and never released their grip. Once again, BHHS rolled up almost five hundred yards of total offense, split evenly between the passing yardage of Tommy Bolton and the large chunks of rushing yardage collected by Horace King, Henry Morse, and Henry Terrell. The Yellow Jackets raced their way to a 40–0 halftime lead before easing the brakes and cruising to a 56–0 rout. The bad news for Burney-Harris was that Gainesville had also easily handled South Hall that evening. Unless BHHS beat Newton County and Gainesville lost to Winder-Barrow in their regular season finales, the Yellow Jackets' season would end the next weekend.

╂╂╂╂

After Athens High had knocked off a couple more regional lightweights, Cross Keys and Briarcliff, Weyman Sellers prepared his team for a crucial matchup with the fifth-ranked team in the state, the Tucker Tigers. The winner of this matchup would be the favorite to win the region title.

As Burney-Harris routed Winder-Barrow on Halloween night, Athens High and Tucker battled just up the hill at Death Valley, in a game dominated by defense. Relying almost strictly on its ground game, AHS could muster only a thirteen-yard Rand Lambert field goal in the first half. The Tigers matched that with a nineteen-yard field goal of their own just before the halftime buzzer, and the two teams went into their locker rooms tied 3–3.

The game was still tied going into the fourth quarter, but the worn-down Tucker defense finally began springing leaks. Andy Johnson, Benny Edmondson, and Terry Smart took turns carrying the ball on consecutive sixty-seven-yard and fifty-five-yard touchdown drives. When the final horn sounded, AHS had secured a 17–3 signature victory that likely clinched the region crown.[25]

The Trojans would not have to wait long to be declared

region champs. The next week, AHS easily defeated the Decatur Bulldogs in a game that officially captured the region title after Lakeside, the only other team with a chance of coming in first in the region, lost its game against Tucker.

╫╫╫

Throughout the fall of 1969, as Athens High and Burney-Harris racked up gridiron victories, the Clarke County Board of Education held public hearings to discuss plans to complete the integration of the school system. The junior high and elementary schools had already been integrated for the 1969 school year, and plans called for Burney-Harris's and Athens High's eleventh and twelfth graders to attend classes together at the Athens High building for the 1970–1971 academic year. The Burney-Harris building off Dearing Extension would house tenth-grade students. Perhaps encouraged by the relatively drama-free integration of the elementary and middle schools in Athens—by 1969, more than 85 percent of the three-thousand-plus Black students in the Athens-Clarke County public school system were attending integrated schools—parents initially raised very little concern about the school board's plans for moving forward with integrating the high schools.[26]

╫╫╫

As the discussion over integration continued in school board and town hall meetings, Burney-Harris traveled to Covington to play the Newton County Rams in its final regular season game.

Continuing their recent trend, the Yellow Jackets steamrolled their opponent 67–6. Walter Jackson was able to empty his bench early as the Yellow Jackets racked up 522 total yards, a high for the season. "I just don't see how Gainesville beat them," Newton County coach Wilbur Fisher remarked in awe after the game.[27] Unfortunately, there was disappointing news from Gainesville—the Red Elephants had defeated Winder-Barrow 35–14. There would be no three-way tie for the region crown; Gainesville had won it outright. The Burney-Harris season was over, and the Yellow Jackets would never again suit up to play football.

BHHS finished the year 7–2, its only two losses coming at the hands of eventual state-title finalists, and the team dominated in all of its wins, playing a highly entertaining brand of football that combined a stout defense with a powerful offense that perfectly blended its equally potent running and passing attacks. Five Yellow Jacket players made the *Atlanta Journal-Constitution*'s AA all-state team: Horace King, Tommy Bolton, Larry Sheats, Henry Terrell, and Richard Harris. Two of those players—Bolton and Terrell—received scholarship offers to play football at Southern University, an HBCU in Baton Rouge, Louisiana.

卌

While Burney-Harris's march through the regular season had ended prematurely with a second-place finish in its subregion, the Athens High squad was shifting its focus to the playoffs. Although Athens had two weeks to rest and reload for its final regular-season game against Lakeside, the team already knew that its first-round playoff game would be against Avondale High School, yet another DeKalb County team. The "bye" week, followed by the meaningless regular-season finale against Lakeside—which the Trojans would win 41–28—gave the players an opportunity to rest and recuperate from injuries.

As the Athens High Trojans prepared for the GHSA playoffs, the Clarke County Board of Education finalized its plans to consolidate Burney-Harris and Athens High into the latter's building off South Milledge Avenue for the 1970–1971 school year. Although the reactions during the hearings over the course of the fall had been muted, school authorities knew that merging the two schools—both of which were the source of immense pride among different sectors of the community—would raise temperatures, and a series of biracial meetings were held to help address the deep divisions, which had been widened in the previous two years by the nascent but intense sports rivalry that had developed between Athens and Burney-Harris.

More than fifty years later, the players on the Athens High squad did not remember the official announcement of consolidation being much of a distraction. Many were seniors and would be moving on to college or other endeavors after graduating in the spring of 1970, and others were simply lost in the moment of advancing through the football playoffs.

The night after Thanksgiving, in near-freezing temperatures, AHS squared off against the Avondale Blue Devils, who had won state championships in both 1958 and 1963. The Blue Devils featured a speedy Black wide receiver named Danny Buggs, who went on to star at West Virginia under Coach Bobby Bowden before launching a ten-year professional career in the NFL and the Canadian Football League. Although the game was played at an ostensibly neutral site, DeKalb Memorial Stadium in Clarkston, Rand Lambert remembered seeing celebratory signs in the hallways to the locker room prematurely congratulating the Blue Devils for their victory, which gave the Trojans a little extra incentive.

After the Trojans allowed a first-quarter field goal, nose guard Mike Epps recovered a Blue Devils fumble, and Athens High drove seventy-nine yards for a touchdown, capped by a twelve-yard Andy Johnson run. Athens took a 7–3 lead into halftime, and after a scoreless third quarter, AHS drove down the field once again to score on a twenty-yard Rusty Russell run.

The Trojans had managed to hem in Danny Buggs for most of the game. When Buggs lined up as wide receiver, Mac Coile—one of the sophomores elevated to the varsity after the Trojans' early-season loss to Gainesville—would jam him before he could start his route, and then Andy Johnson would continue the coverage on the speedster farther downfield. This strategy worked, but no one was going to stop Buggs on the kickoff return after Athens took a 14–3 lead—he took the ball seventy-six yards for a touchdown while the AHS fans were still cheering their own score, and the scoreboard flashed "14–10" with plenty of time left in the game.

Athens recovered from the gut punch of yielding a special teams touchdown and marched down the field in another businesslike seventy-five-yard drive, culminating in a three-yard touchdown run by Johnson, which was the final nail in the Trojans' 21–10 upset win. Athens dominated the game statistically, racking up 371 yards in total offense compared to a meager 139 managed by the Blue Devils.[28]

╫╫╫

The Trojans' opponent for the North Georgia championship game was the Dykes Colts, from Atlanta's tony Buckhead neighborhood. The fact that the Colts had reached the state semifinals was a surprise to almost everyone, including the *Daily News*, which declared in its early Saturday edition that heavily favored South Cobb had defeated the Colts 28–6, when the exact opposite was true. After a winless record in 1967, his first year as coach at Dykes, Bud Theodocion had quickly transformed the Colts into a serious challenger in AAA—they won Region 6-AAA in 1969, and the only blemish on their record was a six-point loss to ultimate AA state champion North Springs.

The state semifinal game took place on a Saturday night at Grady Stadium in Atlanta's Midtown. More than fifty years later, players still remembered the harshest weather conditions imaginable. The temperature was just above freezing, and rain poured the entire afternoon and evening. Mac Coile recalled warming up and seeing a reflection of the stadium lights bouncing off the deep puddles that had formed on the field. In a moment of pregame merriment—and beyond Weyman Sellers's watchful eye—Trojans players tried to stay warm by jumping up and down on a trampoline they found in the Grady High School gym.

The game was played in a thick, muddy mosh pit, and the Trojans' all-white uniforms were soon completely covered in a cold, black sludge. Athens exploded to a 21–7 halftime lead, fueled by Andy Johnson's seventy-yard punt return for a touchdown and Johnson's fifteen-yard touchdown pass to Rusty Carter. Benny Edmondson added to the Trojans' total with a short two-yard scamper at the end of a forty-eight-yard drive.

Johnson started the second half with another long touchdown run that was called back because of a holding penalty on a Trojans guard. The uniforms were so muddy that Coach Sellers could not identify the number of the miscreant, and both guards—Gary Travis and Doc Eldridge—agreed that they would run to the opposite side of the field if Sellers summoned them to the sidelines for a chew-out session.

Terry Smart capped the scoring with a thirteen-yard touchdown run in the fourth quarter, and the Trojans emerged from the muck as 28–7 winners and were officially crowned the champions of North Georgia. But the news from South Georgia was troubling, if not unexpected. Valdosta had whipped Savannah 20–0, and the Trojans would have to travel to Cleveland Field for a date with the Wildcats that would determine the AAA state championship.[29]

CHAPTER 6

THE GAME

Athens's offense could be summed up in two words:
Andy Johnson.

—*Joe Litsch*, Atlanta Journal-Constitution, *December 14, 1969*

After a life-reaffirming shower and a bus ride back to Athens, the Trojans players woke up on a clear, cold early December Sunday morning with a warm glow. They had, after all, made it to the finals after a disastrous early-season loss and a short-lived player rebellion. There were other distractions—the injuries to players that all teams deal with over the course of a season and the uncertainty related to the school itself. Although all signs pointed toward the integration of AHS with Burney-Harris, the how, when, and where were still far from determined.

The enormity of the next challenge was also slowly beginning to sink in. The Trojans would be traveling to Valdosta, fifteen miles north of the Georgia-Florida state line, to take on an integrated Wildcats team that had assembled the most impressive résumé in that school's unparalleled history of gridiron accomplishments. Through ten regular season and two playoff games, the Wildcats had racked up a 12–0 record and a scoring differential of +400 (407–7)—the lone score against them was a touchdown surrendered to Tift County after Valdosta had fumbled the ball away on its own eleven-yard line on the way to a 28–7 win.

That year's Wildcats squad was in every sense a product of the football-mad culture of a city that ESPN would later dub "TitleTown USA." The team had a few players who were highly sought after by colleges—quarterback Don Golden, linebacker Tom Holt, and fullback Danny O'Neal—but it was not, in the words of future Wildcat and UGA star Buck Belue, "a roster filled with five-stars."[1] It was an extremely organized system team; an assemblage that inexorably exerted its will on all challengers; a group that kept its own mistakes to a minimum and ruthlessly exploited the missteps and weaknesses of its opponents.

In addition to exerting physical domination, the team, with the help of the larger community, had also mastered the science of psychological intimidation. For home games, the Wildcats would dress out as many as one hundred players, including the entire junior varsity. For away games, a fleet of Greyhound buses—carrying the players, cheerleaders, and band—would travel as a convoy, serving notice to the local townspeople that the Wildcats had arrived to steamroll their boys.

Visitors were informed that they had entered the city limits of "Winnersville," with roadside signs broadcasting Valdosta's multitude of state and national titles. Cleveland Field seated almost twelve thousand and was known colloquially as "the Pit." The transfer of Wildcats season tickets was the subject of much wrangling in divorces and wills. The city of thirty-five thousand was, in every sense, a "Friday Night Lights" type of town in which King Football ruled.

Legendary Valdosta head coach Wright Bazemore was a trailblazer of sorts, having three years earlier accepted the team's first three Black players, who had transferred to Valdosta High from Pinevale High (an all-Black school) under freedom of choice. Bazemore downplayed any tensions related to the inclusion of African American players on his squad and famously observed that instructing left-handed quarterbacks was more difficult than coaching minorities.[2] John "Lightning" Copeland was the most celebrated of the three original African American players coached by Bazemore, largely due to the starting running back's crucial touchdown in the 1966 state championship game.

But by 1969, fissures were appearing within the student body. By then, four hundred Black students attended Valdosta, and they understandably resented the Wildcat marching band playing "Dixie" at football games. There was also a huge controversy around the vote for homecoming queen in the fall of 1969. A Black candidate recorded the most votes, but the administration overruled the decision and named a White candidate the winner, claiming that the Black students had voted as a bloc for the single African American in the competition; this was deemed unfair since presumably the White vote was diffused among many different aspirants to the crown. In protest, Black students staged a walkout, and several Black football players, including the starting safety, Curtis Lee, joined the protest and sat out that Friday's game against Moultrie, the number-two-ranked team in AAA. Valdosta won 21–0.[3]

The Athens media always found Trojans coach Weyman Sellers to be accessible and voluble, and the week before the Valdosta game was no exception. After decrypting the "coachspeak," it was clear that he was relying on his defense to keep the Trojans in the game—Sellers acknowledged the big size advantage the Wildcats enjoyed over his team but was hopeful that the Valdosta edge in heft would be offset by the Trojans' "quickness and determination." The defensive strategy of the Trojans would be to avoid the "big play," to keep the action in front of them; the Valdosta offense relied on knockout punches in the form of long bombs or explosive runs that put them out of reach of their opponents by halftime.[4]

The excitement in Athens grew by the minute in the week leading up to the game. Terry Smart remembered ministers from most of the local churches coming by practices to pray with the players and bask in their reflected glory. There was no official line on the game, but informally, local bookies were making the Trojans two- or three-touchdown underdogs.

The Trojan Booster Club was working furiously behind the scenes to charter three planes to fly to Valdosta—one for the players and two for the fans. The driving distance between the two cities is 250 miles, and large segments of Highway I-75 between Atlanta and the Florida state line were still under construction in the 1960s, forcing traffic onto slower state highways; a lengthy bus ride risked tiring out players before the game had even started. Buses were chartered for the band, the drill team, and any fans who could not claim a seat on one of the Southern Airways DC-3 propeller-driven "tail draggers." Others made plans to carpool to the game.

The Friday before the Saturday night game, Athens High held the biggest pep rally in the school's history. Invited guests included Mayor Julius Bishop and the 1955 state champion Trojans, who had defeated 'Dosta 41–20. Fran Tarkenton, who quarterbacked the 1955 team and was finishing up an NFL season with the New York Giants, phoned in his support: "I remember how thrilled we were when we won the state championship in '55," the future Hall of Famer recalled. "So I'll be pulling for Athens all the way on Saturday night!"[5] Paul Gilbert, quarterback of the 1965 team that fell agonizingly short in the state championship game against Valdosta, drove the one mile from UGA—where he played for the Bulldogs—and pumped up the crowd. The AHS cheerleaders, dressed in white woolen sweaters, crimson-and-white knee socks, and houndstooth skirts, led the crowd in cheers.

Later that day, the Clarke County Board of Education—to surprisingly little fanfare—voted 6–2 to merge Athens High and Burney-Harris for the 1970–1971 school year. The news, which was expected, was largely drowned out by the pre-game hype.[6]

The game was deemed big enough that *two* local radio stations would be broadcasting it: WGAU, the Trojans' flagship station, with Hope Hines—who went on to become a respected TV broadcaster in Tennessee—handling the play-by-play; and WRFC, best known locally as a Top 40 station, which would feature Bill Hartman in the broadcast booth. Hartman's budding broadcast career had come full circle with Athens High—as a senior at AHS, he performed the public address duties at Death Valley for the 1965 championship game, and now as a senior at UGA, he had been selected to perform play-by-play duties in another Athens-Valdosta state championship clash.[7] This game was especially meaningful for Hartman, because he had always felt that he bore partial responsibility for Chuck Perry's fateful extra-point miss in the 1965—before the PAT attempt, Hartman had announced to the frenzied crowd that *if* the Trojans tied the game, they would be co–state champions, which might have ramped up the already tremendous pressure felt by Perry.

As is the case with many teams given little chance to win, the pressure was largely off the AHS players. After the close call in the opener against Burney-Harris and the glaring misstep against Gainesville the following week, the Trojans had dispatched the remaining opponents on their schedule with relative ease. They had gone on the road and won two playoff games in Atlanta. No one would have thought less of them if the impregnable Wildcats beat them soundly. This serenity was reflected in Coach Sellers, who was as philosophical as a student who had crammed for a final exam and now just had to take the test: "It's a little late to teach 'em something new. After all, if they don't know it by now ... we're confident.

If we weren't, there wouldn't be much point in going down there." Assistant coach Frank Malinowski reminded Rand Lambert that he had better be prepared to block star Valdosta linebacker Tom Holt. "I'll show 'em," Lambert laughed in response.[8]

The local press feasted on the storylines for the game. It was the "rubber match" between Athens and Valdosta, the "kingpins of North and South Georgia," who were deadlocked at 1–1 in state championship games. It was a battle of the quarterbacks between Andy Johnson and Don Golden, who was also highly sought after as a college recruit. It was a story of the smallish thirty-three-member Trojans team marching into the jaws of the juggernaut, a physically larger and faster squad that would outnumber them in players dressed out by a margin of 4–1.

On the bright, cold morning of December 13, 1969, the members of the Trojans team—dressed in suits and ties—arrived at Ben Epps Field in East Athens and boarded one of the Southern Airways DC-3s waiting on the tarmac. For many, it was their first flight, and they swallowed Dramamine as a precaution against airsickness. Bill Hartman and the WRFC radio crew boarded another plane filled with fans—who had paid $26 each for the round-trip airfare—for what Hartman remembered as a "raucous journey to South Georgia." The seats on DC-3s angled backwards, and passengers did not level out into a normal sitting position until the plane was airborne. Although it was a clear and virtually windless morning, Trojans player Dickie Davis recalled the small prop plane "bouncing from cloud to cloud."[9]

Meanwhile, the Trojans faithful who had traveled by bus or car were assembling in Valdosta and establishing the Holiday Inn as their unofficial party headquarters. Parents and alumni mixed with students as pregame festivities cranked up. Georgia was still a few years away from lowering the drinking age to eighteen, but the adults looked the other way as the beer and liquor flowed freely.

The team was met at the airport by an ancient school bus with the seats removed—Wright Bazemore had wasted no time introducing the Trojans to the gamesmanship for which Valdosta was so well known. The bus conveniently got lost on the way to Cleveland Field, where the Trojans would conduct a pregame walk-through to accustom themselves to their surroundings. All along the route, Valdosta fans held up signs and jeered the Trojans and laughed at the dilapidated bus, which was "saved from a junkyard." One zealous Wildcat fan had crafted an oversized yellow thumb that he directed downward as the Trojans caravan passed by.[10]

The Trojans, still dressed in their street clothes, conducted their walk-through in the midafternoon. The Valdosta players were already dressed in their uniforms, minus helmets and shoulder pads, and looked on from the grandstands. "Hey Johnson," yelled Don Golden at the Athens quarterback, "you just need to lay on the ground, cuz that is where you are going to be all night!" Mike Nash, the big AHS lineman, who had returned late in the season from an ankle injury suffered in the Burney-Harris game, responded, "Nah, Golden, that is going to be you!"[11]

The Trojans players and coaches gathered for their pregame meal at the Holiday Inn. The restaurant manager, seeing the small group of less than physically imposing players, asked Coach Sellers if the linemen would be eating separately. "No," responded Sellers, "you are looking at the whole team."

The kickoff was set for 8 p.m. in "the Pit," and Benjamin Belue decided to take his son Buck, who would be turning ten the next week. Benjamin made sure to take Buck by the door leading out of the Trojans dressing room so he could see Andy Johnson—"Keep your eyes on number 14," he told his young son. "He is special."[12]

The teams' dressing rooms were fifty yards apart, with the Trojans assigned the visitor's locker room in the ancient gymnasium better known as "the Barn." Terry Smart remembered the thunderous clamor from Valdosta's locker room—the Wildcats were slamming their helmets against the corrugated metal ceiling of the walkway leading out of their dressing room, which was situated under the stadium.[13] The steady rumble, reminiscent of a brewing summer storm, was the first sign that the Trojans were getting ready to enter the Gates of Hell.

The Trojans ran out first, accompanied by their band playing the school song, played to the tune of the University of Michigan's fight song, "Hail to the Victors." The Wildcats then made their entrance—flanked by two lines of the drill team—to a thundering roar from the crowd. Smart remembered, "They just kept coming, and coming, and coming."[14] The 120 boys who dressed out took so long to reach the sidelines that Belue remembered, only half-jokingly, that "the Wildcat band had to play the school song twice that night."[15] Woody Chastain, a fan and former AHS player who had flown down on one of the DC-3s, remembered the impressive size of the Valdosta players: "Those big boys came out wearing those gold helmets and pants and white shirts with black numbers and looked like Georgia Tech."[16]

The weather was, certainly by South Georgia standards, cold that evening, with temperatures hovering around forty degrees. The only footage of the game—preserved by the Valdosta Touchdown Club from the original 8mm film, which was later converted to VHS tape and finally to DVD format—shows condensation vapor pouring from the players' mouths.

An uproarious crowd was on hand to watch the proceedings. Valdosta had cleverly split up the Athens fans, who were distributed into small, isolated pockets throughout the stadium, where their cheers would be diffused. Valdosta fans stomped their feet on the metal bleachers to create a deafening din.

The two teams' captains met at midfield for the coin toss. Andy Johnson and big tackle Alex Allen came out for the

Trojans, who wore their home uniforms: crimson helmets with white stripes down the middle and the player's number placed on one side of the helmet, and crimson jerseys that featured two angled white stripes along the edges of the shoulder pads, as was the football fashion in the 1960s.

The Wildcats stretched from sideline to sideline, in stark contrast to the Trojans, who comfortably fit between the thirty-yard lines on their side of the field.

AHS won the toss and opted to receive the football. The kickoff bounced around dangerously before Benny Edmondson scooped it up and was tackled on the Trojans' sixteen-yard line. Johnson's first pass from scrimmage was a throw deep downfield that was almost intercepted by a Wildcats defender. After a bootleg by Johnson was stopped for no gain, AHS was faced with its first big challenge— third and long, backed up deep in its own territory. Johnson sprinted out to the right on what today would be called an RPO (run-pass option). Just before running out of bounds, he threw a perfect pass to the opposite side of the field to receiver Morry Collins, who gained thirty-seven yards.

On first down from the Wildcats' forty-three, Valdosta was penalized five yards. On second and five, Johnson took a deep shotgun snap and managed a two-yard gain. The next play shocked everyone. Fullback Benny Edmondson from East Athens took the handoff and ran through a huge hole opened by the left side of the Trojan line. He avoided a linebacker with a nifty cut to the right and ran untouched for thirty-six yards and a touchdown.

On the extra-point attempt, the Wildcats were offside, which moved the ball to the one-and-a-half-yard line. The short distance persuaded Coach Sellers to try for the two-point conversion using a fake play, which misfired when Johnson, as the holder on the kick, took the snap and overthrew his receiver. The missed opportunity to add points would have huge implications later in the game.

Still, the Trojans had taken the opening kickoff and marched eighty-four yards in six plays to take a 6–0 lead. Only two minutes into the game, the Valdosta Wildcats were behind for the first time all season. Even more importantly, Sellers had moved the ball down the field by mixing the pass with the run, which kept the Wildcats' defense off-balance. This had been achieved against a Valdosta defense that was intensely proud and talented and had surrendered only one other score the entire season. "No one," recalled Terry Smart, "was as surprised as we were."[17]

Bill Hartman remembered his excitement in the radio booth, where he was not only performing the play-by-play but also urging the Trojans on as a cheerleader. "I am glad there is no tape of that broadcast," Hartman mentioned more than fifty years later. "I am sure I came across as an excited 'homer.'"[18]

Bill King did not make it to Valdosta—his father, who worked as branch manager at the C&S Bank on Prince Avenue, held the office Christmas party at the King home that Saturday night, a much-anticipated event that King's mother, Mollie, carefully planned and prepared special holiday treats for. King's father did allow Bill to play the broadcast of the game in the kitchen, and he and several guests sneaked off to listen to Hartman's excited play-by-play.

Following the Trojans' opening score and ensuing kickoff, Valdosta ground out ten yards on three running plays to barely eke out a first down. By this time, the AHS defense was committed to stopping the run, and Valdosta quarterback Don Golden ran a play fake to the fullback, which froze the Trojan defense. Golden turned to his right and fired a swing pass to Willie Jones, a fast African American wide receiver, who outran the entire AHS secondary to the end zone for a touchdown of sixty-three yards. The score remained 6–6 with 8:03 remaining in the first quarter after Valdosta was wide on its extra-point attempt.

Like boxers who had exchanged a flurry of punches in the first round, the teams settled down and exchanged punts on the next two possessions.

In its third possession Athens moved the ball inside the Valdosta twenty-yard line, relying on misdirection and Johnson's deft management of the option-oriented offense. Delayed draws, "counter play" handoffs, and other quick-hitting runs, mixed in with the occasional deep pass, were keeping Valdosta off-balance. And it was not simply the play selection; it was also the use of different formations in the backfield, where the Trojans ran Johnson as the only deep back in a shotgun or used him to direct reads out of wish-bone, veer, or wing-T sets.

It was clear that Weyman Sellers had closely studied the Wildcats on film, and he was able to spot and exploit weak-nesses with their oversized defensive line, which was proving to be vulnerable to the Trojans' superior quickness. While the drive ultimately stalled on a tipped-pass interception by Don Golden (who also played safety on defense), Athens had already shown twice in the first half that it was more than capable of carving up the vaunted Wildcat defense.

The Trojans' play in the first half had left the Wildcats gasping for breath. Valdosta had won its previous games that season by such large margins that their defensive starters had not had to stay on the field for a long, sustained drive the entire year. And while this last drive had failed, Sellers felt that his team's superior conditioning would assert itself if the Trojans were still within striking distance late in the game.

Following an Andy Johnson punt after another short Trojans drive, the Wildcats' offense took over on their own sixteen-yard line. Don Golden engineered an eleven-play, eighty-four-yard drive that ended when he scored on a fifteen-yard option keeper. With 2:23 remaining in the half, Valdosta led 13–6. Things suddenly seemed to be slipping away from the Trojans—all eleven plays on the drive were on the ground, as the Wildcats took control of the line of scrimmage. Mike Epps remembered that he had little luck finding gaps big enough for him to slip through the Wildcats' huge and disciplined offensive line. His task was made more difficult by the poor condition of the field, which was mainly grassless that late in the season, thereby making it nearly impossible for the players to dig in their cleats and gain leverage.

Both teams failed to move the ball in their subsequent possessions, and the Wildcats punted the ball over to the Trojans with twenty-three seconds remaining in the half. Athens took over at its own thirty-five, and there was a discussion about running the clock out and heading to the locker room with the moral victory of trailing Valdosta by only seven points at halftime. But Johnson prevailed and convinced his team to try and move the ball. The first play was a disaster, with Johnson—who by now was receiving a pounding from the Valdosta defense on both his running and passing attempts—getting sacked for a deep loss. But a flag was on the field: Valdosta was offside, and a five-yard penalty was called. The next play was a slow-developing screen pass that fell incomplete as time ran out on the half. But once again the referees threw a flag: Valdosta had twelve men on the field, resulting in another five-yard penalty, and Athens was awarded an untimed down with no time left on the clock. The Valdosta fans were incensed—they had complained about the officiating since the first flag was thrown against their beloved Wildcats earlier in the game; one fan screamed, "Those refs got some of that Yankee money!"[19] In the eyes of at least some of the Wildcats' faithful supporters, living in North Georgia sufficiently qualified Athenians as Yankees.

Mike Epps had already started to run off the field before he realized that the Trojans had elected to run one more play; he was astonished and wondered why the team did not simply decline the penalty and head to the locker room to regroup. But Johnson had convinced his teammates to take one more shot at the Wildcats before halftime. The play call was a variation of a "Hail Mary" pass play in which Johnson rolled to the right before launching a bomb downfield. Instead, the Trojans quarterback would seek a hole in the Wildcats' defense after rolling right so that he could use his sprinter's speed to bust through an opening and race down the field.

Johnson took the shotgun snap and rolled to his right. Near the sideline, he spotted a hole and pivoted upfield while Gary Travis delivered a devastating block to clear the path. Johnson shed a couple of arm tackles and took off down the field in his easy gait—head down slightly, shoulders squared, running with the ease of a thoroughbred to the goal line for a sixty-five-yard touchdown. Athens had cut the margin to 13–12. The two-point try was no good, and the teams headed to their locker rooms.

Blake Giles, an Athens High grad and a sports reporter for the *Athens Banner-Herald*, said, "Coach Sellers later told me that Andy was the only player he ever had who had scored as part of the halftime show."[20]

Steve Ray had taken a bus from Athens that day with a group from Prince Avenue Baptist Church. He remembered Johnson's run as "the best and most determined run I have ever seen . . . seemed like every defender hit him on that run." The Trojans fan behind Ray became so excited over Johnson's run that he spilled liquor all over Ray and a fellow church member sitting next to him, and Ray "had to ride home on [the] church bus smelling like a distillery."[21]

Jim Kitchens, the team's center and one of the cocaptains on that Trojans team, remembered: "[The Wildcats] may have been disoriented because of the penalty, but Andy got loose and outran the fastest guy they had." Johnson had an eerie confidence in his ability to perform and inspire his team, even in seemingly hopeless situations. "He was in perfect control to do something amazing," Kitchens added.[22]

On their opening drive of the second half, the Wildcats

quickly regained their composure, driving down the field on a series of runs and scoring on a Don Golden option keeper with 8:16 left in the third quarter to make the score 20–12 after the successful extra-point attempt.

Athens quickly responded with a long drive of its own, as Johnson again mixed run and pass to perfection, including a perfectly executed long pass to end Rusty Carter on a difficult throw—Johnson, a right-hander, rolled out and threw it left, but he still managed to hit his receiver in stride. The Trojans scored a seven-yard touchdown running the same play that ended the first half, a designed Johnson rollout to the right, where his line opened a huge hole. He was once again high trying to hit his receiver on the two-point attempt, and the Wildcats clung to a two-point lead, 20–18.

Valdosta responded quickly, driving the length of the field in the final minutes of the third quarter. But as the quarter came to a close, they squandered a golden opportunity by fumbling the ball away to the Trojans near the goal line.

While Athens had dodged a bullet, the size of the Valdosta lines was starting to take its toll, as Golden and running backs LaVictor Lipscomb and Danny O'Neal ran through gaping holes in the Trojans' undersized defensive line. On offense, the Trojans were having a difficult time blocking all-state linebacker Tom Holt, who was requiring a double-team from Gary Travis and Rusty Russell.

The Wildcats eased ahead 26–18 in the fourth quarter but missed the extra point when the ball bounced off the crossbar of the goalposts. That lead appeared to be safe as the Wildcats pushed inside the Trojans' thirty-yard line with less than two minutes to go in the contest.

Fifty years ago, a team that had the lead deep in the fourth quarter did not assume the "victory formation," wherein the quarterback would take the snap and take a knee. Instead, Golden took a snap and bootlegged to the left. Near the sideline, he absorbed a vicious hit from Gary Travis, and the ball sprang loose. On film, the players who were huddled near the sideline block the view of the ball, but based on the angle, the football took a fortuitous bounce or roll, especially since Golden was carrying the ball in his left hand, the side closest to the out-of-bounds line. After a pileup, Bruce Williams emerged with the football on the Athens twenty-six-yard line, and the Trojans took possession with 1:10 remaining on the clock. Years later, Travis felt like the Wildcats had been trying to pad their lead—they were playing not only for the state title, but also for the mythical national title. Or maybe winning the state championship with the opponent within one score of a tie would somehow be a blow to Wright Bazemore's pride. Or perhaps there was still some residual anger over the three-touchdown loss Athens High had inflicted on Valdosta in the 1955 state title game. In any case, the Wildcats' choice of an aggressive play call so late in the game backfired and gave the Trojans one final hope.

Blake Giles recalled that after the Athens fumble recovery, Sellers told Andy Johnson that the Trojans were going to score. "I know," the quarterback responded.[23]

The first two play calls—both designed run plays for Johnson—were curious selections by Sellers, given the amount of real estate that had to be covered and the limited amount of time left in the game, and they left the Trojans with a third and seven with under a minute to play. With forty seconds left, the Trojans rolled the dice and resorted to trickery, using a "tackle eligible" play that had gained big yardage in their quarterfinal win against Avondale. The tackle-eligible formation allows an offensive lineman to become an eligible receiver and to reposition off the line of scrimmage as either a fullback or a tight end. The play is still seldom called in the NFL or in college, because it requires the offensive team to inform the referee of the lineman's eligibility as a receiver. The referee then informs the defensive team that the offensive lineman is an eligible receiver. The play is now almost universally banned on the high school level.

"Pygmy 64" was the play call, a pass for Gary Travis—Sellers had dubbed offensive guard Travis "Pygmy" because of his small stature, and his uniform number was 64. Johnson went back to pass and was able to release the ball a split second before being leveled by a Wildcat end who had crashed in, unblocked, from Johnson's blind side. The perfectly thrown ball found Travis wide open in the left flats. Travis, who had played running back on the JV team, told himself, "Just don't fumble."[24] He rambled for forty-two yards to the Valdosta twenty-nine-yard line with thirty-one seconds left on the clock.

"Sally 50" was a tackle-eligible play designed for number 50, Rand Lambert, whom Sellers had nicknamed "Sally" after Sally Rand, a famous burlesque dancer in midcentury America. This time, the Wildcats were not caught off guard—Lambert was covered on his route to the right flats, and a Wildcats defender stretched out and barely missed deflecting the ball from its intended target. But Lambert collected the perfectly thrown toss and ran into the end zone untouched. He slammed the ball to the ground in celebration as Sellers sent in the play for a two-point conversion.

The ball was put on the three-yard line, and the Trojans ran a play fake to Benny Edmondson, who attracted the attention of three Valdosta tacklers. If Edmondson had taken the ball, he would have been stopped short of the goal line. But the play fake froze the Wildcat secondary, and Johnson found Gray Sellers in the back of the end zone all alone for the pass and the two points that made it a tie, 26–26.

Athens kicked off with twenty-five seconds left, and an addled Wildcat offense was unable to move the ball. Valdosta actually came close to scoring two points for Athens on a safety when Golden was sacked on about the five-yard line as time expired. The game was over, ending in a 26–26 tie, with the two teams sharing the state championship. And remarkably, the stat line was also a tie, as each team had gained 362 total yards, a particularly astonishing achievement by Athens, considering that Valdosta had held its opponents to a combined 798 yards in the twelve games it had played prior to the state final.

In the competitive landscape of contemporary America, it is difficult to understand how satisfying a tie (or "draw," which is my preferred British term for a match that ends deadlocked) often was fifty or more years ago. The famous 1966 football game featuring number-one-ranked Notre Dame versus number-two-ranked Michigan State that ended in a 10–10 tie is still billed as the "Game of the Century," with the Fighting Irish's 0–0 draw against Army in 1946 ranking a close second. In 1969, underdog Harvard scored sixteen points in the last minute against its longtime rival Yale to snare a 29–29 "victory" that is still celebrated as the most memorable contest in a series that dates to 1875.

The Athens players met at midfield and were jubilant, jumping up and down and congratulating each other. In contrast, the Valdosta players walked around aimlessly, as if they were in a daze. Children who had been gathered on the edge of the field spilled into the end zone as soon as the final horn sounded; their silhouettes can be seen in the deteriorated film from that dark evening, playing their impromptu version of touch football in the shadow of the celebrating Athens players.

Years later, Bill Hartman remembered: "I've done play-by-play for a number of games, including the Bulldogs and the Falcons, but none was more exciting than the '69 championship game."[25]

In a bizarre coda, a new Cadillac was driven out to midfield and presented to Wright Bazemore by the Valdosta Touchdown Club. He had won another state title for the Wildcats, although he of course had to share the crown with Athens. He wore a frozen grin as he and his wife climbed inside to check out the features of their new automobile. He looked every bit as shaken as a golfer who had just double-bogeyed the eighteenth hole on Sunday at the Masters to lose by one stroke.

The Trojans' celebration continued in the locker room, where Vince Dooley joined them and congratulated AHS for its performance. Pat Dye, the former UGA star and an assistant coach for Bear Bryant at Alabama, shook Rand Lambert's hand and mentioned the upcoming recruiting trip planned for Lambert in Tuscaloosa.

While the Athens players and fans were beside themselves with joy, Valdosta supporters were in a state of shock; Trojan fans remembered seeing them at breakfast the next morning in local restaurants, sitting at their chairs "moaning and groaning."[26] Mac Coile, who played on special teams and defense that evening, revisited Valdosta several weeks later for a family Christmas celebration, and one cousin refused to talk to him.

Buck Belue never forgot the performance Andy Johnson put on that evening and pledged that he, too, would one day be a two-sport star like his hero. On visits to his grandmother in Athens, Buck and his father would watch Johnson play football at Sanford Stadium in the fall and baseball with the Bulldogs in the spring.[27]

As the team boarded its plane back to Athens, a booster presented a bottle of champagne to Coach Sellers, who basked in the glow of his moment of redemption after the gut-wrenching 14–13 loss to Valdosta in 1965. His record against Wright Bazemore in state finals now stood at 1–1–1, and his team, as heavy underdogs, had just stunned the Wildcats in front of their raucous fans. And he would soon learn some more good news—AHS's allotted portion of the ticket sales from the overflow crowd at Cleveland Field would amount to $10,000, in those days a staggering sum of money for a high school game.[28]

For Weyman Sellers, the co–state championship was vindication. He had won on his own terms, against all odds, with a small, all-White roster against opponents who had, to varying degrees, accepted integration. At least for the moment, he had silenced the naysayers and skeptics who second-guessed player selection and other coaching decisions on even the most successful of teams. Most importantly, he had almost certainly secured the head football coaching position of the soon-to-be-consolidated high schools, despite the well-founded misgivings of the Black community in Athens. There was virtually zero chance—his baggage be damned—that a White football coach who was the recent winner of a state title would not be picked to lead the new school on the gridiron. And perhaps in the estimation of Coach Sellers, the championship that he had helped bring to his team and community had banked him an inexhaustible amount of goodwill that would protect him against the undeniable integration challenges that lay ahead. A tie represents equilibrium, a perfect balance between two opposing outcomes—victory and defeat—and Coach Sellers would rightfully enjoy the complex fruits of this duality in the postgame celebration and in the celebratory banquets, awards, and accolades that would follow. But the seeds of hubris also were planted, and the harvest would prove to be bitter in the new decade.

The players whooped and hollered as their plane zoomed through the frigid December night back to northeast Georgia. David Lester remembered that a friendly Southern Airways stewardess slipped Rand Lambert a small bottle of champagne, and he and several teammates raised a toast to their team, to the "victory," and to Cobern Kelley, their beloved Athens YMCA coach and mentor, who had passed away unexpectedly a year earlier.

Many of the Athens High fans stayed in Valdosta that night to celebrate at the Holiday Inn, as students joined older alumni in a moving party that covered ten or so rooms.

The plane carrying the Trojans players landed at Epps Field, where they were met by a cheering group of families, students, and fans. Many of the players continued the celebration at the home of Bruce Williams in the Forest Heights neighborhood off Tallassee Road—Williams's parents had stayed back in Valdosta, which gave the boys and their girl-friends free rein to celebrate into the early morning and be-yond; the tales of that night remain closely held secrets more than five decades later.

卌

Early the next morning, Rand Lambert boarded a plane at Ben Epps Field and took his second airplane flight in as many days. He flew to Winston-Salem, North Carolina, where Wake Forest University had invited him on a recruit-ing visit. On Monday afternoon, he flew back to Athens and played an entire game for the Trojans basketball team. On Tuesday, he flew to Tuscaloosa for his recruiting visit with Al-abama. On Wednesday, he committed to the Crimson Tide.

Vince Dooley's Christmas came a little early that year, on December 24. UGA was in El Paso, Texas, preparing for its Sun Bowl game against Nebraska, when Andy Johnson called the Georgia coach and gave him the happy news that he was going to sign with the hometown Bulldogs.

News of the Athens-Valdosta championship game spread quickly, and the instant classic was the lead story in the sports section of the Sunday edition of the *Atlanta Journal-Constitution*, an astounding splash of coverage for a high school game in a big city already jaded by its three profes-sional sports teams.

Athens merchants were ebulliently predicting a 15 per-cent increase over the previous year's record Christmas sea-son sales. With December 25 less than two weeks away, the city basked in the holiday spirit enhanced by the Tro-jans' "victory." Mike Epps recalled the Booster Club giving each Trojan player a wristwatch and an embroidered Tro-jans blanket. The editorial page of the *Daily News* saluted the Trojans' triumph as a heroic upset by an outmanned team that never relinquished hope. The mayor of Valdosta was magnanimous enough to declare the game "the greatest in this city's long football history."[29] The flagging spirits of Valdosta received a much-needed boost when they were declared co–national champions in high school football, sharing the title with Coral Gables (Florida) High School.

The week after the game, large crowds of people assembled at the Mell Auditorium at Athens High, where they paid two dollars each to watch a replay of the state final. Weyman Sellers narrated the game film and sprinkled in player nicknames and other humorous observations to the delight of the crowd.

It was a bittersweet experience. As the decade of the 1960s entered its twilight phase, the audience knew that the final embers of Trojan pride were also burning out and would soon be gone forever. All that had been emotionally invested in AHS over the decades would soon be found only in dusty trophy cases, yellowed newspaper clippings, and fading memories. Bill King remembered that time as "wistful and melancholy."[30]

卌

This disorienting sense of ennui felt by much of the White citizenry—the realization that not only Athens High but also the city of Athens that many had known and loved would soon be part of a bygone era—was heightened by the rapid change that had blown through the Classic City in the late 1960s. The University of Georgia would once again be in the forefront of the transformation, and Pete McCommons would once again bear witness to and participate in the remarkable changes during the closing years of the tumultuous 1960s.

After graduating from UGA in 1962, McCommons left Athens and moved to New York to attend graduate school at Columbia University. He discovered that graduate school was "not for him" and dropped out to work a series of part-time jobs: mail room clerk at NYU, typist for a real estate company in Greenwich Village, and, most interestingly, midnight transcriber for Karlis Osis, a psychologist investigating deathbed experiences. During his time in New York, he met his wife, an artist from Georgia, and the couple moved back to Athens in 1968 so that she could pursue a master's in art at UGA while McCommons began working at UGA's Institute of Government.

McCommons recalled his surprise at the transformation of both Athens and the university during his six-year hiatus: "The instructors at UGA were younger and more liberal—many of them were from the North, from states like Michigan and Wisconsin. The place was literally fermenting with youthful energy and new ideas."[31] The composition of the student body was also slowly changing, largely due to an infusion of disillusioned Vietnam War veterans attending UGA on the G.I. Bill and more left-leaning students attracted by an increasingly more tolerant atmosphere in Athens.

By the mid-1960s, downtown Athens had reached its nadir, with businesses fleeing to the more lucrative shopping centers on the edge of town and beyond. The Athens Chamber of Commerce commissioned a study in 1965 that found that downtown property values were plummeting and buildings were deteriorating. Modern development, as exemplified by the Robert G. Stephens Federal Building—a dreadful brutalist concrete eyesore that was seemingly modeled after a high-security prison—threatened the historic heart of downtown. But by the late 1960s the seeds of a downtown renaissance had been planted.

Many former students were staying in Athens and starting businesses after they were finished with school, abandoning the traditional path of leaving the Classic City for good—except for reunions and football games—after graduating from UGA. A large portion of these small downtown businesses that opened in the late 1960s or early 1970s reflected the bohemian values of their younger owners: the

Hobbit Habit, a counterculture bookstore; El Dorado Café, the city's first vegetarian restaurant; Underground Records, a retailer of alternative vinyl recordings; the Middle Earth Light and Power Company, a College Avenue rock music club that featured live bands playing cover songs; the Onion Dome East, which sold incense, blacklight posters, and other hippie paraphernalia; and the Glass of Hill Wall "head shop." Athens was also very affordable, especially for those graduates delaying marriage, children, and professional jobs. Rents and food were cheap, and one could eke out a living working a series of minimum-wage jobs.

An avalanche of cash under the administration of the reform-minded governor Carl Sanders had helped usher in a new era at UGA; the amount of state funding *quadrupled* between 1962 and 1968, and 450 new professors were hired in 1967 alone.[32] Inevitably, the new, more liberal-minded assistant and associate professors clashed with the "old guard"—the older and more conservative professoriate who remained as heads of most academic departments.

By 1967, the "New Left" organization Students for a Democratic Society (SDS) had gained a foothold at UGA, and though its membership represented only a small minority of what remained a deeply conservative student body, it immediately made its impact felt by organizing a protest against the Vietnam War during Vice President Hubert Humphrey's visit to the campus. Weekly anti-war peace vigils were later held outside Memorial Hall, and SDS members were involved in the integration of the Rail Bar and Alice's Cafe, two Athens establishments that were still refusing to serve Black people in the late 1960s. SDS-fueled activism ultimately led to the abolition of the university's requirement that all male students from Georgia participate in a two-year ROTC program. In a more menacing but comic twist, several SDS members were arrested in an unsuccessful attempt to burn down the on-campus ROTC building. While attempting to burn the building down, the would-be arsonists also stole a copy machine, which they shipped to the SDS office in Atlanta, a theft to which they later confessed. "They brought the wrong matches," Pete McCommons wryly recalled decades later.[33]

The most visible SDS-inspired success was the updating of antiquated coed dress codes—women were finally permitted to wear slacks and shorts on campus. The 11:15 p.m. curfew for women was also eliminated, and the prohibition against female consumption of alcohol was finally removed, as Dean William Tate's *in loco parentis* policy guiding student conduct was all but declared dead.

Illegal narcotic use was sweeping the nation in the 1960s, and Athens was no exception. No one seemed to know the extent of drug use on campus, but Dean Tate was concerned enough to contact Robert Kane, an Atlanta-based FBI agent, who kept Tate informed of surveillance activities his team conducted in the Athens area. Of particular interest was a "hippy colony" living in a house off Milledge Avenue and "a commune that had recently organized on a farm in Madison County."[34]

In early 1970, the *Athens Banner-Herald* interviewed a "former marijuana pusher," who estimated that 20–30 percent of Athens High School students were smoking pot and said that "she ought to know because she had sold it to them." Both Athens High Principal Don Hight and Athens police authorities disputed that estimate, and Hight revealed that some students had been under surveillance for suspected drug use, but nothing had turned up.[35]

Drugs—typically marijuana, LSD, and amphetamines— had spread beyond the original counterculture users to a broader swath of more recreational users among the general student population at UGA, including fraternity and sorority members. The acceptance of counterculture fashion and norm-breaking attitudes—particularly the adoption of casual sex and more comfortable, hip clothing—also spread to the fraternities and sororities, manifesting itself most prominently in the "Greek-Freaks." The Greek-Freaks, noted UGA student Doug Monroe, were "dressing hip, growing hair, and consuming drugs with the gusto they formerly reserved for grain alcohol. However, they still retain the crass material-ism, shallow conceits, and vapidity that identified them as traditional Greeks."[36]

Inevitably, the use of illegal narcotics spread to the greater Athens community. Two sixteen-year-olds were hospitalized in the fall of 1969 after bad LSD trips, and marijuana was available "by the bundles," according to the Clarke County Sheriff's Department. Amphetamines—whose most com-mon form was Dexedrine or "Black Beauties"—were abun-dant in Athens, having been either manufactured in local pill labs or smuggled in from Mexico by the Dixie Mafia.

Shifting mores were also apparent in the films appear-ing in Athens. While a local newspaper headline huffed that "Nudity [is here] to Stay" in film, the X-rated sex comedy *The Libertine* was showing at Alps Road Minicinema.

The distant war in Indochina had an impact locally. Two former Burney-Harris students were killed in action in early 1969: Thomas Clark, a marine private first class with a young son, fell in battle in South Vietnam just before his twenty-first birthday; a few weeks later, nineteen-year-old marine lance corporal Jeff Whitehead, who had graduated a year behind Clark, also died in combat. Both were buried at East Lawn Cemetery in Athens.

Bill King remembered that a handful of AHS students wore black armbands to school as part of the Vietnam War protest movement that swept the nation in 1969. Unlike at many schools across the nation, this silent form of protest did not result in suspension for the students involved.

Local journalists also cast a more critical eye on the stark divide between the races, as illustrated by the persistently deplorable living conditions endured by many Black resi-dents of Athens. Despite almost a decade of urban renewal efforts, the sad state of much of the Classic City's housing stock continued to be an embarrassment to civic leaders. An estimated three thousand homes—clustered mainly in East Athens, Rocksprings, "the Bottom," and the Hancock Avenue corridor—were deemed "dilapidated." The wood-framed homes that had gone decades without repair were, "for the most part, occupied by Negroes who live there not by choice, but simply because there is no place else to go."[37]

In the late sixties, Sharon Bailey, a bold reporter for the *Daily News*, visited one of Athens's many boarding homes, including a six-room structure that housed eighteen mainly elderly and orphaned residents. A photographer captured harrowing images of vacant-eyed residents living amid trash, peeling walls, and broken furniture.[38] The lack of electricity and sunlight, the swarms of flies, the unspeakable stench, and the invasion of the flimsy boarding home by hordes of rats and roaches were all part of a shocking peek at an underside of Athens that few had seen.

Meanwhile, the Department of Housing and Urban Development was rolling out the Model Cities program across the country, and $2.6 million had been allocated to the Classic City. The program had been developed as a plank in President Lyndon Johnson's War on Poverty, and Athens mayor Julius Bishop planned on spending the first chunk of funds allocated to Athens on a new bridge over the North Oconee River that would connect Broad Street in downtown with East Athens.[39] The new span would replace an ancient one-lane "horse and buggy bridge" that had been built in 1906. A groundswell of enthusiasm for reform and renewal was sweeping through the growing number of progressive citizens in the Classic City, and a feeling of optimism took hold that the problems of poverty, racism, and crumbling housing and infrastructure could all be tackled as the new decade loomed. Exemplifying this buoyant attitude of change was the excitement generated over one city council race in particular.

Running on a platform of higher infrastructure spending, a crackdown on police brutality, improved garbage collection, and higher pay for city employees, Ed Turner was viewed by many pundits as the first Black candidate to have a real chance at winning a seat on the Athens City Council. There had been several failed attempts by African American candidates in the past, but the twenty-six-year-old Turner, a native Athenian and UGA graduate, was a smart and energetic challenger. Turner would have to defeat the incumbent White councilman David Seagraves in the November 1970 election.[40]

But before that race would be decided ten months into the new decade, the long-awaited and nervously anticipated consolidation of the city's two public high schools would finally come to pass.

Maxie Foster (first row, far left), cocaptain of the Athens High School varsity basketball team. Foster would go on to become the first African American to earn an athletic scholarship at the University of Georgia. *Trojan 1968*, accessed via the Athens-Clarke County Library Heritage Room.

Bonnie Hampton (first row, far right) was one of the "Forgotten Five," five Black students who integrated the Athens-Clarke County school system in 1963. She is pictured here at Athens High School as a member of DECA. *Trojan 1968*, accessed via the Athens-Clarke County Library Heritage Room.

History is made—the all-White Athens High football team squares off against all-Black Burney-Harris High School on September 13, 1968, in the first battle for the "City Title." Athens High would prevail in a 58–32 shootout. © Athens Banner-Herald–USA TODAY NETWORK.

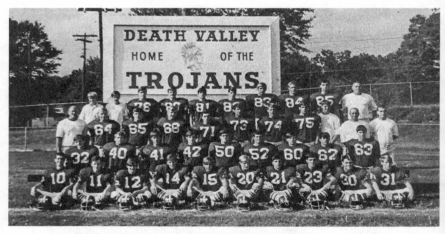

Athens High School Trojans team photo, 1969 season. The last football team to ever suit up for the Trojans featured thirty-two players, only one of whom weighed over two hundred pounds. *Trojan 1970*, accessed via the Athens-Clarke County Library Heritage Room.

Athens High Trojans give the thumbs-up the week before their clash with Valdosta for the 1969 state title in AAA. From right to left, Rusty Carter, Andy Johnson, Benny Edmondson, and Terry Smart. Photo courtesy of Terry Smart.

"The Greatest High School Football Game Ever"—Athens High and Valdosta meet for the 1969 AAA state football championship. Trojan players Mike Epps (number 11) and Rusty Carter (number 84) chase Valdosta quarterback Don Golden. *Trojan 1970*, accessed via the Athens-Clarke County Library Heritage Room.

Athens High School letterman jacket, 1969. Courtesy of David Lester. Photo by Ken Young.

Athens High quarterback Andy Johnson rumbles for yardage. Johnson was a legendary prep player in North Georgia and went on to start at quarterback at the University of Georgia before playing in the NFL for nine years. *Trojan 1970*, accessed via the Athens-Clarke County Library Heritage Room.

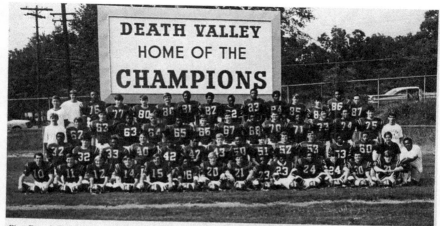

First Row, L-R: Skip Creasy, Mike Epps, Perry Strickland, Steve Lambert, Gray Sellers, Saxon Craft, Dickie Davis, Mark Zornig, Michael Thurmond, Eugene Hunter, Horace King, Jack McCue, Paul Giddings, Gene Powers, Tojo Crawford, Second Row, L-R: Clarence Pope, Bob Snipes, Dwight Marshall, Rusty Russell, Clifford Wise, Johnny Shell, Terry Tiller, Willie Davis, John Duke, Doc Eldridge, Howard Guest, Maurice Hawes, Bruce Holt, Spider Doolittle, Third Row, L-R: Trim Almond, Bud Bulter, Bruce Weekly, Benny Taylor, Jim Stuchell, George Wingfield, Randy Jackson, Hugh O'Farrell, John Luke, Bob Thornton, Joe Bell, Alex Allen, Bobby Sewell, Mark Thomas, Steve Bell, Fourth Row, L-R: Bill McDougald, Slim Almond, Nathaniel Craddick, Kevin Stoll, Pat Flanders, Mac Coile, Harold Moon, Roger Moss, Howard Long, Richard Appleby, O'Neal Luke, Mike Tillman, Jose Rodriqeuz, Bobby Crook, Frank Fleming.

Clarke Central Gladiators 1970 football team. The first integrated high school football team in Athens featured the combined squads of Athens High School and Burney-Harris High School. *Gladius 1971*, accessed via the Athens-Clarke County Library Heritage Room.

Clarke Central prepares for its inaugural 1970 season. Pictured, from left to right, are running back Horace King, Coach Weyman Sellers, and Sellers's son and quarterback, Gray Sellers. Photo courtesy of Gannett Company, Inc. The photographer was Mike Windham. © Athens Banner-Herald–USA TODAY NETWORK.

Don Hight, principal at Athens High School and later at Clarke Central High School. *Gladius 1971*, accessed via the Athens-Clarke County Library Heritage Room.

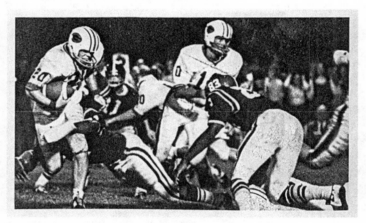

Clarke Central's Richard Appleby (number 83) reaches out to make the tackle on Gainesville running back Reggie Sexton in Clarke Central's first football game. The Gladiators would lose to the Gainesville Red Elephants 17–15. *Gladius 1971*, accessed via the Athens-Clarke County Library Heritage Room.

Michael Thurmond in his senior-year photograph at Clarke Central High School. Thurmond played running back for the football team and was copresident of the student council. *Gladius 1971*, accessed via the Athens-Clarke County Library Heritage Room.

CHAPTER 7

THE GLADIATORS

We need them [the Black players] to promote the
kind of spirit that can be instrumental in building
the kind of program we all would like to have.

—*Dr. Charles McDaniel, Clarke County superintendent of schools*

Athens shivered as prolonged cold snaps brought several
sleet and snowstorms in the first weeks of January 1970, and
the Classic City recorded an all-time low temperature of four
degrees.

The new decade also ushered in a cold reality at Burney-
Harris High School, as the previous autumn's casual acceptance of integration—when the idea was more of an abstraction—gave way to the inescapable fact that the Black
community's beloved school would soon cease to exist.

As details of the consolidation of Athens High School and
Burney-Harris High School emerged, members of the Black
community became increasingly worried about the plans
laid out by Clarke County school superintendent Charles
McDaniel. Their concerns centered on both cultural and
practical issues. In terms of cultural issues, there were deep
misgivings about whether the proud symbols of Burney-

Harris—the sports teams, student groups, the school newspaper—would be preserved, or whether they would be subsumed into a predominantly White high school. On the practical side, Black community leaders, students, and parents wanted assurances that Black teachers and administrators would have some protection form the job redundancies that would inevitably result from the merger. It boiled down to a numbers game: the student body at AHS outnumbered Burney-Harris's by a ratio of more than three to one, and it was easy to envision a future in which all vestiges of the Yellow Jackets' proud past would sink without a trace, as had happened with Black schools in both Gainesville (E. E. Butler) and Valdosta (Pinevale) when they merged with their majority-White counterparts.

Many in the Black community recognized that merging the two schools was a painful but necessary step toward redressing a century of uneven outcomes created by "separate but equal" schools. Athens High had vastly superior resources and offered more than twenty subjects not on the curriculum at Burney-Harris, such as Latin, German, and calculus. A few years earlier, Calvin Trillin had interviewed then–Clarke County school superintendent Sam Wood, who acknowledged the wide gulf that separated the two schools as related to standardized test scores and academic rigor. The two men also discussed cultural disadvantages such as the absence of a significant Black middle class in Athens, and the fact that White students were often the children of college professors. Wood relayed to Trillin a conversation he had recently had with H. T. Edwards, the principal of the Black high school: "I said, 'Remember last year when I came out to your school to induct ten of your seniors into the National Honor Society? Now, just how many of those seniors do you think would have made the National Honor Society at Athens High—with that competition?' And he said, 'Not the first one.'"[1]

Five decades later, Dr. Mary Blackwell-Diallo, the first

Black Athenian to graduate from UGA, energetically challenged Trillin's assertions that the education offered by the city's Black high school was in any way inferior and that Burney-Harris was capable of producing only "one or two students able to meet the relatively undemanding minimum requirements for admission to the University of Georgia."[2] According to Dr. Blackwell-Diallo, the dearth of Black applicants to UGA was attributable to a lack of confidence and a pervasive fear among local Black teachers and students who had been conditioned by generations of reprisals and rejection. She cited Dr. Walter Allen Sr. as the only Black high school teacher willing to openly assist her and other African American students in applying to UGA, and Blackwell-Diallo felt that Dr. Allen's support potentially put his own job in peril.[3] Dr. Allen's quiet, behind-the-scenes work also succeeded in securing an estimated 160 college scholarships (mainly in music) for Black students from Burney-Harris.[4]

The debate over the preservation of a Black high school more than fifty years ago in many ways mirrors the continued justification for historically Black colleges and universities—the HBCUs, though often underfunded and underresourced, offer a culturally supportive and confidence-building environment in which to prepare minority students for life beyond the classroom, in a society that is often indifferent or hostile to their background and unique set of experiences.

Aware that students from both schools would be sailing into uncharted waters, Burney-Harris and AHS set up unsupervised student committees early in 1970 to try to anticipate and hash out any differences well in advance of the planned September 1970 merger. The groups met each week, alternating their meeting locations between AHS and BHHS, and group members also attended classes at each other's schools. According to Bill King's article in the AHS student newspaper, the *Thumb Tack Tribune*, in January 1970, the main concerns for students from both schools centered on the name of the new school, extracurricular activities such as clubs, and the mascot and colors for the new school's athletic teams. These concerns repeatedly resurfaced as points of contention over the course of the coming months.

Mistrust between the Black and White communities had been brewing and barely kept contained for years, and Black citizens, conditioned by a long history of disappointment in dealing with Athens's White power structure, felt that they would inevitably get the short end of the stick in any compromise. There was also deep resentment over the planned use of the revered Burney-Harris building to house the tenth grade of the consolidated high school, while the AHS facility would be utilized for juniors and seniors; many in the Black community felt that this plan consigned their beloved alma mater to a subordinate status. Clarence Pope, a rising senior in the summer of 1970, summed up the misgivings of the Black community perfectly: "It looked as if Burney-Harris and everything that was associated with it was going to be swallowed up in the merger. We had everything to lose and nothing to gain."[5] Uncertainty related to the new school's name and mascot, the school colors, and the future of the Burney-Harris coaches was not just troublesome to athletes but also of grave concern to the members of the greater Black community, who had invested three generations of pride in their Yellow Jackets. Rising senior Horace King remembered, "I didn't want to wear the cardinal and white."[6]

More signs of trouble emerged in early April during an intramural basketball tournament at Athens High. An all-Black freshman team consisting of ninth-grade players from Athens Junior High played a heated game against a senior squad of White players, including Andy Johnson. The crowds supporting the two teams began hurling insults at each other, and someone threw a drink out onto the court. After the game (which the seniors won), a melee ensued. In the words of African American Athens High student Nathaniel Fox: "Words were exchanged, fights broke out. It was a powder keg."[7]

Bill King—who had joined ROTC to avoid Weyman Sellers's PE classes—made a beeline to the ROTC room located in the basement of Athens High. King and a few other ROTC members banged on the locked doors and were granted admittance by the senior commander, who promptly relocked the doors to prevent the rioters from making a "run for the gun rack." King, an aspiring journalist who had already done some work for the *Athens Banner-Herald*, phoned the newspaper's city desk to report the incident; several days later, Athens High principal Don Hight called King into his office and grilled him on why he thought it was necessary to notify the local media of the incident—"I thought that it [the riot] would be newsworthy" was his pithy response.[8]

Word soon spread to concerned parents, who arrived en masse to pick up their sons and daughters. Green-beret-wearing ROTC cadets directed traffic as the cars crowded into the AHS parking lot.

Over the weekend, Principal Hight called "responsible students," including Bill King, and asked for their help. The following Monday, King was tasked with telling students entering the school to go directly to their homeroom and to not loiter in the lobby or hallways. Rumors quickly spread that Hosea Williams, the renowned Atlanta civil rights activist, was in Athens and was leading a march on AHS. The rumor proved to be unfounded, but it caused a near panic at the school.

Amid this dizzyingly eventful spring of 1970, Pete McCommons—as part of a group guided by Presbyterian minister Frank Hutchison—started a weekly newsletter called the *United Free Press*. Hutchison was sent to Athens by the northern United Presbyterian Church, which rented him, his wife, Anne, and their daughters a house in Five Points. The mission-oriented church was focused on social action rather than on erecting a building for worship and ancillary activities, which meant that church services were held in the living room of the Hutchisons' home.

The racially mixed church group hatched the idea for the newsletter because its members and other like-minded people in the congregation felt that Athens's main daily newspaper, the *Athens Banner-Herald*, was not properly addressing the issues and root causes that had led to the eruption of protests and violence. (In late 1967, the Morris family, which owned the *Athens Banner-Herald*, purchased the city's other daily newspaper, the feisty *Athens Daily News*, and merged the two papers' editorial staffs, which turned the *Daily News* into a much more staid version of its formerly freewheeling self.)

A group of congregants, both Black and White, would meet at the Hutchisons' home and write articles for the newsletter, mimeograph and assemble the pages, and then staple them together—all while drinking beer and dancing around the table as Aretha Franklin blared from the stereo. "We were classic, well-meaning liberals," McCommons recalled.[9] "They [the Hutchisons] came here at the perfect moment for Athens. There were a lot of us strongly opposed to what was happening in our nation and in our community but with no discernable path of action."[10]

In the first edition of the newsletter, which was distributed to area churches and other organizations, the *United Free Press* detailed the list of demands that Black students had presented to Superintendent McDaniel. The demands included job security for Black custodians, administrators, and teachers; a requirement of consent from African American students before any policies could be implemented that would affect them; establishment of a Black Studies program within the school's curriculum; and assurances that there would be equal status for African American athletes and coaches in the new school's athletic program. Other demands included the removal of a plaque from the lobby of Athens High honoring the AHS male senior athlete who had best exemplified the values of Cobern Kelley, the renowned youth group leader at the all-White Athens YMCA who had passed away in 1968.[11] Kelley had resisted integrating the YMCA during his long tenure as youth group leader.

It was almost inevitable that the tensions spilled over into violence again, when students at Burney-Harris and Athens High clashed on April 16, 1970, a day later dubbed "Rowdy Thursday." A group of Black students, accompanied by a few sympathetic White classmates, walked out of Athens High and gathered in the Mell Auditorium parking lot, ostensibly to talk to "the newspaper people" about an article the day before discussing the trouble brewing along racial lines at AHS. *Athens Banner-Herald* reporter Chuck Cooper had filed a story in which he reported on a meeting that Athens High principal Don Hight held with an equal number of Black and White student leaders; in the meeting, each group outlined its list of concerns. The Black students were frustrated by discrimination—most notably, they felt blocked from joining clubs and organizations, and they believed that White teachers treated them unfairly. The White students countered that Black teachers at AHS were discriminating against *them*. In his article, Cooper referred to the Black student leaders as "militants," which further incensed them.[12]

Separately, 150 frustrated students at Burney-Harris—including Clarence Pope, Richard Appleby, and Michael Thurmond—had gathered after the first-period class change and walked outside in protest. BHHS principal E. T. Roberson demanded that the students either return to class or leave the school's premises. They then decided to march to Athens High School, and Roberson phoned his counterpart at AHS, Don Hight, to warn him that the students were en route. As the group crossed Rocksprings and Broad, Andy Johnson and Terry Smart—who had senior "open campus" privileges—were stopped at a red light in Johnson's Triumph Spitfire. Smart later said he sensed the seething anger of the Burney-Harris students and feared that he and Johnson would be dragged out of the car and beaten up, but the students just walked past them.

When the Burney-Harris students arrived at AHS, they joined up with the Black and White protesters from Athens High who were already gathered in the parking lot. By that time, Athens police had arrived on the scene, as principals Roberson and Hight talked to the leaders of the group. Talks broke down, and a group of Black students rushed past the police and into the building.

Years later, Burney-Harris student Marcus Thomas recalled the harrowing events that ensued:

> [S]tudents just rushed [Athens High]. . . . It was just bizarre, unlike anything I had ever seen before in my life. They were running up and down the hall pushing and punching. People were screaming and calling cops. I remember the cops came and it was horrible. I was just around. I remember being in the hallway because I wasn't familiar with the school. I had never been in Athens High and I was just there. I remember one moment this police officer pulled his gun out because this other guy had squared off with the policeman . . . and you see something happening in slow motion and you think he's about to get killed. The assistant chief came and grabbed his gun and said "put that damn gun away." I never will forget that. Someone could have died right there.[13]

Athens High assistant principal Dr. Walter Allen Sr., a Black man who had previously served as bandleader at Burney-Harris High School before earning a college degree in school administration, was struck in the back. More than fifty years later, at the age of ninety-two, Allen recalled the event: "Don Hight was hiding in the closet while I was getting beat up."[14]

Some White students were attacked—including an AHS student who was hit in the face with a baseball bat—and several Black AHS students, trying to restore order, were also beaten. "We did not follow the nonviolent lessons of

Reverend King that day," Richard Appleby remembered years later, "and I regret that."[15] News of the violence spread quickly, and a White Athens High parent who drove to the school later to pick up his daughter brandished a pistol at a Black protester, putting it away only after being asked to by Don Hight and two policemen. Later, Black students demanded that Hight take out a warrant on the man, but no action was taken.[16]

David Lester remembered that he was participating in an indoor physical education class for football players monitored by Weyman Sellers when word spread of the riot, and Sellers locked the doors of the gymnasium to prevent entry.

The Black students who had earlier left Burney-Harris for Athens High returned to their school and vandalized the building, smashing flowerpots, breaking windows, and discharging fire extinguishers. The local criminal justice system reacted quickly: later that afternoon, superior court judge James Barrow issued an injunction against thirteen named Black students—including BHHS student Michael Thurmond, AHS student Nathaniel Fox, and BHHS basketball standout Terry Green—and one hundred other "John Does," restraining them from any acts that might interrupt normal school operations.[17]

As a safeguard against further violent activity, the next school day—Friday, April 17—saw both schools open under a heavy police presence. There was no violence that day, but both schools saw absenteeism rates soar—Don Hight estimated that 35–40 percent of AHS students stayed home, while at Burney-Harris, a large group of students assembled across from the school to protest the restraining order issued by Judge Barrow. Superintendent McDaniel met with the protesting students at the Burney-Harris gymnasium and talked to them for roughly an hour about the need to maintain a police presence. After the meeting concluded, some students went to class, while others left the school premises.

The anger felt by many Black students at both Burney-Harris and Athens High spread to the greater African American community in West Athens. Several nighttime marches from the Rocksprings area to downtown led to clashes with police after demonstrators blocked traffic, and small businesses suffered broken windows from rocks hurled by the crowd. Police took aggressive action, firing tear gas and charging into the demonstrators to disperse any gathering of more than two people. Early morning arson attacks by rioters hurling Molotov cocktails damaged several more businesses.

Close to one hundred people were arrested over two nights of rioting, and the city simmered with resentment and rage. Mayor Julius Bishop commended the police for their "restraint" and pleaded with Black leaders to restrain the younger members of their community: "We have a fine, responsible Black community in Athens," Bishop said. "I urge all of them [the leaders] to use every means at their command to convince the young people involved in last night's disturbance that no possible good can come to the community through this type of action."[18] For their part, Black leaders condemned overaggressive tactics used by the police—which included a sweep through an African American neighborhood near West Broad Elementary that resulted in the arrest of eighty people—and highlighted the lack of a Black presence in the Athens Police Department. The Reverend Frank Hutchison, who had encouraged the members of his church to take an active role in pushing for social justice, was arrested, along with a group of his congregants, for protesting the tough police reaction to the demonstrations.

By late April, attendance figures had returned to normal at Athens High, but absenteeism continued to be a lingering problem at Burney-Harris, where a staggering 40 percent of the student population was absent at the end of the month.

On May 4, news of the infamous Kent State shootings rippled through the nation after Ohio National Guard soldiers shot and killed four White students who were protesting President Richard Nixon's decision to invade Cambodia. Campuses across the nation witnessed a huge spike in student protests, and UGA was no exception.

On May 6, with emotions still smoldering in Athens from the consolidation riots, UGA student activists sprang into action, first surrounding the ROTC building and then marching on the administration building on North Campus. The crowd grew to more than a thousand and included antiwar demonstrators, conservative counterprotesters, and interested onlookers. The activists' list of demands included the closure of classes at UGA as a memorial to the slain Kent State students; they also wanted UGA president Fred Davison to sign a letter to the *New York Times* condemning the Kent State killings.

The UGA administration ultimately agreed to the closure of classes for two days, but Davison did not offer further support; he refused to sign the *New York Times* letter and—unlike Mayor Bishop—elected not to attend the memorial service held in honor of the Kent State students. Several dozen UGA students entered the school's administration building and smashed windows, and arrests were made.

The protests spilled out onto the streets of Athens, with students and their supporters marching through downtown and continuing to President Davison's home on Prince Avenue, where they sat on the front lawn and demanded an audience with the beleaguered head of the university.

The crowd grew increasingly restless at night when Davison did not appear and began to chant, "Bullshit! Bullshit!" Dean Tate donned love beads and grabbed a bullhorn to yell, "Let's cut the bullshit!"; this elicited peals of laughter from the crowd. As he had done almost ten years earlier when a riot broke out at Center Myers, Tate mingled with the students and even splurged on breakfast for the hardy few who stayed the entire night.[19]

Behind the scenes, Davison was desperately trying to

convince Governor Lester Maddox not to send the National Guard to Athens. But Mayor Bishop, concerned about another upsurge in Black protests and violence—including five separate reports of arson—requested assistance from Governor Maddox; two hundred National Guard soldiers soon arrived from Augusta and bivouacked at the fairgrounds off Hawthorne Avenue.[20]

Town and gown once again intersected in mid-May when racial protests resumed. May 11 would go down in the annals of Athens history as "Black Monday," a day when two hundred African American protesters, in coordination with UGA's Black Awareness Week, marched to the downtown courthouse and then peacefully dispersed. Two hundred and fifty Black high school students missed school that day—many of them to participate in the march—and Superintendent McDaniel suspended them for three days.

The Black community's frustration with the school consolidation was by now extended to police brutality and the lack of fair employment opportunities in Athens. There was also great disparity in the treatment of protesters—two thousand UGA students had marched through the streets of Athens to protest the Kent State killings, and no one had been arrested, while African Americans protesting consolidation had been arrested in the hundreds, many times with extreme force. Pete McCommons recalled the differences between the mainly White protesters marching after Kent State and the mostly Black demonstrators protesting racial injustice: "The Kent State march was one night's walk from the campus to Five Points to the president's house, with a sit-in in the street, accompanied, of course, by Dean Tate. The school integration marches down Milledge occurred over several nights and were louder and more upsetting. But the 'Blackness' of the school [merger] marches was no doubt a trigger, especially considering the cops of that era."[21]

While Athens had integrated its police force in 1962, it remained divided along racial lines. Frank Platt, who later became the first Black lieutenant in the Athens Police Department, recalled that Black officers could not patrol White neighborhoods until 1971, and Black cops were routinely asked to wash the squad cars of their White colleagues. During the May 1970 protests, White police officers, accompanied by National Guard soldiers, drove through the Rocksprings neighborhood and sprayed tear gas with impunity.

The racial violence and deaths among Black protesters that had occurred that spring in Augusta, Georgia, and Jackson, Mississippi, further inflamed local passions. UGA students and professors joined Black Athenians in marching from Ebenezer Baptist Church West to the intersection of Milledge Avenue and Broad Street, next to the Varsity. The marchers smeared ointment on their faces as protection against tear gas attacks and sat down at the busy intersection. Although they were peaceful, nearly three hundred protesters—including one hundred UGA students—were arrested and driven off to jail in National Guard trucks. "They were hauling off people in paddy wagons," recalled Richard Appleby, "including my sister."[22] As reported in the *United Free Press*—but disputed by the Athens Police Department—the mainly Black protesters were held in overcrowded cellblocks, and police sprayed mace beneath the doors of the poorly ventilated holding tanks; the detained protesters pressed their faces against the concrete floor as the fumes spread.[23]

Amid the consolidation-related turmoil swirling through the Classic City, the Clarke County Board of Education barely defeated, by a 5–4 vote, a resolution that would have delayed consolidation of Athens High and Burney-Harris for another year.

Meanwhile, the athletic programs of both high schools continued to function as usual, other than a switch in venue for an AHS baseball game against Briarcliff, which was moved to Atlanta in the wake of the riots. The Trojans baseball team was beginning its final push toward the region playoffs, with Andy Johnson's batting average hovering around .500. The right-handed third baseman batted left-handed in one game for the first time ever and promptly blooped a single. There were whispers that Johnson might pass up the opportunity to play football for UGA and instead enter that spring's Major League Baseball draft; a few weeks later, much to the relief of Vince Dooley, he decided to forego the draft and play football at UGA. Burney-Harris had started a baseball team a year earlier, and the school was still looking for its first victory in that sport.

In football, plans were made for an expanded spring practice with the combined squads of both schools. Although the name, mascot, and team colors of the soon-to-be-merged schools had yet to be determined, Weyman Sellers was named head coach of the football team. The local chapter of the NAACP had asked that Sellers resign and suggested replacing him with two "co-head coaches": an assistant coach from Burney-Harris and another from AHS.[24] While the Black community was deeply concerned about Sellers's history of mistreating African American players, there was little chance that administrators would let Sellers go in the wake of the Trojans' recent odds-defying state championship run. Decades later, in a phone interview from his home in Hawaii, Richard Appleby expressed disappointment in the decision to keep Sellers and stated that he "wished he could have graduated from Burney-Harris."[25] Appleby did acknowledge, though, that he had hoped to benefit from Sellers's well-earned emphasis on physical conditioning and discipline. Former BHHS head coach Walter Jackson and his assistants James Crawford and James Holston agreed to join Sellers's staff, joining White AHS assistant coaches Don Warlick and Richard Saye.

With the expanded fan base resulting from the combination of schools and teams, improvements were approved for Death Valley, including the addition of seating capacity to accommodate the 1,500 to 2,000 new fans that Burney-Harris was expected to contribute. Seats were removed from the Burney-Harris stadium and added to the Death Valley bleachers, and new stadium lights and improvements to the scoreboard were also approved.[26]

In mid-May, a biracial committee of ten Black and ten White students selected red and gold as the school's new colors—a combination of the Athens High crimson and white and the Burney-Harris blue and gold. The twelve cheerleaders selected for the varsity football squad included two Black students, and five of the eight cheerleaders selected for varsity basketball were Black.[27] Shortly afterward came the announcement of the new mascot, which it was hoped would please both factions: the name "Golden Gladiators" paid homage to the gold colors worn by Burney-Harris (though the "Golden" was later dropped), and the image of a shield-and-sword-wielding gladiator represented a reasonable facsimile of the old Athens High mascot. "We weren't real happy with the Gladiator name, because it was too close to a Trojan," Richard Appleby recalled years later, "but we decided to let it go."[28] Also galling to many of the Black students was the fact that the "gold" color selected was closer to a bright sunflower hue, in contrast to the more subdued gold worn by the Yellow Jackets. *Banner-Herald* sports editor and columnist Chuck Perry wondered if the girls' teams would be referred to as the "Golden Gladiolas," and he quipped that Weyman Sellers would have to change the name of his business from Trojan Dry Cleaning and Laundry to Golden Gladiator Dry Cleaning and Laundry.

An agreement was also reached to combine the names of the two schools' student newspapers—Athens High's *Thumb Tack Tribune* and the Burney-Harris paper the *Highlight*—into *Highlights of the Thumb Tack Tribune*.

As spring football practice commenced, Coach Weyman Sellers vowed that the racial problems that had engulfed the greater Athens community would not affect his team: "Oh, there will be problems, I'm sure, just like any year, but I don't foresee any difficulty in getting this group of boys together. We can't have any cliques on this team of Blacks and Whites separated. This is a team, and it must play as a team."[29]

Michael Thurmond, who weeks earlier had been named in the "Rowdy Thursday" restraining order, was turning heads in spring practice: "I really like his attitude," Coach Sellers said about his undersized tailback. "He'll come back from a 20-yard run apologizing for not getting more." James Crawford, Thurmond's former coach at BHHS, added: "He's so quick that he'll get ten yards before the defense can react to him."[30] Thurmond and Rusty Russell, a returnee from the AHS championship squad, were fighting it out for one tailback position, while Horace King—who had gained 740 yards rushing for Burney-Harris the previous season—was the favorite for the other starting running back slot.

Sellers was faced with a conundrum as he weighed the challenge of merging two former rivals into one team. He obviously would need to increase the size of his roster; he preferred to coach fewer than forty players, but Burney-Harris traditionally dressed out more players than AHS, so Sellers was looking at potentially more than doubling the number of players under his charge. The benefit to an expanded roster was the possibility of a two-platoon system, wherein few or no players would have to play both offense and defense; the downside would be some loss of control with a larger-sized squad. Sellers settled on forty-four as the perfect number of players for the Gladiators: "That's the ideal number, but if we have more than 44 football players, then we will carry more on the team."[31]

Unbeknownst to the rest of the team, Sellers had also received some unsettling news: his chief assistant of eleven years, Frank Malinowski, would be resigning at the end of May to take a position as principal at Winterville Elementary School. The native of Queens, New York, was a personable "player's coach" who helped smooth out some of Sellers's rougher edges.

Meanwhile, controversy was brewing at the quarterback position.

Bobby Cross was a rising senior from Burney-Harris who could, according to teammate Clarence Pope, "throw it from one goal line to the other."[32] While that was a slight exaggeration—the 5'10" Cross confirmed many years later that he could throw it about eighty yards at that time[33]—Cross clearly possessed a stronger arm than the other leading candidate for the position, Sellers's son, Gray.

Gray Sellers had played an important role in the Trojans' success in the previous season as a halfback and linebacker. He caught the game-tying two-point conversion pass from Andy Johnson against Valdosta, and like his father, he spent hours in the weight room—with his muscular build, Gray Sellers had more of a linebacker or tight end's physique. At best, he was a "game manager" type of quarterback, and he had an awkward shot-put-style throwing motion that limited his range to short, ten-to-twenty-yard passes.

No matter who played quarterback for the Gladiators, he would represent, in terms of both athletic and leadership skills, a downgrade from the recently departed generational talent Andy Johnson. But in the early 1970s, as high school and college teams in the South slowly began to integrate, the quarterback position was considered the special preserve of White athletes. There were exceptions in which a Black player won the starting role, like Condredge Holloway at the University of Tennessee—and Eddie McAshan, a Black quarterback who played for Georgia Tech's freshman team in 1969 and so thoroughly impressed legendary Yellow Jackets coach Bobby Dodd that he anointed McAshan as the most accurate passer he had ever seen in the almost forty years he had spent at Tech.[34] The next season, McAshan would become the first Black quarterback to play for a major southeastern university and would lead the varsity Yellow Jackets to a 17–7 win over the Bulldogs in Athens, a performance that was celebrated by many in Athens's Black community.

But White coaches typically downgraded Black quarterbacks for intangible qualities such as poor decision-making skills or a lack of calmness under pressure. Even in the NFL, it was considered a breakthrough when Doug Williams of the Washington Redskins became the first Black quarterback to win a Super Bowl in 1988.

Weyman Sellers's comments during spring practice, when he compared the relative skill sets of the two players vying for the quarterback position, illustrated the misgivings of most White coaches. Regarding his son, he told a local reporter:

> Gray is an excellent ball handler. He has good hands and is a fine runner. He is a better runner from the quarterback position than he is from the halfback position. . . . The quarterback has to do a lot of cutting, and he cuts real well. His passing has improved 50 per cent, but he has a lot more work to do in throwing the ball.

Offenses were generally much more run oriented in 1970 than they are today, so the advantage of having a running quarterback was indeed meaningful. What is not clear is why Sellers did not at least consider a dual quarterback system to utilize Cross's unquestioned superiority passing the ball as an added weapon in his offensive arsenal.

Sellers even admitted, "Bobby Cross is probably the quickest and best passer we have on the team. But he doesn't know the offense yet. He is timid in calling his plays. He just needs to gain a little confidence in himself. He has gotten off to a slow start and that is to be expected since he is going to an entirely new system. He is extremely quick on avoiding the pass rush and can hurt you back there."[35] More than fifty years later, Cross confirmed his understandable lack of familiarity with the playbook—"I wasn't going to know the playbook after a week."[36] The offensive philosophy adopted by the Gladiators was the same conservative one run by Athens High—a run-first, option-oriented attack, which contrasted with Burney-Harris's offense that relied much more on the passing game.

On the surface, it remains difficult to discern which way Sellers was leaning in awarding the starting quarterback role for the upcoming season. He had a classic "field general" quarterback who struggled with the forward pass but was a solid runner that had played in the system for three years—and who also happened to be his son. With Bobby Cross, he had both an accurate long-range passing threat and an adept scrambler who was also able to buy time to find an open receiver or tuck and run the ball under a heavy rush. Cross had developed under the much more explosive, high risk/high reward Burney-Harris offensive system.

Frustrated by the prospect of playing behind the coach's son during his senior year, Bobby Cross quit the team during spring practice. In a break from his previous policy of not allowing players who quit the team to return, Sellers relented when Cross requested reinstatement a few days later. In allowing Cross to return, Sellers had to have been concerned about the public relations impact of a talented Black quarterback leaving the team in the already overheated racial climate of Athens in the spring of 1970.

Always chatty with the local press, Sellers was effusive in his praise for the Black players that he would be coaching in the fall. "Somebody told me [Horace] King wouldn't put the hat on it, but he'll stick it in there. He never says die," Sellers gushed.[37] Sellers had also taken a liking to big defensive tackle Nathaniel Craddick, a Burney-Harris standout who spent spring practice sacking quarterbacks and creating general havoc behind the line of scrimmage. Even the best blocker on the offensive line, Alex "Cadillac" Allen—who would go on to play at the University of Texas—could not stop the player that Sellers dubbed "the Viking."

As spring practice concluded with the "Red versus Gold" intrasquad game, Sellers knew that the "merged team" he would be fielding in 1970 would be the strongest assemblage of talent he had ever coached. Wide receiver Richard Appleby had played only one season on offense, but the 6'3" receiver won all-state honors in 1969 despite his limited experience at that position. Horace King was a tough and speedy halfback, who, like Appleby, was also a skilled passer. Lightning-quick Michael Thurmond figured to be a situational change-of-pace scatback runner, and Bobby Cross showed his special talent in the spring game by throwing a forty-yard pass after leaping in the air while avoiding a strong rush. Former Yellow Jackets Clarence Pope at linebacker and Joe Bell and Nathaniel Craddick on the defensive line figured to anchor a strong Gladiator defense, and seniors such as Rusty Russell, Mike Epps, Alex Allen, and Doc Eldridge were crucial components of AHS's 1969 championship team and figured to be even better in the Gladiators' inaugural season.

╫╫╫

On Monday, August 31, 1970, the newly named consolidated high school—the school district had agreed to "Clarke Central High School" over the summer—opened its doors for its first day of classes. Due to the overflow situation and the limited space available at both facilities, sophomores attended class at the old Burney-Harris High School, while juniors and seniors walked the hallways of the former Athens High School.

The day went smoothly, and a relieved Superintendent Charles McDaniel exclaimed, "It's been a very good day and I am delighted." No disturbances or disciplinary issues had been reported on the anxiously awaited opening day of school.[38]

The Gladiators' fall practices held earlier in August were

much more of a mixed bag. The team fielded fifty-three players, twenty more than Sellers had coached in the previous season, and the White players slightly outnumbered their African American teammates.

The amount of conditioning and discipline demanded by Sellers was not a surprise to the Black players—Sellers had a well-deserved reputation in Athens as a stern taskmaster—but the reality of having to participate in the actual drills was still a difficult adjustment.

Gray Sellers showed up for the first day of practice as the anointed first-team quarterback. Coach Sellers had spent the summer running drills with his son to improve his passing and ball-handling skills. This development, which was counter to Sellers's philosophy of players earning their first-team status on the practice field, shocked most of the players, Black and White alike. "He had small hands," one Black player recalled. "You can't play quarterback with small hands." One of Gray's White teammates sensed that even Gray was uncomfortable with the situation. "I am sure it was difficult being the son of Coach Sellers," he recollected.

A recently graduated Trojans player recounted, "I knew that [naming Gray as starting quarterback] would raise some eyebrows. Coach Sellers wanted Gray to be a quarterback, but he didn't have the skills or leadership ability to be one. But what Sellers wanted he always got, even at the expense of losing some gifted players."

Gray's nickname among the players was "Soda Cracker," because they felt he was—contrary to his father's assessment—not a very tough runner and, like the snack, "easy to break."

Bobby Cross, the team's Black quarterback, who had showcased his passing talents in spring practice and in the intrasquad game, quit the team for the second and final time after it became clear that Gray Sellers would be the starter. Years later, Cross looked back at the lost opportunity with equanimity and attributed nepotism rather than racism as the motivating factor for Coach Sellers's decision to make his son the starting quarterback: "[Coach Sellers] was just doing what any father would do: protecting his son. I would have done the same if I had been in his shoes. I was raised in a Christian family, and I learned to just let things go, to move on."[39]

Racial tension was building, however, among the Black players during preseason practices. The three African American assistant coaches that Sellers had been forced to accept as part of the consolidation—Walter Jackson, James Holston, and James Crawford—had all coached the Black players at Burney-Harris. But they were much more than coaches; they were nurturing, highly esteemed father figures. "They were teachers," remembered Clarence Pope, "who always placed an emphasis on doing the right thing; they watched over you and were always there for you." They placed the responsibility of molding young men to succeed in life above wins and losses on the football field. Michael Thurmond remembered someone once asking James Holston how good the Burney-Harris team would be for an upcoming season; "I will let you know in twenty years," he responded.[40]

Sellers belittled the African American coaches in front of the players and assigned them menial roles, such as painting and grounds keeping. Pope remembered one incident in which Sellers threw a towel in Walter Jackson's face and ordered him "to take the boys to the showers, that is the only thing you are good for."[41] In private, the Black coaches counseled their former players from BHHS to look beyond the slights and focus on improving themselves on the field. But it was hard for the players to overlook the mistreatment of their cherished coaches, and it was a shared pain they carried with them throughout the season.

Concurrent with the troubling developments on the football field, a disproportionate number of African American schoolteachers and administrators were displaced by integration, realizing the worst fears of the Black community. Former BHHS principal E. T. Roberson was assigned to a new position as head of adult education in the Athens-Clarke County school system. Many other Black educators took early retirement or accepted lower-level positions. Prior to integration, it was not uncommon for African American teachers to teach subjects that they had obtained a practical expertise in over the years, even if they were not "credentialed" with a degree in that specific subject matter, but Paul Troutman, a former industrial arts teacher at BHHS who had taught shop classes for decades, lost his job because he had earned a degree in a different discipline. Robert Hawkins remembered that the loss of so many Black teachers "crushed the Black community. Teachers were the top of the social pyramid, and they were tossed to the side."[42]

This sentiment expressed by Hawkins—that Black teachers rested on the top rung of the African American social strata—was true in the Jim Crow South because Black aspirants were largely blocked from professional careers in business, law, medicine, and government. While there is no question that most Black teachers during this era were dedicated and took their role as both instructor and mentor seriously, they were also a protected class that was sheltered from competition by the segregated school systems. For this reason, many Black teachers were either ambivalent about or opposed to the idea of integration as promoted by the NAACP; they preferred instead the idea of "equalization," or gradual improvement in the quality of Black schools, which would continue not only to instruct students but also to build confidence and instill community pride.

Those instructors' ambivalence about or outright opposition to integration reflected the values of many in the greater Black community, which was more concerned about righting the wrongs of segregation through even-handed treatment in the justice system, the protection of voting rights, and equal access to both housing and higher-paying jobs.[43]

Hawkins's observation that African American educators were being "tossed to the side" would be borne out in the coming years in the form of harsh statistics: the number of Black teachers in the Athens-Clarke County public school system dropped from 113 in 1969 to 95 in 1974, while White instructors saw their numbers grow from 333 to 364. This disproportionate increase in White teachers occurred over a period that also saw White families abandoning the public school system in increasing numbers; White enrollment dropped from more than 67 percent to 63 percent over the same time span.[44] These same trends—an increase in Black students and a concurrent decrease in Black teachers within the public school system—were echoed throughout the Deep South.

Oblivious to the racial tensions gripping the new school, the *Atlanta Journal* looked at the talent of the Gladiators football team and ranked them number one in its preseason poll of AAA contenders. Joe Litsch, the *Journal*'s prep editor, predicted a state title matchup between Clarke Central and Valdosta—though Litsch was apparently unaware of the school's name change and referred to Clarke Central as "Athens High"—and correctly noted that "Coach Weyman Sellers has more talent than ever before in his seventeen years of coaching."[45]

Chuck Perry of the *Athens Banner-Herald* went even further, claiming that the Gladiators had the most impressive aggregation of high school football talent in the state since the Valdosta 1961 squad that went 12–0 and won its state title game by three touchdowns. Perry went on to predict that up to eight members of Clarke Central's inaugural team could win all-state honors. "They are loaded," Perry raved.[46]

Perry also dismissed any notion that racial discord might damage the team: "There is no race problem on the field. Harmony and mutual respect abound. It's smooth. [Horace] King wants blockers in front of him. He doesn't care what color they are. [Alex] Allen wants runners following his blocks. He doesn't care what color they are. The Golden Gladiators are indeed, one big happy family of football players."[47]

Coach Sellers did not make any attempt to poor mouth his stacked team: "We have no glaring weaknesses," he said. Unlike the previous year's undersized Trojans, Clarke Central would match or exceed the physicality of its opponents: "For the first time, we have the kind of team that can line up head-to-head and beat people. We won't have to stunt or do any fancy stuff like that."[48]

In the final week of preparation before their opener, the Gladiators held a scrimmage in which an offensive tackle missed a block and the quarterback was sacked. As punishment, Sellers forced the offending lineman to stand in a stationary position holding the football over his head—the classic "Statue of Liberty" stance. Three defensive linemen crashed through the line unopposed and smashed into the unprotected player, turning "the statue [into] mere snowflakes under a hot iron."[49] This brutal drill, which had long been utilized by Sellers to punish players who missed blocks, would have an even more impactful reprise later in the season.

The Gladiators' opening game was against Gainesville High at City Park in Gainesville. The Red Elephants, who had beaten both Athens High and Burney-Harris by seventeen points the previous year, had finished the 1969 season losing by a touchdown to North Springs to finish runner-up in AA. They were picked number one in the state in the *Atlanta Journal*'s preseason AA poll, so the matchup was an early-season clash of the highest-ranked teams in the two top classifications in Georgia high school football. Clarke Central was favored, but both Weyman Sellers and Red Elephants coach Bobby Gruhn expected a tough game. Sellers remembered the rain-soaked 1969 game when Gainesville had surprised his Trojans 20–3. "That game really shook us," he ruefully recalled." I still think we could have won it. We fumbled so many times down near their goal line. We could have won it."[50]

The Gladiators ran out on the field as a team for the first time, wearing newly designed uniforms with crimson jerseys highlighted with yellow numbers and piping. The helmets, like those of Athens High, featured players' numerals on the side.

The game, like all gridiron matchups between Gainesville and Athens-based teams, was very physical. Red Elephants starting cornerback Nat Strong suffered a season-ending torn ACL on a cross-body block delivered by Mac Coile on the opening kickoff. Later in the game, Mike Epps, the Gladiators' 150-pound nose tackle, attempted a stunt to penetrate a gap in the Gainesville offensive line and met the Red Elephants' talented running back, Tommy West, head-on. The crown of West's helmet smashed through Epps's two-bar face mask, which cost the nose tackle three front teeth. The blow also tore apart Epps's leather chinstrap, which forced him to the sidelines, where a furious Weyman Sellers screamed at him for leaving the game due to an injury. Decades before CTE and "targeting" became widespread concerns, the stadium reverberated with the thud of pads and the loud crack of helmet-to-helmet hits that induced fumbles and left players dazed.

Gainesville's strategy was to stymie the Gladiators' ground game and force Clarke Central to win with the arm of Gray Sellers. The plan worked—Horace King and the other Gladiator running backs were hemmed in by a strong Gainesville defensive line led by tackle Eddie Dean Lipscomb, who recorded ten tackles and recovered two fumbles.

When the Gladiators moved the ball through the air, it was through the efforts of King, who took option pitchouts from Sellers and faked end runs before stopping and throwing to open receivers downfield. After Gainesville stunned the Gladiators with two scores to take a 10–0 lead, Clarke Central struck back on the last play of the first half after

Gray Sellers took the snap and pitched the ball out to King, who stopped and completed a bomb to a streaking Richard Appleby for a sixty-three-yard touchdown. Sellers ran the ball in for the two-point conversion, and the Red Elephant lead was trimmed to 10–8 at halftime.

In the third quarter, Gainesville extended its lead after a breakdown in coverage by the Gladiators' defense allowed a fifty-three-yard touchdown pass. The lead stood at 17–8 until midway through the fourth quarter, when King once again connected with Appleby, this time on a seventy-five-yard touchdown pass. With five minutes to go in the game, Gainesville led by only two points, but other than the two long halfback touchdown passes, it had stuffed the vaunted, high-powered Clarke Central offense.

After recovering a fumble near midfield with just over a minute left, the Gladiators had one final chance to win, and it appeared that they might steal a victory after driving inside the Red Elephants' five-yard line. The next play call raised eyebrows among the Gladiators faithful: King took another pitchout and swept toward the right, but Gainesville immediately recognized the play and clogged the stand-out tailback's path to the end zone. King then reversed field and retreated backward and was finally brought down for a fifteen-yard loss. After the game, Sellers remarked, "Most of the times in that situation, I would have called a dive. But we hadn't got a dive to go anywhere."[51] Confusion reigned as the final seconds ticked down, as jubilant Gainesville fans, thinking the game was over, began to overrun the field. But the Gladiators were able to squeeze in one final play, a King pass to former Burney-Harris teammate O'Neal Luke, who rambled inside the five-yard line before Gainesville tacklers swarmed him and brought him down just short of the goal line as time expired.

In his postgame interview, Sellers blamed poor blocking for the defeat: "There was a lot to be desired in the line blocking. They weren't blocking their men well, and they were missing assignments all night. . . . It is almost impossible to get a play off when they have men in the backfield before you can make a move." Indeed, the only offensive play that worked all evening was the halfback pass from King to Appleby; the pitch-and-catch combination between the two former teammates at Burney-Harris accounted for the only two touchdowns the Gladiators scored, and Appleby finished the game with four receptions for 148 yards.[52]

Clarke Central had failed to achieve "double revenge" for the losses the two Athens schools had suffered at City Park in 1969. And Gainesville had once again knocked an Athens team off its number one pedestal in mid-September.

As the shock of the upset loss gradually wore off, the Gladiators realized that their goal for the season, to play in the state championship game, was still within reach. They would have to successfully run the nine-game gauntlet in Region 8-AAA to win the playoff spot awarded to the region champion. On the surface, this seemed to be a less daunting challenge than Athens High had faced the previous year. Traditional region foe Tucker was not ranked and, due to graduation losses, was presumed to be less imposing than the 1969 version. Up-and-coming Lakeside was also unranked, and the Gladiators would play both Tucker and Lakeside in Death Valley.

Both players and coaches vowed to correct the mistakes made against Gainesville. "I think we have the kind of kids who want to come back and work a little harder, to do better. History does repeat itself," Coach Sellers reflected after the game.[53] Horace King, who put on a dazzling passing display but fumbled the ball three times against the Red Elephants, expressed similar sentiments: "Just because we are rated high does not mean that teams are just going to stand there and let us beat them. We are going to have to go after them . . . all nine of them."[54]

Following the blueprint established by the 1969 AHS team, the Gladiators easily dispatched its next four opponents—Cross Keys, Briarcliff, Tucker, and Sequoyah; the narrowest margin of victory over that span was eighteen points. The Gladiators showed signs of jelling as a team on both sides of the ball. Although the aerial attack remained disjointed—with Gray Sellers sharing passing duties with both Horace King and backup quarterback Perry Strickland—the Gladiators were moving the ball effectively. The staunch linebacker corps, consisting of Clarence "Bear" Pope, Alex "Cadillac" Allen, and Mike Saunders, anchored a steadily improving defense. The stage was set for a crucial game against the Lakeside Vikings at Death Valley on October 23.

Lakeside's first-year head coach was Wayman Creel, who had just completed a highly successful nineteen-year run at Northside High School of Atlanta. The Vikings were led by all-state quarterback Jack Fuqua and were undefeated at 5–0. Both teams were a perfect 4–0 in region play.

Lakeside took advantage of a short field on its opening possession, driving forty yards to take a 7–0 lead. The game quickly evolved into a defensive struggle, with Clarke Central unable to manage a first down in the first quarter. Late in the first half, Horace King sprang loose for a sixty-one-yard run to the Vikings' five-yard line. Two plays later, the Gladiators punched it in for a touchdown, knotting the score at 7–7 after Doc Eldridge converted the extra point.

The Gladiators' offensive success was short-lived, as they managed only two first downs in the second half, but their stout defense kept Clarke Central in the game until late in the fourth quarter. Fueled by a thirty-yard Fuqua pass, the Vikings drove deep into Gladiator territory and scored on a six-yard run with 4:11 left in the game.

Then the bottom fell out.

On the first play after the ensuing kickoff, a bad shotgun snap forced Gray Sellers into the end zone to recover the ball. He was tackled for a safety, and Lakeside extended its lead to 15–7. On the Gladiators' final drive, Sellers attempted a screen pass that was intercepted and returned for a touch-down.[55] When the Lakeside players boarded the bus back to Atlanta, they knew that their upset win in Athens had secured them a stranglehold on the region crown.

The loss was no fluke, as the Vikings dominated every statistical category—they led in first downs 14–5, and in total yardage 243–121. The most shockingly abysmal statistics were compiled in the passing game, where Clarke Central completed only three of eleven attempts for thirty yards, with three interceptions. The Gladiators had been whipped in every phase of the game. A disconsolate Coach Sellers knew the loss had almost certainly snuffed out any playoff hopes: "This leaves us out in the cold. . . . They outcoached us, out-charged us, out-blocked us, out-tackled us, they just plain dominated the game. Who is going to beat them twice?"[56] His last question acknowledged the harsh math that would require the Gladiators to win their remaining games while hoping that two of Lakeside's last four region opponents would somehow defeat the Vikings.

The bitter loss to Lakeside occurred amid a groundswell of resentment over the treatment of Black players that was subsequently made public after the season, when African American student leaders submitted a list of grievances to the Clarke County Board of Education centered on Sellers's alleged mistreatment of African American players. The complaints included charges that he drove the Black players much harder than the White players during practice and called Black players terms they considered offensive, such as "clown" and "hot dog."[57] Sellers also continued to wear his old Athens High School sweatshirts and windbreakers and referred to the new school as "Athens," which further irked the African American players. During a physical education class, the Gladiators head coach asked a Black student who had been imitating an animal, "Why don't you go back to the jungle?" Sellers admitted to this last offense and later apologized to the Black student assembly in the Mell Auditorium.[58] African American assistant principal Dr. Walter Allen Sr. remembered stunning displays of juvenile obnoxiousness by the football coach; for example, when Sellers spotted Allen in the hallway, he would flap his arms and squawk like a chicken. "Just trying to demean me, make me feel less than human," Allen thought.[59]

For his part, Sellers denied any racial insensitivity on the football field, and years later, Mike Epps supported his former coach's view: "I may have been naïve, but I didn't see it. Coach Sellers was mean and abrupt to everyone, and I don't think the Black players were used to that. They took it personally."[60] Mac Coile remembered Sellers requiring every player on the team, both Black and White, to attend the funeral of the mother of African American player Bruce Holt.[61]

During the Sunday film session after the Lakeside defeat, Sellers blamed the loss on several Black players, including Horace King, who had suffered a sprained ankle and sat out most of the second half, and Richard Appleby, who had dropped a crucial pass. Black players felt like they had been unfairly singled out, while several White players backed up Sellers's version of the story—that many players, both Black and White, had received harsh criticism from the head coach.

On Monday, October 26, all twenty-three Black players walked down to the practice field in their uniforms (minus shoulder pads) and then walked off in unison. They retreated to a corner of the practice field and waited for Sellers to meet with them; when their head coach ignored them, they walked to the dressing room, changed into street clothes, and left. The remaining members of the team— twenty-eight White players—stayed on the field and completed practice.[62]

Behind the scenes, both groups of players appointed leaders: the White players selected center (and future Athens mayor) Doc Eldridge, and the Black players picked running back Michael Thurmond, who would go on to become Georgia's first African American labor commissioner and later the CEO of the state's second most populous county, DeKalb. Eldridge and Thurmond reached an agreement for the Black players to return—with only a month left in the season and the Gladiators virtually eliminated from playoff consideration, defusing the crisis by having the African American players return to the team would also lower the temperature at the new school, which was seething with racial resentment.

Sellers allowed the Black players to return, but they were forced to participate in additional drills and running as penance for their insubordination. Even Horace King, still hobbled by his sprained ankle, had to take part in the additional work.

Michael Thurmond felt that his role as spokesman for the Black players angered Sellers and sparked him to seek retribution against the diminutive running back on the practice field. Thurmond, who had started in several games, was singled out, screamed at, and forced into extra running, as Sellers, in Thurmond's words, "tried to run me off."[63] The head coach's grudge reached its boiling point on the practice field one day, when Thurmond missed a block that allowed Nathaniel Craddick to crash in and sack Gray Sellers.

Sellers screamed for the "Statue of Liberty" drill, where Thurmond was forced to stand alone, with no blocking, as linemen gang-tackled him. The 125-pound running back was buried under a half ton of weight but slowly rose to his feet.

"*Michael, please stay down,*" his friend and former Burney-Harris teammate Clarence Pope begged him.

But Thurmond slowly climbed back to his feet, and Sellers ordered another rush. Once again, he was crushed by the combined bulk of his teammates; his shoulder pads were knocked to the side, and his helmet was twisted over his face to the point that he could almost see through the earhole.

"Michael, please stay down," Pope again begged.

But Thurmond again slowly crawled to his feet and resumed the Statue of Liberty position. After he was crushed by rushers once more, an assistant coach—a White coach whose name no one can recall—shouted, "That's enough."

The remainder of the season was remembered by Thurmond as a battle of wills between him and his head coach. Sellers benched him, insulted him in front of the team, and subjected him to extra drills, but Thurmond would not flinch. No matter what humiliation he had to endure, he was determined to finish the season as a member of the team and not let his coach break him.[64]

In the final game of the season, as the Gladiators ran out the clock at Death Valley in a 40–7 rout of Druid Hills, Thurmond, accompanied by other Black seniors, ran off the field before the final horn sounded. As they made their way up the hill and through the pines, Clarence Pope remembered, "We were free—it felt like the Jubilee!"[65]

卌

In November, as Clarke Central wound down its disappointing season, Ed Turner won his race to become councilman for the first ward of the city of Athens. In a district that was split evenly between Black and White voters, Turner won election through a strong "get out the vote" campaign and a platform that emphasized his advocacy for poorer constituents. His victory was the first time an African American had won public office in the Classic City.

Shortly after the season ended, Walter Jackson, the former head coach at Burney-Harris who had served as an assistant to Weyman Sellers, announced that he was retiring due to health reasons.

The first year of school at Clarke Central was a cauldron that burned steadily and occasionally boiled over into sporadic fights and other acts of violence. Mike Epps remembered announcements over the school's intercom system for teachers to lock their classroom doors after fights had broken out in the hallway.

Richard Appleby sought the refuge of the Black community after class. He established some casual friendships among his new White classmates, he remembered, "but I couldn't wait to get back to my neighborhood after school. I wanted to be around Black music, Black food, Black culture."[66]

Bill King, who by now was an underclassman at UGA, returned to his old high school building to help set up an area called "The Place," an unused cafeteria space where Clarke Central students could hang out and socialize free from the temptation of drugs. Administrators knew that Clarke Central would hold the combined junior and senior classes for all Black and White public school students in the county when it opened—with crowding eased only after the opening of Cedar Shoals High School in 1972—and thus had anticipated a need for two cafeterias. But White students, particularly the seniors who had "open campus" privileges, typically had cars and could come and go as they pleased. Black students, on the other hand, were much more dependent on buses to arrive and depart from school and thus were much more reliant on school-provided meals.[67] Cafeteria meals are perhaps the most important ritual of forced socialization within any large student body; the fact that they became largely limited to Black students at Clarke Central only further exacerbated the sense of separation between the two races.

In the school's first yearbook, Mike Epps, the White football player, was voted "Best All Around," while Kim Basinger, the future Hollywood star and Academy Award winner and the daughter of a local businessman, placed third. Richard Appleby was rated as "Wittiest."

Michael Thurmond was copresident of the student council—as a racial compromise, the students had voted to have a Black student and a White student share the role. Years later, he remembered White students applauding after he delivered a speech in the auditorium. "I didn't know what to do," he said. "I had never had Whites applaud me before."

By the end of the school year, Thurmond was exhausted—"We were children, trying to resolve adult issues."[68] Although accepted at UGA, Thurmond chose to attend Paine College, the HBCU in Augusta.

He needed a break from Athens.

EPILOGUE

In December 1970, just weeks after the end of the high school and college football regular seasons, three beaming, suit-and-tie-clad young Black men with carefully sculpted Afros sat at a table. Behind them were ("Big") Mike Castronis Sr., the UGA assistant tasked with recruiting Athens-area prep footballers, and Georgia's head football coach, Vince Dooley. The five men were gathered to take part in a historic signing ceremony.

The three Lyons Middle School, Burney-Harris, and Clarke Central teammates—Horace Edwards King, Clarence Alfonza Pope, and Richard Appleby—became part of the "First Five": the first Black scholarship athletes to play football for the University of Georgia. They would be joining a fellow Athenian, quarterback Andy Johnson, whom they had played against when they were at Burney-Harris and he was at Athens High. Appleby, King, and Johnson would form the spearhead of the Bulldogs' potent early-1970s offensive attack.

On September 30, 1972, Horace King lined up as tailback in a goal-line situation against North Carolina State University and soared "over the top" before tumbling headfirst into the end zone. On that sweltering early autumn afternoon in Sanford Stadium, the little boy who once sold Coca-Colas at UGA games and dared to dream of someday playing for the Bulldogs became the first African American to score a touchdown for the University of Georgia.

Richard Appleby is eternally linked to one of the most treasured memories in Georgia football history—an end-around play in which he took the ball, stopped and planted his feet, and hurled a perfect bomb for a touchdown to defeat a heavily favored Florida team during the Bulldogs' 1975 season. Clarence Pope started at linebacker for UGA for one season until an even more talented Black player, Sylvester Boler, supplanted him.

╫╫╫

When the end came, it was no surprise. After Clarke Central's disappointing 1970 campaign ended with an 8–2 record and no playoff appearance, the 1971 squad again went 8–2, slipped to third place in 8-AAA, and missed the playoffs for the second straight year.

In 1972, the program hit rock bottom, finishing 1–9. For the first time in his twenty-year career, Weyman Sellers had a team quit on him. By the end of the season, the roster had shrunk to nineteen players, only four of whom were Black.

Racial tensions had not eased over Clarke Central's short two-and-a-half-year existence. Principal Don Hight had begun carrying a handgun on school grounds, and Assistant Principal John Tillitski had been attacked twice and carried mace with him while on the job.

As the pressure mounted and it became increasingly apparent that Hight was not prepared to extend Sellers's contract, the head football coach grew more defiant. "I think it is two things," he told a reporter from the *Atlanta Constitution*. "I think he [Hight] is trying to appease our Black students, and now he and John Tillitski are paying for it by being beaten up in their own school and being intimidated in the halls."[1]

Sellers continued to brush off accusations of racism while criticizing Hight's permissive dress code for students, which Sellers called "obscene," and he defended his decision to wear "a football jacket with the old Athens High School emblem on it." The school's administration labeled Sellers as "uncooperative and difficult to work with."[2]

The town was split on Sellers's future—many among the White "old guard" sported buttons proclaiming "I Support the Coach," while those in favor of his ouster countered with buttons that stated "I Support the Principal."

On the night of December 8, 1972, the lights remained on in one ground-level office at the Clarke County Board of Education. Almost three years to the date after the legendary "victory" against Valdosta, Weyman Sellers's fate was to be decided by the ten-member board. By a 9–1 vote, the board supported Principal Hight's decision not to retain the controversial coach.

One former Athens High player maintained a lonely vigil outside the board of education building on that rainy night, standing up in his Volkswagen convertible and staring through the windows at the meeting taking place inside. Police questioned the man, who had driven around for two hours looking for the parking space in front of the meeting to open up and had two shotguns and a pistol in his car. He told the police he was a marine and was planning on going duck hunting the next day.

When asked why he was there, he replied that he wanted "to see what was going on" with his former coach and called him "one of the greatest persons around." He added that he had joined the Marines to see if they were as tough as Sellers. "Were they?" he was asked. "No," he replied, before getting back inside his car and driving off into the night.[3]

After Weyman Sellers's departure in late 1972, Clarke Central was beset with challenges. The moneyed interests, many of whom had once played for the fired coach, were upset and threatened to withhold contributions to the strapped athletic department. More and more White families were sending their children to area private schools or were considering the brand-new public high school across the North Oconee River, Cedar Shoals.

Clarke Central remained divided along racial lines, with each of the warring sides still upset over the loss of its treasured legacy high school and ready to pounce on any signs of mistreatment or favoritism by the school's administration.

A self-effacing, hardworking, and empathetic head coach named Billy Henderson took over the ruins of the football program and immediately set out to bring the two sides together. He worked tirelessly in community outreach and made certain that parents, teachers, players, and community leaders felt connected to the program. The crew-cut-wearing coach was renowned for his 7:00 a.m. meetings, at which anyone interested was assigned a role within the program, from volunteer concessions work to ticket sales to sponsorships.

He held Thanksgiving meals for his players and their families in the Clarke Central gymnasium. "We bowed our heads for the invocation, but I did not close my eyes," Henderson recounted in a *Georgia Trend* magazine article in 2005. "I looked around the gym and saw white hands holding black hands, hands of the rich and prominent holding hands with poor kids from the other side of the track. And I was thinking, 'If all human beings did something like this, there would be few problems in this world.'"[4]

‖‖‖

On another cold December night, this time in 1977, Clarke Central faced off with Valdosta in Death Valley for the state title. Buck Belue—who as a young boy had attended the 1969 state championship game between Valdosta and Athens High with his father—led the Wildcats at quarterback.

Clarke Central jumped to a 16-0 lead, but Belue engineered a furious comeback to bring the Wildcats within two. In the waning minutes of the game, Belue drove his team deep into Gladiator territory, but the last-minute drive failed when the Wildcats missed on a short field goal attempt that would have won the game. The Gladiators had won their first state title 16–14. Clarke Central, under Henderson's leadership, went on to win two more state titles over the next eight years. An Athens-based "Colossus of the North" had been restored.

┼┼┼┼

On Valentine's Day night in 1977, a tremor rattled through the Classic City, when a band performed in an old house at the corner of Prince and Milledge Avenues. The B-52's—which included AHS graduate Cindy Wilson, her brother Ricky, who attended Clarke Central, and their friends Keith Strickland, Kate Pierson, and Fred Schneider—played two raucous sets in front of a small group of friends. The rumblings from that performance radiated out across Athens, and the tremor gradually turned into an earthquake, as the Athens music scene exploded through the city, the region, the nation, and the world.

The sudden arrival of Athens as an alternative music mecca, spearheaded by such acts as R.E.M., Pylon, and Love Tractor, required a local ecosystem to nurture and support the burgeoning acts; otherwise, talented groups would follow the example of the B-52's, who outgrew Athens and moved on to New York. This support system needed to be anchored by a reputable publication that would provide record reviews, interviews with musicians, and concert calendars.

In October 1987, a newsweekly named *Flagpole* ("Color-bearer of Athens Alternative Music") was launched, and it quickly became the voice of the Athens music scene. After Pete McCommons joined *Flagpole* in 1993, ultimately becoming both editor and copublisher (along with Alicia Nickles), it grew its circulation to more than fifteen thousand, and under McCommons's and Nickles's leadership, *Flagpole* became a constant progressive thorn in the side of the city's developer-friendly business and political establishment, which, if left unchallenged, would have turned their beloved Athens into a facsimile of a soulless Atlanta suburb.

In 2018, the University of Georgia's Grady College of Journalism and Mass Communication established the annual Rollin M. "Pete" McCommons Award for Distinguished Community Journalism, with the dean of the college hailing McCommons for instituting *Flagpole* as an "important countercultural voice of progressivism in the city."[5]

╫╫╫

At Athens High School class reunions, Black and White alumni maintained a polite distance from each other for decades. In the early part of the new millennium, that began to change—White former classmates would approach Robert Hawkins, Maxie Foster, and Bonnie Hampton Travis to acknowledge and apologize for instances of their own previous indifference to or participation in racist behavior.

Bonnie Travis always graciously accepts the apologies and acknowledges that "those were the times" but follows up with a direct question: "How have you taught your children?" This usually catches people off guard, and they answer with a "not to discriminate" response. "Whether this is true or not, I don't judge," she shrugged.[6]

After being forced out at Clarke Central, Weyman Sellers served as head coach at Jonesboro High School and then at Pebblebrook High School. His integrated teams at those schools enjoyed some success but never reached the lofty heights attained by his Athens High squads. He retired from head coaching in 1986 and was inducted into the Athens Athletic Hall of Fame in 2002 after not being included in the inaugural class of 2000, which included Andy Johnson, Fran Tarkenton, longtime Burney-Harris women's basketball coach Elizabeth King, and Billy Henderson. With the résumé he had amassed while coaching Athens High for almost twenty years, it was inevitable that Sellers would eventually be selected. But the old wounds still had not healed in the decades since he had left the Classic City, and at least one key Black member of the hall's board blocked Sellers's initial entry to send a message to the controversial coach.

When Sellers died in 2011, his two standout quarterbacks from the 1960s—Andy Johnson and Paul Gilbert—served as pallbearers at his funeral.

━━━━

"Superman is not supposed to get cancer," Doc Eldridge remembered saying when he received the news that his longtime friend and local hero Andy Johnson had been diagnosed with thyroid cancer.

Johnson finished his career at Georgia as a three-year starter at quarterback, where he earned a permanent place in the Bulldog pantheon of heroes after leading the red and black to a last-second comeback win against Georgia Tech on a Thanksgiving night that was eerily similar to the miraculous drive he engineered against Valdosta two years earlier.

After completing a ten-year professional football career in Boston, Johnson returned to Athens, where he raised a family and worked in insurance. When he was in his mid-fifties, he received the call from his doctor with the cancer diagnosis while loading golf clubs in his car before beginning a family trip to Florida.

Andy Johnson had always been Terry Smart's best friend and mentor. But Smart had his own personal challenge to deal with—Janet, his wife of forty-two years, was reaching the end of her painful journey with a terminal illness. Between caring for his wife and holding down a full-time job, Smart had little time to check in on his old friend.

Janet Smart passed away on May 4, 2018, and a bedridden Johnson called his devastated friend and asked if there was anything he could do for him. Twelve days later, Johnson's wife, Chot, called Smart and urged him to come over, as Andy was fading fast. When Smart arrived that evening, Johnson—his muscular build and great looks ravaged by cancer—struggled to talk, and Smart tried to provide hopeful and uplifting words to his friend, as Johnson had done for him so many times over his life.

After almost an hour, Smart had to leave to tend to his two daughters, who were still grieving the recent loss of their mother. The two men hugged, Smart kissed him on the forehead and told him he loved him, and Johnson reclined back in his bed and whispered, "I'll see you tomorrow."

Andy Johnson passed away that evening at the age of sixty-five.

Johnson's funeral was unofficially one of the most heavily attended in the history of Athens, with dozens of former teammates showing up to pay tribute. He was buried in the "Bulldog Haven" section of Oconee Hills Cemetery, between Sanford Stadium and the North Oconee River.

⧛⧛⧛

Now in their seventies, Mike Castronis Jr. and Allen Morse recently met up for the first time in over fifty years on the campus of Clarke Central, so they could "walk down the pines" and reminisce. In 1966, the two briefly were teammates during the preseason practices at Athens High, before the highly talented Morse was told by his coach that "there weren't enough uniforms" for Morse to dress out for the Trojans.

Haunted over the intervening decades by the guilt of having not spoken up in defense of his Black teammate, Castronis apologized to Morse, who graciously accepted the apology—"It was the times," he reflected.[7]

⠊⠊⠊⠊⠊

On a sunny weekend in late September, more than fifty years after their arrival at UGA, the "First Five"—the Black pioneers who broke the color barrier in football at the University of Georgia—were honored at Sanford Stadium, and Richard Appleby was invited to speak to the Bulldog players in the dressing room before Georgia's game that evening. "I couldn't believe all the brothers on the team!" he recalled with joy three weeks later, when he was back home in Hawaii.

Nearing age seventy and recovered from a long battle with COVID-19, Appleby, in front of almost one hundred thousand spectators, narrated the pregame "hype video" playing on the dazzling fifty-two-foot-high, one-hundred-foot-wide screen above the west end zone; he spoke in the deep, soulful tones molded by the rich soil of the Piedmont, where he was raised: *"Let us not forget where we have been, the tests we faced, and the scars on our skin . . ."*

⠊⠊⠊⠊⠊

Fifty years after playing his final game at Clarke Central, Michael Thurmond, the chief executive officer of DeKalb County, was invited to deliver a pregame speech to the Gladiators.

The racial makeup of Clarke Central had undergone a profound transformation since Thurmond graduated from the school in 1971. The majority-White student body of the early 1970s had gradually shifted over the intervening decades, to the point that minority students—including a surging Hispanic student population—had reached 73 percent of the total enrollment.

But Thurmond went back in time and spoke to the assembled players of the hardships of that first year of integration, when racial divisions prevented an immensely talented team from achieving its lofty goals. He spoke of Billy Henderson, who later inherited and healed a fractured program and instilled it with unity and pride. He spoke of the traditions, of walking down the pines, of the storied history of Death Valley, and of a sense of community that was reinforced by the Gladiators' successes on the gridiron.

He told them that no matter what they did later in life, they should never forget the sacrifices and the proud legacy of those who came before them and should always be proud that they wore the *crimson and gold*.

NOTES

Chapter 1. The Schools

The epigraph is from Frank Lebby Stanton, "Keep A-Goin'!," *Atlanta Constitution*, ca. 1920.

1. Ashton G. Ellett, "Not Another Little Rock: Massive Resistance, Desegregation, and the Athens White Business Establishment, 1960–61," *Georgia Historical Quarterly* 97, no. 2 (Summer 2013): 184, https://www.jstor.org/stable/24636699.

2. Michael L. Thurmond, *A Story Untold: Black Men & Women in Athens History* (Athens, Ga.: Deeds Publishing, 2019), 78.

3. Thurmond, *Story Untold*, 67.

4. Interview with Elizabeth Platt on November 2, 2021.

5. Betsy Bean, "How Black History Is Lost," *Boom Magazine*, November 11, 2016, https://boomathens.com/black-history-lost/.

6. Monica Dellenberger Knight, "Seeking Education for Liberation: The Development of Black Schools in Athens, Georgia from Emancipation through Desegregation" (PhD diss., University of Georgia, 2007), 167, https://getd.libs.uga.edu/pdfs/knight_monica_d_200708_phd.pdf.

7. Platt interview.

8. Jackie Wright, "The Sharecropper's Son: Michael Thurmond Makes History," *Blueprints Magazine*, February 27, 2020, http://cedarblueprints.com/2020/02/27/the-sharecroppers-son-michael-thurmond-makes-history/.

9. Interview with Alexander Stephens on November 3, 2021.

10. "Walter Allen, Sr., Music Teachers' Stories," interview by Roy Legette, November 17, 2020, Richard B. Russell Library for Political Research and Studies, University of Georgia Oral History Collections.

11. Interview with Horace King on April 13, 2021.

12. Interview with Bobby Cross on November 5, 2021.

13. Platt interview.

14. King interview.

15. Knight, "Seeking Education for Liberation," 180.

16. Knight, 180.

17. Knight, 179.

18. Knight, 181.

19. James Fair, *A Salute to Athletes from Athens High & Industrial and Burney Harris High Schools* (self-pub., 2014), 14.

20. Interview with Clarence Pope on May 6, 2021.

21. Interview with Paul Gilbert on May 22, 2021.

22. Fair, "Salute to Athletes," 106.

23. Fair, 14.

24. Walter Allen Jr., "Athens High 1965: Integrating High School Athletics in Athens," *Boom Magazine* 2, no. 4 (August 10, 2018), https://boomathens.com/athens-high-1965-integrating-high-school-athletics-in-athens/.

25. Fair, "Salute to Athletes," 115.

26. Interview with Charlie Strong on November 6, 2021.

27. Interview with Ken Dious on April 30, 2023.

28. Patrick Garbin, "UGA Football's Pre-Pioneers," UGASports.com, February 10, 2021, https://uga.rivals.com/news/uga-football-s-pre-pioneers.

29. Amelia Monroe Andrews et al., *The Tangible Past in Athens, Georgia*, ed. Charlotte Thomas Marshall (Athens: Charlotte Thomas Marshall, 2014), 289.

30. Bill King, "College Life in the New South: A Freshman's First Quarter at the University of Georgia in 1970," *Quick Cuts with Bill King* (blog), August 22, 2020, https://billkingquickcuts.wordpress.com/2020/08/22/college-life-in-the-new-south-a-freshmans-first-quarter-at-the-university-of-georgia-in-1970/.

31. Interview with Mike Epps on November 3, 2021.

32. Interview with Bobby Poss on May 6, 2021.

33. Interview with Woody Chastain on May 4, 2021.

34. Doug Gorman, "Remembering a Legend," *Clayton News-Daily*, January 18, 2011, https://www.news-daily.com/news/remembering-a-legend/article_765d6fb7-fc52-5135-afe3-b2b30b8546e1.html.

35. Lewis Grizzard, "Weyman Sellers: It's All He Has Ever Done," *Atlanta Journal-Constitution*, December 3, 1977, 28.

36. Trojan Laundry advertisement, *Red and Black*, February 9, 1966, 3.

37. Ralph McGill, "The Georgias and the Techs," *Atlanta Constitution*,

November 26, 1960, reprinted in *The Best of Ralph McGill: Selected Columns*, comp. Michael Strickland, Harry Davis, and Jeff Strickland (Atlanta: Cherokee Publishing, 1980), 66–67.

38. Ed Thilenius and Jim Koger, *No Ifs, No Ands, a Lot of Butts: 21 Years of Georgia Football* (Atlanta: Foote and Davies, 1960), 10.

39. Jim Klobuchar and Fran Tarkenton, *Tarkenton* (New York: Harper & Row, 1976), 40–41.

40. Klobuchar and Tarkenton, 41.

41. Interview with Gary Travis on May 5, 2021.

42. Poss interview.

43. Klobuchar and Tarkenton, *Tarkenton*, 37.

44. Epps interview.

45. Poss interview.

46. Interview with Doc Eldridge on March 9, 2021.

47. Gilbert interview.

48. Interview with Terry Smart on May 23, 2023.

49. Grizzard, "Weyman Sellers."

Chapter 2. The Town

The epigraph is from an interview with Pete McCommons on March 16, 2021.

1. McCommons interview.

2. "History," Athens YMCA, https://athensymca.org/history.

3. Valerie Beynon, "Morton Theatre," New Georgia Encyclopedia, last modified March 1, 2021, https://www.georgiaencyclopedia.org/articles /arts-culture/morton-theatre.

4. Blake Aued, "Black-Owned Businesses Are Endangered in Athens," *Flagpole*, March 22, 2017, https://flagpole.com/news/city-dope/2017/03 /22/black-owned-businesses-are-endangered-in-athens/.

5. Charles Hayslett, "Lucky Bethel Project Was There—Hodgson," *Athens Daily News*, July 25, 1970, 1.

6. "Our Georgia Commitment," Class Notes, *University of Georgia Magazine*, Fall 2017, 47.

7. George T. Counter, "From Ashes to Diamonds," Net54baseball post, March 2009, https://www.net54baseball.com/showthread.php?t =251258.

8. Cora McCaffrey, Georganna Kolar, and Cindy Hahamovitch, "Child Labor and the Athens Manufacturing Company," Clio: Your Guide to History, August 25, 2023, https://www.theclio.com/entry/88155.

9. Kristen Morales, "New Book 'Over the River' Details the History of East Athens," *Flagpole*, July 17, 2019.

10. Calvin Trillin, *An Education in Georgia: Charlayne Hunter, Hamilton Holmes, and the Integration of the University of Georgia* (Athens: University of Georgia Press, 1991), 135.

11. Ashton G. Ellett, "Not Another Little Rock: Massive Resistance, Desegregation, and the Athens White Business Establishment, 1960–61," *Georgia Historical Quarterly* 97, no. 2 (Summer 2013): 191–92, https://www.jstor.org/stable/24636699.

12. Ellett, "Not Another Little Rock," 176.

13. Ellett, 186.

14. Ellett, 203.

15. B. J. Williams, "Arcade: 'We Have an Eye toward the Future,'" AccessWDUN, January 31, 2020, https://accesswdun.com/article/2020/1/871752/arcade-we-have-an-eye-toward-the-future.

16. Sean Kipe, "Of Monsters and Men" (chapter 2, season 1), August 25, 2020, in *In the Red Clay*, produced by Sean Kipe, podcast, MP3 audio, 37:44, https://www.intheredclaypodcast.com/podcast/episode/65adf315/of-monsters-and-men-or-chapter-2-season-1.

17. Interview with Jimmy Klein on March 2, 2021.

18. Interview with Bobby Poss on May 6, 2021.

19. Jim Galloway, "Remembering the Assassination of Floyd Hoard, 50 Years Later," *Atlanta Journal-Constitution*, August 5, 2017, https://www.ajc.com/blog/politics/remembering-the-assassination-floyd-hoard-years-lateru9hLPqHzyJiBZoDNr3D1wI/.

20. Wayne Ford, "50-Year-Old Car-Bomb Murder of Prosecutor to Be Remembered in Jefferson," *Athens Banner-Herald*, August 4, 2017, https://www.onlineathens.com/local-news/2017-08-04/50-year-old-car-bomb-murder-prosecutor-be-remembered-jefferson.

21. Interview with Lawton Stephens on May 8, 2021.

22. Jack Nelson, *Scoop: The Evolution of a Southern Reporter*, ed. Barbara Matusow (Jackson: University Press of Mississippi, 2013), 73–77.

23. Nelson, 73.

24. Nelson, 73–77.

25. John W. English and Rob Williams, *When Men Were Boys: An Informal Portrait of Dean William Tate* (Lakemont, Ga.: Copple House Books, 1984), 135–137.

26. Poss interview.

27. Nelson, *Scoop*, 77.

28. Interview with Richard Appleby on October 15, 2021.

29. James F. Cornelison, "Present at the Creation," *Flagpole*, April 14, 2010, https://issuu.com/flagpolemagazine/docs/fp100414/10.

30. Interview with Pete McCommons on October 26, 2021.

31. Obituary of Fred Birchmore, *Athens Banner-Herald*, April 17, 2012,

https://www.legacy.com/us/obituaries/onlineathens/name/fred
-birchmore-obituary?pid=157079333.

32. Poss interview.

33. Frank Graham Jr., *Great No-Hit Games of the Major Leagues* (New York: Random House, 1968), 83–97.

Chapter 3. The Gown

The epigraph is from a statement from President Aderhold to students. UA 97–100: Box 76, O. C. Aderhold Collection, Hargrett Rare Book and Manuscript Library, University of Georgia (hereafter Aderhold Collection).

1. "Dr. Aderhold Did Much for Georgia, Georgians," *Athens Banner-Herald*, undated clipping, UA 97–100, box 76, Aderhold Collection.

2. Calvin Trillin, *An Education in Georgia: Charlayne Hunter, Hamilton Holmes, and the Integration of the University of Georgia* (Athens: University of Georgia Press, 1991), 53.

3. Edward A. Hatfield, "Desegregation of Higher Education," New Georgia Encyclopedia, last modified February 25, 2021, https://www .georgiaencyclopedia.org/articles/history-archaeology/desegregation -higher-education.

4. Trillin, *Education in Georgia*, 73.

5. Loran Smith, "Miss State Invades Leaking Woodruff Hall," *Athens Daily News*, February 20, 1961, 2.

6. Rebecca McCarthy, "40 Years Ago, the Face of Higher Education Altered," *Atlanta Journal-Constitution*, January 7, 2001, https://www.ajc .com/lifestyles/years-ago-higher-education-face-altered /bgJoLJT5Uw9ZqozJreBE2K/.

7. Interview with Pete McCommons, March 16, 2021.

8. Jim Cobb, "Here's to You, (Generally) Beloved Ink-Stained Scribe!," *Cobbloviate*, February 11, 2014.

9. Interview with Winston Stephens on October 14, 2021.

10. Stephens interview.

11. McCommons interview.

12. Trillin, *Education in Georgia*, 58.

13. Monica Dellenberger Knight, "Seeking Education for Liberation: The Development of Black Schools in Athens, Georgia from Emancipation through Desegregation" (PhD diss., University of Georgia, 2007), 216, https://getd.libs.uga.edu/pdfs/knight_monica_d_200708_phd.pdf.

14. Pratt, *We Shall Not Be Moved*, 103.

15. McCommons interview.

16. Trillin, *Education in Georgia*, 47.

17. "Alumni Spotlight: Br. Dean William Tate," Phi Kappa Literary Society, March 23, 2015, http://phikappa.squarespace.com/news/2015/3/23/alumni-spotlight-br-dean-william-tate.html.

18. Trillin, *Education in Georgia*, 53.

19. John W. English and Rob Williams, *When Men Were Boys: An Informal Portrait of Dean William Tate* (Lakemont, Ga.: Copple House Books, 1984), 173.

20. Trillin, *Education in Georgia*, 61.

21. Trillin, 58.

22. Trillin, 44–45.

23. Tommy Johnson, "Calm Returns Here after Administration Orders Restrictions," *Red and Black*, January 19, 1961, 1.

24. Jim Thompson, "Killian Remembered as Tireless and Fearless Crusader for Justice and Fairness," *Athens Banner-Herald*, November 1, 2016, https://www.onlineathens.com/local-news/2016-11-01/killian-remembered-tireless-and-fearless-crusader-justice-and-fairness.

25. Blake Aued, "R.I.P. Rev. Archibald Killian, Athens' First Black Police Officer," *Flagpole*, November 2, 2016, https://flagpole.com/news/news-features/2016/11/02/r-i-p-rev-archibald-killian-athens-first-black-police-officer/.

26. Interview with Maxie Foster on May 7, 2021.

27. Trillin, *Education in Georgia*, 133.

28. Trillin, 45.

29. Telegram from President Aderhold to Roy Harris dated January 13, 1961, UA 97–100, box 76, Aderhold Collection.

30. Telegram to O. C. Aderhold, UA 97–100, box 76, Aderhold Collection.

31. Transcript of editorial broadcast by Billy Woodall, Radio Station WDMD, January 17, 1961, UA 97–100, box 76, Aderhold Collection.

32. "Education: Shame in Georgia," *Time Magazine*, January 20, 1961, https://content.time.com/time/subscriber/article/0,33009,871979,00.html.

33. Letter from President Aderhold to Chancellor Harry Ransom, University of Texas, October 27, 1961, UA 97–100, box 76, Aderhold Collection.

Chapter 4. Violence and Hope

The epigraph is from Steve Teasley's article "Sellers, Trojans Open Season Monday," *Athens Banner-Herald*, August 7, 1966, 13.

1. Lauren Patterson, "The Modern Classic City: Analyzing Commercial Development in Athens, Georgia from 1930 to 1981" (PhD diss., Univer-

sity of Georgia, 2019), 55, https://getd.libs.uga.edu/pdfs/patterson
_lauren_e_201905_mhp.pdf.

2. Patterson, "Modern Classic City," 56.

3. Patterson, 66.

4. Frances Taliaferro Thomas, *A Portrait of Historic Athens and Clarke
County* (Athens: University of Georgia Press, 1992), 210–11.

5. Hattie Thomas Whitehead, *Giving Voice to Linnentown* (Grayson,
Ga.: Tiny Tots & Tikes, 2021).

6. Interview with Alexander Stephens on November 2, 2021.

7. Whitehead, *Giving Voice to Linnentown*, 76.

8. Fleming Smith, "50 Years Ago Today, Flooding in Athens Took 8
Lives," *Athens Banner-Herald*, June 27, 2013, https://www.onlineathens
.com/story/news/state/2013/06/28/50-years-ago-today-flooding-athens
-took-8-lives/15566539007/#:~:text=The%20rains%20caused%20the
%20North,Eight%20passengers%20drowned.

9. Adam Fairclough, "The Costs of Brown: Black Teachers and School
Integration," *Journal of American History* 91, no. 1 (June 2004).

10. Monica Dellenberger Knight, "Seeking Education for Liberation:
The Development of Black Schools in Athens, Georgia from Emancipation through Desegregation" (PhD diss., University of Georgia, 2007),
200, https://getd.libs.uga.edu/pdfs/knight_monica_d_200708_phd
.pdf.

11. Knight, "Seeking Education," 203–4.

12. Knight, 205.

13. Interview with Bonnie Hampton Travis on October 9, 2021.

14. Travis interview.

15. Bill Shipp, *Murder at Broad River Bridge* (Atlanta: Peachtree Publishers, 1981), 28.

16. Shipp, *Murder at Broad River Bridge*, 13.

17. David J. Krajicek, "Ku Klux Klan Thugs Chase Down and Kill African American Soldier on Desolate Georgia Road in 1964," *New York Daily
News*, February 15, 2014.

18. Robert A. Pratt, *We Shall Not Be Moved: The Desegregation of the
University of Georgia* (Athens: University of Georgia Press, 2005), 126.

19. Shipp, *Murder at Broad River Bridge*, 28–29.

20. Shipp, 29–30.

21. Shipp, 30–31.

22. "Seven Negroes Convicted Here of Criminal Trespassing," *Athens
Banner-Herald*, May 22, 1964, 1.

23. John T. Edge, *The Potlikker Papers: A Food History of the Modern
South* (New York: Penguin Press, 2017), 37.

24. Shipp, *Murder at Broad River Bridge*, 14.

25. Jack Nelson, *Scoop: The Evolution of a Southern Reporter*, ed. Barbara Matusow (Jackson: University Press of Mississippi, 2013), 89.

26. Shipp, *Murder at Broad River Bridge*, 87.

27. Interview with Clarence Pope on May 5, 2021.

28. Jackie Wright, "The Sharecropper's Son: Michael Thurmond Makes History," *Blueprints Magazine*, February 27, 2020, http://cedarblueprints.com/2020/02/27/the-sharecroppers-son-michael-thurmond-makes-history/.

29. Interview with Horace King on April 13, 2021.

30. King interview.

31. Interview with Richard Appleby on October 15, 2021.

32. Interview with Doc Eldridge on March 9, 2021.

33. Eldridge interview.

34. Interview with Pete McCommons on June 14, 2023.

35. Interview with Bill King on October 28, 2021.

36. Lewis Grizzard Jr., "Athens-Lee Clash Set at Trojan Field," *Athens Daily News*, November 14, 1965, 4.

37. Interview with Mike Epps on November 3, 2021.

38. Lewis Grizzard Jr., "Devore, Parsons to Miss Valdosta Tilt," *Athens Daily News*, November 30, 1965, 3.

39. Chuck Perry, "Missed Kick . . . Doesn't Mean Much Now," *Athens Banner-Herald*, December 12, 1969, 12.

40. Johnny Futch, "Bazemore Feels 'Real Good' at Midfield Victory Party," *Athens Daily News*, December 5, 1965, 4.

41. Wade Saye, "Sellers Takes Longest Walk as Heartbreak Looms Heavy," *Athens Daily News*, December 5, 1965, 4.

42. Interview with Maxie Foster on May 7, 2021.

43. Interview with Robert Hawkins on June 25, 2021.

44. Betsy Bean, "Coulda, Woulda, Shoulda," *Boom Magazine*, January 3, 2022, https://boomathens.com/coulda-woulda-shoulda/.

45. Hawkins interview.

46. Foster interview.

47. Interview with Elizabeth Platt on November 2, 2021.

48. Appleby interview.

49. Hawkins interview.

50. Walter Allen Jr., "Athens High 1965: Integrating High School Athletics in Athens," *Boom Magazine* 2, no. 4 (August 10, 2018), https://boomathens.com/athens-high-1965-integrating-high-school-athletics-in-athens/.

51. Hawkins interview.

52. Interview with Bobby Poss on May 6, 2021.

53. Associated Press, "KKK Klavern Backing Maddox for Governor," *Athens Banner-Herald*, August 18, 1966, 2.

54. Robert D. Jacobus, *Black Man in the Huddle: Stories from the Integration of Texas Football* (College Station: Texas A&M University Press, 2019), 203.

55. "Reserve in Trojans Line May Be a Problem—Sellers," *Athens Daily News*, August 12, 1966.

56. Allen, "Athens High 1965."

57. Allen.

58. Bean, "Coulda, Woulda, Shoulda."

59. Bean.

60. Bean.

61. Robert L. Robinson, "More Than Just a Game: The Impact of Sports on Racial Segregation in One Southern Town" (PhD diss., University of Alabama, 2017), 74.

62. Mike Castronis, *A Football Story* (self-pub., 2017), Kindle.

Chapter 5. The Season

The epigraph is from Blake Giles's article "City Championship Costly for Athens," *Athens Banner-Herald/Daily News*, September 14, 1969, 13.

1. Interview with Bill King on October 28, 2021.

2. Michael L. Thurmond, *A Story Untold: Black Men & Women in Athens History* (Athens, Ga.: Deeds Publishing, 2019), 91.

3. Richard Moore, "Offense, Pride: Defense, Concern," *Athens Banner-Herald/Daily News*, September 15, 1968, 15.

4. Charles Hayslett, "Jackson's Jackets Eye Josey," *Athens Daily News*, September 30, 1969, 5.

5. Patrick Garbin, "Catching Up with Clarence Pope," UGASports.com, December 6, 2020, https://uga.rivals.com/news/catching-up-with -clarence-pope.

6. Bill King, "UGA Football: Dawg-Gone Legend Harry Dog Was Front-Page News in Athens," *DawgNation*, June 25, 2017, https://www .dawgnation.com/football/opinion/uga-football-this-dawg-gone-legend -was-front-page-news-in-athens/.

7. Interview with David Lester on May 25, 2023.

8. Interview with Mac Coile on September 28, 2021.

9. Blake Giles, "City Championship Costly for Athens," *Athens Banner-Herald/Daily News*, September 14, 1969, 13.

10. Interview with Clarence Pope on May 5, 2021.

11. Giles, "City Championship," 13.

12. Interview with Horace King on April 13, 2021.

13. Phil Jackson, "Tough Red Elephants Trounce Athens, 20–3," *Gainesville Daily Times*, September 20, 1969.

14. Interview with Doc Eldridge on March 9, 2021.

15. Interview with Terry Smart on March 11, 2021.

16. Coile interview.

17. Plott Brice, "Athens, B-H Finished?," *Athens Daily News*, September 26, 1969, 4.

18. Charles Hayslett, "Burney-Harris Fined after Grid Flare-Up," *Athens Daily News*, October 25, 1969, 9.

19. Chuck Perry, "Jackets Unable to Deliver Knockout Punch on Trojans," *Athens Banner-Herald/Daily News*, September 14, 1969, 13.

20. Charles Hayslett, "Jackets Are Best Says Knight Coach," *Athens Daily News*, October 10, 1969, 4.

21. Charles Hayslett, "AHS Passing Up; Jackets Eyeing 2,000," *Athens Daily News*, October 15, 1969, 4.

22. Horace King interview.

23. Interview with Michael Thurmond on April 2, 2021.

24. Charles Hayslett, "Bolton Says 'Dogs Tough,'" *Athens Daily News*, October 24, 1969, 4.

25. Plott Brice, "Athens Drills Tucker's 'Mighty' Tigers, 17–3," *Athens Daily News*, November 1, 1969, 9.

26. Sharon Bailey, "Fair, Equitable Plan Sought," *Athens Daily News*, December 16, 1969, 1.

27. "B-H, 67–6," *Athens Daily News*, November 8, 1969, 10.

28. Plott Brice, "Trojans Axe Imps, 21–10, to Start State Title Run," *Athens Daily News*, November 29, 1969, 4.

29. Plott Brice, "Trojans Rule North!," *Athens Daily News*, December 7, 1969, 15.

Chapter 6. The Game

The epigraph is from Joe Litsch's article "Athens Ties Valdosta in Last Minute, 26–26," *Atlanta Journal-Constitution*, December 14, 1969, 1H.

1. Interview with Buck Belue on May 4, 2021.

2. Gabe Burns, "The King of Titletown," *Valdosta Daily Times*, July 11, 2016, https://www.valdostadailytimes.com/sports/local_sports/burns-column-the-king-of-titletown/article_e746864f-0ce2-54a1-b4b4-f3dfe83dd502.html.

3. Robert L. Robinson, "More Than Just a Game: The Impact of Sports on Racial Segregation in One Southern Town" (PhD diss., University of Alabama, 2017), 80–81.

4. Charles Hayslett, "Athens 'Stoppers' Have Jobs Cut Out," *Athens Daily News*, December 11, 1969, 4.

5. Plott Brice, "Athens High Charged with Trojan Support," *Athens Daily News*, December 13, 1969, 9.

6. Sharon Bailey, "School Mix Plan Approved by Unit," *Athens Daily News*, December 12, 1969, 1.

7. Bill King, "50 Years Ago: Oh, What a Night!," *Quick Cuts with Bill King* (blog), December 13, 2019, https://billkingquickcuts.wordpress.com/2019/12/13/50-years-ago-oh-what-a-night/.

8. Charles Hayslett, "Trojans Eye 'Dosta," *Athens Daily News*, December 13, 1969, 1, 4.

9. Bill King, "50 Years Ago."

10. Clissa Spratlin, "A Victory Celebrated," *Thumb Tack Tribune*, December 19, 1969, 7.

11. Interview with Gary Travis on May 5, 2021.

12. Belue interview.

13. Interview with Terry Smart, March 11, 2021.

14. Smart interview.

15. Belue interview.

16. Interview with Woody Chastain on May 4, 2021.

17. Smart interview.

18. Interview with Bill Hartman on May 20, 2021.

19. Bill Bryant, "Oh, What a Night!," *Thumb Tack Tribune*, December 19, 1969, 7.

20. King, "50 Years Ago."

21. Steve Ray, "Went to the game with a group from Prince Avenue Baptist Church," October 28, 2021, comment on Mark Clegg, "Anyone with any memories of the 1969 state title game played between Athens High and Valdosta?," Facebook, October 28, 2021, https://www.facebook.com/mark.clegg.507/videos/389851476172487?idorvanity=692650161300548.

22. King.

23. King.

24. Travis interview.

25. King, "50 Years Ago."

26. King.

27. Belue interview.

28. Blake Giles, "Athens, Valdosta Bargain for Rematch," *Athens Banner-Herald*, April 1, 1970, 6.

29. Larry Pope, "The Greatest Game Belongs to AHS," *Athens Banner-Herald/Daily News*, December 14, 1969, 14.

30. Interview with Bill King on October 28, 2021.

31. Interview with Pete McCommons on March 16, 2021.

32. Blake Gumprecht, *An American College Town* (Amherst: University of Massachusetts Press, 2018), 195.

33. Interview with Pete McCommons on May 20, 2021.

34. Christopher A. Huff, "Radicals between the Hedges: New Left Activism at the University of Georgia, 1963–1975" (master's thesis, University of Georgia, 2005), 60, https://getd.libs.uga.edu/pdfs/huff_christopher_a_200512_ma.pdf.

35. Chuck Cooper, "Officials Say Pot Use Claims Overestimated," *Athens Banner-Herald*, January 22, 1970, 1.

36. Huff, "Radicals between the Hedges," 91.

37. Hank Johnson, "There's an Ugly Side to the Classic City," *Athens Daily News*, September 8, 1968, 1.

38. Sharon Bailey, "18 Living in 6 Athens Rooms," *Athens Daily News*, September 10, 1968, 1.

39. Hank Johnson, "Original Work Started on Broad Street Bridge," *Athens Banner-Herald*, April 17, 1970, 1, 8.

40. Charles Hayslett, "Dissatisfaction Rules Ed Turner's Candidacy," *Athens Daily News*, September 3, 1970, 13.

Chapter 7. The Gladiators

The epigraph is from Blake Giles's article "Blacks Stage Walkout," *Athens Banner-Herald*, October 27, 1970, 6.

1. Calvin Trillin, *An Education in Georgia: Charlayne Hunter, Hamilton Holmes, and the Integration of the University of Georgia* (Athens: University of Georgia Press, 1991), 117–18.

2. Trillin, 116.

3. "UGA Names Residence Hall after Dr. Mary Blackwell Diallo," *Zebra Magazine* 29, no. 90 (2022): 26–27.

4. Interview with Walter Allen Jr. on April 25, 2023.

5. Michael L. Thurmond, *A Story Untold: Black Men & Women in Athens History* (Athens, Ga.: Deeds Publishing, 2019), 90.

6. Interview with Horace King on April 13, 2021.

7. Thurmond, *Story Untold*, 91.

8. Interview with Bill King on October 28, 2021.

9. Blake Gumprecht, *The American College Town* (Amherst: University of Massachusetts Press, 2008), 195.

10. Pete McCommons, "A Front-Line Preacher: Frank Hutchison 1930–2017," *Flagpole*, April 12, 2017, https://flagpole.com/news/pub-notes/2017/04/12/a-front-line-preacher-frank-hutchison-1930-2017/.

11. "Sequence of Events," *United Free Press* 1, no. 1 (June 1, 1970), 3, 4.

12. Chuck Cooper, "Attempts Are Being Made to Ease Tensions at AHS," *Athens Banner-Herald*, April 15, 1970, 1, 5.

13. Tene A. Harris, "Value, Networks, Desegregation, and Displacement at One of Georgia's Black High Schools, Athens High and Industrial School/Burney-Harris High School, 1913–1970" (PhD diss., Georgia State University, 2012), https://scholarworks.gsu.edu/eps_diss/95.

14. Interview with Dr. Walter Allen Sr. on April 30, 2023.

15. Interview with Richard Appleby on October 15, 2021.

16. Sharon Bailey, "Desegregation: Disorder, Dispute," *Athens Banner-Herald/Daily News*, May 10, 1970, 10.

17. Thurmond, *Story Untold*, 90–92.

18. "Won't Condone Disorder—Mayor," *Athens Banner-Herald*, April 30, 1970, 1.

19. John W. English and Rob Williams, *When Men Were Boys: An Informal Portrait of Dean William Tate* (Lakemont, Ga.: Copple House Books, 1984), 148.

20. Terry Adamson, "Blacks, Whites to March Together Tonight in Athens," *Atlanta Constitution*, May 15, 1970, 11A.

21. Interview with Pete McCommons on November 2, 2021.

22. Appleby interview.

23. "Police Brutality in Athens: Fact or Fiction?," *United Free Press* 1, no. 4 (July 12, 1970), 1.

24. Chuck Perry, "There's Still One Unpaid Bill," *Athens Banner-Herald*, July 14, 1971, 11.

25. Interview with Richard Appleby on October 15, 2021.

26. Blake Giles, "Change Due for Valley," *Athens Banner-Herald*, May 27, 1970, 6.

27. Jan Collins, "AHS School Colors, Cheerleaders Picked," *Athens Banner-Herald*, May 13, 1970, 1.

28. Appleby interview.

29. Blake Giles, "Harmony Prevails at AHS," *Athens Banner-Herald*, May 5, 1970, 6.

30. Charles Hayslett, "Thurmond Making Bid in Crowded Backfield," *Athens Banner-Herald/Daily News*, May 17, 1970, 15.

31. Blake Giles, "Spring Grid Drills: 'No Position Filled Yet,'" *Athens Banner-Herald*, May 3, 1970, 16.

32. Interview with Clarence Pope on May 6, 2021.

33. Interview with Bobby Cross on November 5, 2021.

34. "Dodd Likes Frosh Quarterback," *Athens Daily News*, November 29, 1969, 4.

35. Blake Giles, "Quarterback Now Athens' Problem," *Athens Banner-Herald*, May 19, 1970, 6.

36. Cross interview.

37. Blake Giles, "Harmony Prevails at AHS," *Athens Banner-Herald*, May 5, 1970, 6.

38. Sharon Bailey, "Clarke School Openings Go Smoothly," *Athens Daily News*, September 1, 1970, 1.

39. Cross interview.

40. Interview with Michael Thurmond on April 2, 2021.

41. Pope interview.

42. Interview with Robert Hawkins, July 29, 2021.

43. Adam Fairclough, "The Costs of *Brown*: Black Teachers and School Integration," *Journal of American History* 91, no. 1 (June 2004).

44. Thurmond, *Story Untold*, 93.

45. Joe Litsch, "Athens and Valdosta Probable For Finals," *Atlanta Journal*, September 3, 1970, 6-D.

46. Chuck Perry, "Inherent Problems Are Secondary to Talent," *Athens Banner-Herald*, August 23, 1970, 11.

47. Perry, "Inherent Problems."

48. Plott Brice, "Clarke Flexing Muscles," *Athens Daily News*, September 3, 1970, 4.

49. Plott Brice, "Clarke Starting Slow," *Athens Daily News*, September 9, 1970, 4.

50. Plott Brice, "Revenge Factor Huge in Clarke's Opener," *Athens Daily News*, September 18, 1970, 4.

51. Blake Giles, "History Haunts Gladiators in Loss to Red Elephants," *Athens Banner-Herald*, September 13, 1970, 13.

52. Giles, "History Haunts Gladiators," 13.

53. Giles, 13.

54. Plott Brice, "Clarke Sees 17–15 Replay," *Athens Daily News*, September 22, 1970, 4.

55. Jim Satterly, "Harris, Vikings Clobber Athens," *Atlanta Constitution*, October 24, 1970.

56. Blake Giles, "Gladiators 'Out in the Cold,'" *Athens Banner-Herald—Daily News*, October 25, 1970, 5.

57. "Black Student Grievances," *United Free Press* 2, no. 6 (May 16, 1971), 5.

58. "Principal Hight's Reply to Black Student Representatives," *United Free Press* 2, no. 6 (May 16, 1971), 3.

59. Dr. Walter Allen Sr. interview.

60. Interview with Mike Epps on November 3, 2021.

61. Interview with Mac Coile on September 28, 2021.

62. Blake Giles, "Blacks Stage Walkout," *Athens Banner-Herald*, October 27, 1970, 6.

63. Thurmond interview.
64. Thurmond interview.
65. Pope interview.
66. Appleby interview.
67. Bill King interview.
68. Thurmond interview.

Epilogue

1. Jim Stewart, "Athens Dispute Growing On," *Atlanta Constitution*, November 25, 1972, 1, 12.

2. Stewart, "Athens Dispute."

3. Ken Willis, "Sellers Out at Clarke," *Atlanta Constitution*, December 9, 1970, 1D–3D.

4. Chip Towers, "Billy Henderson's Greatness Extended beyond UGA, Football Accomplishments," *Dawgnation*, February 15, 2018, https://www.dawgnation.com/football/billy-henderson-georgia-football-accomplishments-clarke-county-tribute/.

5. Anna Alyssa McKoy, "Pete McCommons to Receive Inaugural Award for Distinguished Community Journalism," Grady College of Journalism and Mass Communication, February 26, 2018, https://grady.uga.edu/pete-mccommons-receive-inaugural-award-distinguished-community-journalism/.

6. Interview with Bonnie Hampton Travis on October 9, 2021.

7. Betsy Bean, "Coulda, Woulda, Shoulda," *Boom Magazine*, January 3, 2022, https://boomathens.com/coulda-woulda-shoulda/.

BIBLIOGRAPHY

Andrews, Amelia Monroe, Steven A. Brown, Patricia Irvin Cooper, Gary L. Doster, Lee Epting, Theresa M. Flynn, Mary Anne Martin Hodgson, et al. *The Tangible Past in Athens, Georgia.* Athens: Charlotte Thomas Marshall, 2014.

Castronis, Mike. *A Football Story.* Self-published, 2017. Kindle.

Dellenberger, Monica Knight. "Seeking Education for Liberation: The Development of Black Schools in Athens, Georgia from Emancipation through Desegregation." PhD diss., University of Georgia, 2007. https://getd.libs.uga.edu/pdfs/knight_monica_d_200708_phd.pdf.

Edge, John T. *The Potlikker Papers: A Food History of the Modern South.* New York: Penguin Press, 2017.

Ellett, Ashton G. "Not Another Little Rock: Massive Resistance, Desegregation, and the Athens White Business Establishment, 1960–61." *Georgia Historical Quarterly* 97, no. 2 (2013): 176–216. https://www.jstor.org/stable/24636699.

English, John W., and Rob Williams. *When Men Were Boys: An Informal Portrait of Dean William Tate.* Lakemont, Ga.: Copple House Books, 1984.

Harris, Tene A. "Value, Networks, Desegregation, and Displacement at One of Georgia's Black High Schools, Athens High and Industrial School/Burney-Harris High School, 1913–1970." PhD diss., Georgia State University, 2012. https://scholarworks.gsu.edu/eps_diss/95.

Kng, Bill. "50 Years Ago: Oh, What a Night!" *Quick Cuts with Bill King* (blog), December 13, 2019. https://billkingquickcuts.wordpress.com/2019/12/13/50-years-ago-oh-what-a-night/.

Klobuchar, Jim, and Fran Tarkenton. *Tarkenton*. New York: Harper & Row, 1976.

Nelson, Jack. *Scoop: The Evolution of a Southern Reporter*. Edited by Barbara Matusow. Jackson: University Press of Mississippi, 2013.

Patterson, Lauren. "The Modern Classic City: Analyzing Commercial Development in Athens, Georgia from 1930 to 1981." PhD diss., University of Georgia, 2019. https://getd.libs.uga.edu/pdfs/patterson _lauren_e_201905_mhp.pdf.

Pratt, Robert A. *We Shall Not Be Moved: The Desegregation of the University of Georgia*. Athens: University of Georgia Press, 2005.

Shipp, Bill. *Murder at Broad River Bridge*. Atlanta: Peachtree Publishers, 1981.

Strickland, Michael, Harry Davis, and Jeff Strickland. *The Best of Ralph McGill: Selected Columns*. Atlanta: Cherokee Publishing, 1980.

Thurmond, Michael L. *A Story Untold: Black Men & Women in Athens History*. Athens, Ga.: Deeds Publishing, 2019.

Trillin, Calvin. *An Education in Georgia: Charlayne Hunter, Hamilton Holmes, and the Integration of the University of Georgia*. Athens: University of Georgia Press, 1991.

Whitehead, Hattie Thomas. *Giving Voice to Linnentown*. Grayson, Ga.: Tiny Tots & Tikes, 2021.

INDEX

Aderhold, Omer Clyde ("O. C."), 45, 48–50, 63–65
Allen, Alex, 138, 159, 197–98, 202, 207
Allen, Walter, Sr., 4, 8, 122, 181, 186
Alps Road Elementary School, 96
Appleby, Richard: growing up in Athens, 40, 88, 93; at Burney-Harris High School, 10, 113, 127–28, 130, 132–33, 145, 185, 187, 191; at Clarke Central High School, 192–93, 198, 205–6, 209, 212; at University of Georgia, 214–15, 222
Arcade, Ga., 15, 35
Archer High School, 11
Athens, Ga.: architecture, 13, 28–29, 82, 173; early history of public schools, 5–6; music scene, 1, 12, 16, 34, 41, 82, 218–19; neighborhoods, 2, 6, 26, 29–32, 68–73; 82, 93–98, 106–9; restaurants and other businesses, 16, 27–32, 40–44, 43, 68–69, 73, 86, 96, 124, 173–74; tolerance of eccentric behavior, 40–44; topography, 26–27

Athens, Ga.: Inside/Out (film), 12
Athens Athletic Hall of Fame, 12, 220
Athens Banner-Herald, 67, 85, 105, 129, 164, 175, 183–85, 193, 202
Athens–Ben Epps Airfield, 26, 43, 92, 109, 157, 171
Athens Chamber of Commerce, 15, 32, 34
Athens Country Club, 15, 91, 93, 98, 113
Athens Daily News, 105, 113, 129, 139, 150, 171, 177, 184
Athens High and Industrial School (AHIS): 5–8, 63, 91. *See also* Burney-Harris High School
Athens High School: history, 5–6, 13–14; integration of, 74, 76, 106–120; social strata, 14–16
—football team, 17, 17–25, 39, 67, 95; 1965 season, 102, 105–6; 1966 season (first Black football players), 67, 115–19; 1969 season, 121, 124–28, 131–33, 135–39, 141, 146, 151, 154, 156, 158, 160–64, 166–67, 169–70, 172

Athens Observer, 41, 99

Athens YMCA, 28–29, 91, 93, 95–97, 99, 106, 115, 125–26, 137, 170, 185

Atlanta Journal, 136, 202

Atlanta Journal-Constitution, 148, 152, 171

Augusta Chronicle, 51

Avondale High School, 148–49, 166

Bailey, Sharon, 177

Barrow, James, 187

Basinger, Kim, 212

Bazemore, Wright, 104–6, 117, 125, 153–54, 158, 166, 168–69

Beechwood Shopping Center, 68–69, 73, 102, 113

Belue, Buck, 153, 158–59, 169, 218

Benson, Howard: 31; Benson's Bakery, 31, 42

B-52's, 41, 218

Birchmore, Fred, 41–42

Birt, Billy Sunday, 35–36

Bishop, Julius, 70–71, 84–85, 155, 177, 188–90

"Black Monday," 190

Blackwell-Diallo, Mary, 180–81

Blanche's Open House Restaurant, 86

Bolton, Tommy, 127, 132, 142–46, 148

Bondurant, John, 32, 34

Booker T. Washington High School, 5

Bootle, William Augustus ("Gus"), 50, 61

Briarcliff High School, 125, 146, 191, 207

Brown v. Board of Education of Topeka, 59, 75, 122

Buggs, Danny, 149–50

Burney, Annie H., 6

Burney-Harris High School, 174; football team, 2–3, 6, 9–13, 121–23, 126–34, 139–48, 214–15; integration, 112–14, 152, 156, 179–82, 185–88, 191–98; social activities, 6–7; teachers, 6–7, 8, 30; textbooks, 112–14. *See also* Athens High and Industrial School

Butts, Wally, 9, 12, 17–19, 21–22, 115

Carithers, Herschel, 42–43

Carter, Rusty, 151, 165

Castronis, Mike, Jr., 119–20, 221

Castronis, Mike, Sr., 214

Chamblee High School, 124, 141–42

Champion, Leonard, 10, 12, 91

Chase Street Elementary School, 75

Chastain, Woody, 17, 159

Childs Street School, 75–79, 122

Clarke Central High School: football team, 202–11, 214–22; mascot, 182; name, 192–93; student newspaper, 193; violence at, 211–12, 215

Clarke County Board of Education, 109, 147–48, 156, 191, 208, 216

Clarke Junior High School, 79, 95

Clink, John, 85

Clyde Beatty and Cole Brothers Circus, 40

Cocking, Walter, 32

Coile, Mac, 131, 138, 149–50, 169, 204, 208

Coleman, Stan, 117–19, 126

Collins, Morry, 23, 160

Cooper, Chuck, 185

Copeland, John, 117, 154

Craddick, Nathaniel, 197–98, 210

Crawford, James, 128, 192, 194, 200

Creel, Wayman, 207. *See also* Lakeside High School

Cross, Bobby: at Burney-Harris High School, 7; at Clarke Central High School, 195–200

Cross, Spurgeon, 93

Cross Keys High School, 125, 146, 207

Danner, Walter, 48, 53–54, 56
Davis, Dickie, 157
Davis, Glenn, 102–3, 105
Davison, Fred, 189–90
Decatur High School Bulldogs, 124–25, 141
Dious, Ken, 13
Dixie Mafia, 35–36, 176
Dooley, Vince, 9, 13, 100, 116, 169, 171, 192, 214
Druid Hills High School, 125, 138, 141, 211
Du Bois, W. E. B., 5
Dubose, Bolling S., Jr, 108
Dye, Pat, 19, 169
Dykes High School, 150–51

East Athens Elementary School, 89
Eaves, Joel, Jr., 113
Eaves, Joel, Sr., 100, 113
Edge, John T., 86
Edmondson, Benny, 141, 146, 151, 160
Edwards, H. T., 2, 180
E. E. Butler High School, 135. See also Gainesville High School Red Elephants
Effie's, 38–40
Eldridge, Erwin J., III ("Doc"): growing up in Athens, 94–97, 98, 106; at Athens High School, 23, 151; at Clarke Central High School, 198, 206, 209–10; death of Andy Johnson, 220
Epps, Mike: at Athens High School, 15–16, 20, 23, 103, 106, 134, 141, 149; state title game versus Valdosta, 163, 171; at Clarke Central, 198, 204, 209, 211–12

Farr, Alice, 85
"First Five," 10, 214. See also Appleby, Richard; King, Horace; Pope, Clarence
First Presbyterian Church, 54

Flagpole, 219
Forest Park High School, 125
"Forgotten Five," 74, 79, 81, 107; Agnes Green, 74–76, 80; Marjorie Green, 74–75, 79; Wilucia Green, 74, 76, 109; Scott Michael Killian, 74–75. See also Hampton, Bonnie
Forsyth County, Ga.: Forsyth County High School Bulldogs, 127, 143–46; "Sundown City," 144–45
Foster, Maxie: growing up in Athens, 63, 106–8; at Athens High School, 109–12, 117, 119, 219
Four Seasons Restaurant, 62, 75, 84
Fox, Nathaniel, 183, 187
"freedom of choice," 74, 106, 112, 122–23, 126, 154

Gainesville, Ga., 16, 30, 35, 134, 180. See also Gainesville High School Red Elephants
Gainesville High School Red Elephants, 13, 16, 101, 118, 126–27, 134–38, 143–49, 156, 203–6
Geer, Peter Zack, 58
Georgia, University of (UGA): Black football players, 9–10, 12–13, 90, 92, 116–17, 214–15, 222; expansion of, 67–74; integration of, 45–66, 82; student life in 1950s/early 1960s, 12, 14–17, 19, 21; student life in late 1960s 172–178; student protests in 1970, 189–91
GHSA (Georgia High School Association), 43, 117, 126–27, 129–30, 139, 148
GIA (Georgia Interscholastic Association), 11, 126
Gilbert, Paul, 19, 23, 98, 101, 103–5, 155, 220
Giles, Blake, 164–66
Golden, Don, 153, 157–58, 161–62, 165–67

Green, Agnes, 74–76, 80
Green, Marjorie, 74–75, 79
Green, Terry, 12, 128, 132, 187
Green, Wilucia, 74, 76, 109
Greensboro, Ga., 51–52
Grizzard, Lewis: columnist with
    Atlanta Journal-Constitution, 18,
    46, 102; writer with *Athens Daily
    News*, 129
Guest, Herbert, 84, 86, 111

Hally, R. B., 34
Hampton, Bonnie (Travis), 107; at
    Childs Street School, 74–78, 122;
    at Clarke Junior High School, 79;
    at Athens High School, 79, 219
Hardy, E. E., 58, 62, 108
Harris, Richard, 127
Harris, Roy, 63–64
Harris, Samuel F., 6
Hartman, William ("Bill"), Jr.:
    student at Athens High School,
    16, 104, 113; radio announcer for
    WRFC, 156–57, 161, 168
Hawkins, Robert: on African
    American teachers, 7, 201–2; at
    Athens High School, 114, 219
Heard, Aaron, 12, 107
Henderson, Billy, 217–18, 220, 223
Hight, Don, 175, 183, 185–87, 215–16
Hines, Hope, 156
historically Black colleges and
    universities (HBCUs), 12, 181
Hoard, Floyd, 36–37
Hodgson, Pat, 71
Holloman, Bobo, 43
Holmes, Eugene ("Doc"), 7, 9–11, 126
Holmes, Hamilton, 54–55, 57–58,
    61–65, 76, 82
Holston, James, 128, 144, 192, 200
Holt, Bruce, 209
Hunter, Charlayne (Hunter-Gault),
    50, 56–58, 61, 63, 76
Hutchison, Frank, 183–84, 188

"Iron Horse," 52

Jackson, Phil, 136
Jackson, Walter: head coach at
    Burney-Harris High School, 127–
    28, 131, 139, 142, 147; assistant
    coach at Clarke Central High
    School, 192, 200, 211
Johnson, Anderson Sidney ("Andy"):
    growing up in Athens, 93–94,
    98, 106; at Athens High School,
    103; 1969 football season, 125,
    131–33, 136–38, 146, 149–51; 1969
    state title game versus Valdosta
    High School, 152, 157–59, 162,
    164, 166, 171, 182, 185, 192, 195; at
    University of Georgia, 214; death
    of, 220–21
Johnson, Lyndon, 68, 82, 110, 177
Jonesboro High School, 101, 220

Kappa Alpha, 15, 58
Kappa Alpha Theta, 15, 53
Kelly, Cobern, 96–97, 115, 170, 185
Killian, Archibald: Hamilton
    Holmes living at house of,
    62; owner of Four Seasons
    Restaurant, 62, 75, 84; member of
    Athens Police Department, 62, 85
Killian, Scott Michael, 74–75
King, Corky, 54
King, Horace: growing up in Athens,
    88, 91–93; at Burney-Harris High
    School, 8–10, 127–28, 131–33,
    144, 146; at Clarke Central High
    School, 182, 194, 197–98, 202,
    204, 206–7, 209–10; at University
    of Georgia, 214–15
King, Mollie Parry, 98, 161
King, William ("Bill"): growing up
    in Athens, 98–99; student and
    journalist at Athens High School,
    122–23, 129, 161, 172, 176, 181, 183;
    at University of Georgia, 202

Kitchens, Jim, 164
Klein, Jimmy, 36
Ku Klux Klan, 59, 62, 81, 115;
    Athens-Clarke County Klavern,
    81–86

Lackey, James, 86–88
Lakeside High School, 124–26,
    147–48, 206–9
Lambert, Rand, 94, 125, 135, 137,
    146, 149, 157, 167, 169–71
Lester, David, 23, 130, 136, 170, 187
LeVias, Jerry, 116
Lincoln High School (S.C.), 127, 142
Linnentown, 70–73. *See also* Athens,
    Ga.: neighborhoods
Lipscomb, Eddie Dean, 135–35, 165,
    204
Litsch, Joe, 152, 202
Lucy, Auterine, 47
Lucy Laney High School, 11
Luke, O'Neal, 205
Lyons Middle School, 81, 92–93, 109,
    128, 214

Maddox, Lester, 115–16, 190
Malinowski, Frank, 127, 157, 194
Marietta High School, 119
Matthews, Effie, 38, 39
McCommons, Rollin ("Pete"):
    growing up in Greene County, 51;
    student at University of Georgia,
    26–27, 46, 50, 50–58; at *Athens
    Observer*, 99; at University of
    Georgia Institute of Government,
    172–73; at *United Free Press*, 184,
    190; at *Flagpole Magazine*, 219
McDaniel, Charles, 179, 184, 187, 190
Melton, Terry, 41
Middle Oconee River, 26, 97
Model Cities (urban renewal
    program), 70–73, 176–77
Morse, Allen ("Alan"), 67, 108–9,
    111–12, 114, 117–20, 126, 221–22

Morse, Henry (student and football
    player at Burney-Harris High
    School), 132, 146
Morse, Henry A. (father of Allen
    Morse), 108, 111
Morton, Monroe, 29
Motley, Constance Baker, 54
Mulroy, John, 84
Myers, Cecil, 86–87

Nash, Mike, 125, 134, 158
Nelson, Jack, 37, 39, 87
Newton County High School,
    146–47
Newtown Elementary School,
    109
New York Times, 189
Nickles, Alicia, 219
North Athens Elementary School,
    93, 109
Northington, Nate, 13, 117
North Oconee River, 26, 31, 72–73,
    90, 94, 177, 217, 221

Park, Cliff, 36–37
Parthemos, George, 54
Penn, Lemuel, 86–88
Perry, Chuck: football player at
    Athens High School, 104–6, 156;
    writer at *Athens Banner-Herald*,
    193, 203
Platt, Elizabeth, 6–8, 30, 112
Platt, Frank, 190
Pope, Clarence: growing up in
    Athens, 88–90; at Burney-Harris
    High School, 8, 92, 127–28, 132,
    182, 185; at Clarke Central High
    School, 195, 198, 200, 207, 210–11;
    at University of Georgia, 214–15
Popovich, Joseph, 55
Poss, Bobby, 17, 20–21, 23, 36, 101,
    105–6, 115
Potts, James, 84
Powell, Marsha, 56

Raper, Arthur F., 51
Ray, Steve, 164
Red and Black, 56
Reese, Spencer, 36
R.E.M., 82, 218
Rittenberry, Rose, 107–8
Rittenberry, Walter, 12
Roberson, E. T., 185–86, 201
Robinson, Marty, 117
"Rowdy Thursday," 185, 194
Royster, C. W., 36
Russell, Rusty, 134–35, 149, 165, 194, 198

Sanders, Carl, 67, 115, 174
Saye, Richard, 192
Sellers, Gray: football player at Athens High School, 132, 167; Clarke Central football player, 195–96, 199, 204–5, 207, 210
Sellers, Jackie, 18
Sellers, Weyman, 17; Athens High School football coach, 17, 17–25, 39, 67, 95; 1965 season, 102, 105–6; 1966 season interaction with Black football players, 67, 115–19; 1969 season, 121, 124–28, 131–33, 135–39, 141, 146, 151, 154, 156, 158, 160–64, 166–67, 169–70, 172; Clarke Central football coach, 187, 192–97, 200, 203–11; firing from Clarke Central, 215–17; election to Athens Sports Hall of Fame, 220. *See also* Sellers, Gray; Butts, Wally
Sequoyah High School, 125, 141, 207
Sheats, Larry, 127, 131, 148
Shipp, Bill, 82
Sims, Howard, 85–88
Smart, Terry: 24, 95, 98, 106, 127, 136, 138, 146; state title game versus Valdosta, 151, 155, 158, 161, 185; death of Andy Johnson, 221
Smith, Don, 129

Snow, Ralph, 37, 58
South Hall High School, 127, 143, 146
"Statue of Liberty," 20, 210–11, 293
Stephens, Alexander ("Aleck"), 8, 72
Stephens, Mary, 79
Stephens, Robert, 37, 53, 79, 173
Stephens, Winston, 53, 63
Stipe, Michael, 82
Strong, Charlie, 13, 134
Stroud, Armell, 30
Students for a Democratic Society (SDS), 174–75

Tarkenton, Francis ("Fran"): at Athens High School, 17, 19–22, 155, 220; University of Georgia, 19
Tate, William ("Bill"): integration of University of Georgia, 34, 56–58, 61, 64; *in loco parentis*, 38, 175; 1970 protests at University of Georgia during Vietnam War, 189–90
Terrell, Henry, 127, 131, 146, 148
Thomas, Marcus, 185
Thumb Tack Tribune, 99, 181, 183
Thurmond, Michael: growing up in Athens, 88, 90, 94; at Burney-Harris High School, 7, 127, 142, 144; at Clarke Central High School, 194, 198, 200, 210–13, 222–23
Tillitski, John, 215–16
Tillitski, Steve, 126
Travis, Gary, 19, 98, 106, 124, 151, 164–67
Trillin, Calvin ("Bud"), 32, 55–57, 80–81
Troutman, 7, 201
Tucker High School, 119, 124–25, 146–47, 206–7
Turner, Ed, 177–78, 211
Turner High School, 50, 63

Union Baptist Institute, 6, 9
United Free Press, 183–84, 191

Valdosta High School Wildcats, 16,
202; 1955 state title versus Athens
High School, 17; 1965 state title
versus Athens High School,
102–6; integration of, 119–20,
180; 1969 football regular season,
125, 153–54; 1969 state title versus
Athens High School, 155–72, 195,
216; 1977 state title versus Clarke
Central High School, 218
Vandiver, 33, 46, 56–57, 61, 64
Varsity, the (restaurant), 30, 83–85,
191

Walter's Barbecue, 12
Ward, Horace, 47, 50
Washington, Booker T., 5; Booker T.
Washington High School, 5

Weeks, Ed, 41
West Broad Elementary School, 91,
108–9, 188
"Westminster Disciplined Study
Community," 54–55. *See also*
McCommons, Rollin: student at
University of Georgia
Whitehead, Hattie Thomas, 70–72
Whitehead Road Elementary
School, 98
Williams, Bruce, 135, 170
Williams, Chris, 132
Williams, Joseph, 56–58
Wilson, Homer, 83
Winder-Barrow High School,
145–46, 148
Wingfield, George, 93, 131
Wood, Sam, 180